CHE GUEVARA AND THE
MOUNTAIN OF SILVER

Other books by Anne Mustoe

A Bike Ride: 12,000 miles around the world

Lone Traveller: one woman, two wheels and the world

Two Wheels in the Dust: from Kathmandu to Kandy

Cleopatra's Needle: two wheels by the water to Cairo

Amber, Furs and Cockleshells: bike rides with pilgrims and merchants

www.annemustoe.co.uk

CHE GUEVARA AND THE MOUNTAIN OF SILVER

By Bicycle and Train through South America

Anne Mustoe

First published in Great Britain in 2007
by Virgin Books Ltd
Thames Wharf Studios
Rainville Road
London
W6 9HA

A catalogue record for this book is available from the
British Library.

ISBN 978 0 7535 1274 6

The paper used in this book is a natural, recyclable product
made from wood grown in sustainable forests.
The manufacturing process conforms to the regulations of
the country of origin.

Typeset by TW Typesetting, Plymouth, Devon

Printed and bound in Great Britain by CPI Bookmarque Ltd,
Croydon CR0 4TD

1 3 5 7 9 10 8 6 4 2

Extracts quoted from *The Motorcycle Diaries: A Journey
Around South America* by Che Guevara (translated by Ann
Wright, Fourth Estate 1996) and *Travelling with Che
Guevara: The Making of a Revolutionary* by Alberto
Granado (translated by Lucia Alvarez de Toledo, Pimlico
1978 and 2003). Every attempt has been made to trace
copyright holders and seek permission for any quoted
material in the text, but the author apologises for any
omissions and will be happy to give a full credit in future
editions of this book.

CONTENTS

PROLOGUE – THE TWO ANAS IN
HAVANA IN THE SHADOW OF EL CHE

'The two Anas on the town!' said Big Ana triumphantly, as we scrambled out of the battered Oldsmobile and marched arm in arm across Habana Vieja towards the Cuban music bars. I was Little Ana (Ana Pequeña), despite being much taller than Ana Grande and quite a few years older. But she was the boss of a bustling household, while I was just a modest lodger, so size and age had nothing to do with it. Status was all.

I was spending December and January in Cuba, escaping the worst of the English winter as I polished up my South American Spanish. We were a class of two: Oliver from Munich and myself. We had four hours of lessons every morning and were set mountains of homework, which filled our afternoons. It was an excellent course, but the icing on the cake was staying at Ana's. She was plump and smiling, a wonderful cook – and she and her husband spoke not a word of English. So I had total immersion in the Spanish language, as well as the everyday life of post-revolutionary Cuba.

It was ten o'clock in the evening and things were just livening up in El Floridita, the bar where Ernest Hemingway, a long-time resident of Havana, used to stop for his first *mojitos* of the evening. Big Ana and I ordered the same and sighed with satisfaction as we sipped that delicious concoction of white rum, sugar and sparkling water, topped with a sprig of mint. The perfect refreshment for a hot climate. Then we moved down Obispo, where the crowded bars were pulsing to the beat of rumba, mambo, salsa and the love-lorn wails of *son*.

The Cubans are enormously talented musicians. They live and breathe music and dance. Within seconds, Ana was moving to the beat with unselfconscious ease, along with all the other locals in the bar. Only the *gringos* looked awkward and slightly embarrassed. We were clearly on the outside, looking in. I shuffled a little, to show willing, but I felt like a camel in distress. All those languid, sexy Cubans were an integral part of the music, ebbing and flowing on its tides of emotion. There was music inside the bars and music outside, as groups of guitarists roamed the cobbled streets, singing and strumming with innate artistry and fantastic invention. There were at least fifty 'Buena Vista Social Clubs' that night in Obispo, every one with the flair of Segundo and Gonzalez – and Obispo was just one street in the maze of Old Havana.

For Big Ana, it was a wonderful evening out, a brief escape from her difficult life. In every revolution, there are winners and losers. Hilda, my warm, witty Spanish teacher, was a shining beneficiary of Castro's brand of communism. Born a black woman in the poor rural east of the island, her prospects in life had been transformed by the Revolution with its universal suffrage, anti-racist legislation and education for all. She was a lecturer, attached to the University of Havana, a career beyond the wildest dreams of her parents' generation. She had even travelled abroad, on a teachers' exchange to Wolverhampton, a city whose parks and gardens she often described with rapture.

Hilda always joined the annual parade, when Castro himself, now well into his eighties, marched at the head of Havana's multitudes from the Plaza de la Revolución to the US

Special Interests Office. This glass and concrete slab on the seafront has served as the unofficial US embassy since the two countries broke off diplomatic relations in 1961.

'It's a long walk – at least five kilometres – but it's such fun!' she told us. 'We turn up in our thousands and swarm along the avenue to the Malecón, and when we get to the US Office, we all stand behind Castro and shake our fists, shouting defiance at the Americans. It's like Carnival. It's a wonderful day out! And have you seen that hilarious poster opposite the building? Uncle Sam, an awful old man in his Stars and Stripes and top hat, growls at us across the sea, gr-r-r-r-r, while a handsome young Cuban under a palm tree grins at him and shouts "Señores Imperialistas, we're not the least bit scared of you!" That's what the Americans see,' she crowed gleefully, 'every time they look out of their office windows.'

Hilda was bursting with enthusiasm for the three Cs – Cuba, Castro and Che Guevara. She had flourished since the Revolution. But Big Ana and her husband, like most of the professional middle classes, had fared less well. They had seen their standard of living crumble. Their once comfortable existence had been shattered when Ana's husband had to take early retirement from his professorship at the University of Havana. He suffered from a particularly distressing form of Parkinson's disease, which had attacked his vocal cords, making his speech virtually unintelligible. For a man who had lived by his intellect and his powers of communication, this inability to convey his thoughts was a far greater trial than his debilitating tremors. He had held the chair of Economic Geography and was keenly interested in my travels. In my first days as a lodger in the house, he made desperate attempts to talk to me about them, but I could understand scarcely a word he said and the conversations fizzled out in mutual embarrassment.

Ana had given up her work as an expert dealer and restorer of colonial furniture to care for her husband. In the early stages, when his condition could be regulated by Cuban manufactured generic drugs, they had managed quite well, thanks to the state's free medical services. Their troubles began when the disease progressed to the point where he needed a branded drug produced only in Europe. The US Cold War embargo, which was (and still is) needlessly in operation, prevented the Cuban health service from importing foreign drugs. So Ana had to buy the drug in cash dollars from one of the Servimed outlets, set up by the state to provide paying health care for tourists. On his miserable pension of US $25 a month, this was impossible, so Ana had to take in paying guests to earn the necessary cash. She worked from morning to night, cooking breakfast and dinner for three of us and cleaning our rooms, as well as nursing the professor, who was fast approaching the stage where he needed help with his feeding and dressing. It was a very hard life.

American dollars were legal tender in Cuba, along with the Cuban peso and the convertible peso – three types of currency, with three different sets of rules. It was a nightmare for tourists, who were expected to pay for everything in dollars and usually did, because that's the currency they could understand. Since tourism took off in the early 1990s, the ludicrous situation had arisen where taxi drivers, for instance, whose foreign passengers paid their fares in US cash dollars, could earn $35 in a day, as much as a doctor on a state salary earned for a whole month's work. The professions were the losers in a country where the provision of services to affluent tourists was the pathway to wealth.

Fortunately, not being affluent myself, I had Big Ana and Hilda to look after me. I was treated for free, for a minor ailment, by Ana's excellent young woman doctor. While other tourists paid through the nose for their fruit in the dollar supermarkets, Ana showed me the places where I could buy luscious pineapples and oranges for a peso. Hilda told me of threadbare but much loved cinemas, where I could enjoy the latest Hollywood films, the Russian classics of Eisenstein and Tarkovsky and avant-garde Cuban and Spanish films for two pesos. And I learned how to travel with the locals in the lumbering juggernaut buses, called *camellos* for obvious reasons, and the *colectivos*, or shared peso taxis, every one of them a marvellous 1950s Chevrolet or Oldsmobile, crammed from its chromium bumpers to its preposterous tail fins with Habaneros, their babies and their shopping. They were transports of delight – so much so that I never once regretted being in Cuba without my bicycle, particularly as most of the roads had potholes the size of bomb craters. The locals cycled on imported Chinese war horses, whose sturdy, gearless frames were more suited to the road conditions than my slender Condor, but even they rarely ventured out of town.

Big Ana lived in a gracious old colonial-style house, with rooms opening out onto a central tiled courtyard. Thanks to her lodgers' dollars, it was the one freshly painted house in a dilapidated street. There was a roof terrace with an awning, a swing and an array of white, cast-iron garden furniture. Hilda, Oliver and I soon decided that it was far pleasanter to have our lessons up there on the terrace than in the stuffy classroom provided by the language school, especially as Ana could be counted on for trays of good, strong Cuban coffee to keep us going through our four-hour stint. Oliver (pronounced 'Olly Bear' by the Cubans, like a cousin of Teddy Bear) didn't live in the house, but he was a great favourite of Ana's.

'Olly Bear, you must come to dinner one night. I will cook lobster, specially for you.'

A date was fixed and Olly Bear arrived with flowers and two bottles of real French wine from the dollar store. This was the height of luxury, not seen in that house for forty years. And the lobster was delicious.

'Olly Bear, Olly Bear!' Hilda had said mockingly, when Ana disappeared with her tray. 'You notice she didn't invite me for the lobster! Just her lovely Olly Bear.'

The house was conveniently situated in Vedado, the cultural centre of Havana. Its leafy suburban avenues, lined with the crumbling grandeur of once-elegant mansions, were a reminder of the city's wealthy nineteenth-century past. I spent my leisure hours wandering from the Museum of Decorative Arts to the

Museum of Napoleon to the Anthropological Museum and back to the university and my home in Calle Concordia. I lived near the Malecón, the seawall which defends the city from the raging Atlantic. By day, small boys dived from its boulders into the churning waters, old men fished and a few health-conscious Habaneros jogged along its broad pavement. It was all very sedate and a bit down at heel, like most of Havana. But the evenings were party time, when the moonlight obscured the potholes, and peanut-sellers jostled with musicians, lovers, children on bikes and skateboards, and the inevitable prostitutes. It was Havana's free entertainment centre – but it took courage for a *gringo*, and even more for an innocent *gringa*, to venture there alone. We were safer sipping a sunset *mojito* in The National, that grand old lady of Havana's hotels, an Alhambra lookalike in style and opulence. It was perched on a hilltop, high above the Malecón, and had been patronised by every visiting celebrity from Winston Churchill to Naomi Campbell. Or if the funds didn't run to such luxury, there was always an ice cream at the Coppelia, the weird, space-age restaurant in a park off La Rampa. One of Havana's most famous landmarks, it featured in the opening scenes of Tomas Gutierrez Alea's 1993 film, *Fresa y Chocolate* (Strawberry and Chocolate), the two favourite flavours of ice cream. Cubans stand in line for hours to enjoy one of the Coppelia's delicious confections, but tourists can jump the queue by forking out for the dollar-only section.

Big Ana's end of Vedado, between the Malecón and the University of Havana, was the old fashioned pre-Revolutionary end. The state's power resided further inland, in La Plaza de la Revolución. This was a vast windswept desert of flagstones, surrounded by the concrete blocks of the Cuban Communist Party, the government offices and the police. Stalinist brutal in the extreme, the complex was obviously laid out in the heyday of Cuban–Russian relations, before the fall of the Soviet Union. We were told that the square bursts with life at the May Day parades and other such ceremonies, when the flags fly and Fidel Castro takes the salute before millions of cheering Cubans. But for Oliver and me, on our first cultural outing with Hilda, its bleak, empty expanse was seriously depressing.

We paid our respects at the memorial to Jose Martí. Little known outside the country (Oliver and I had never heard of him!), this poet-journalist is considered to be the father of Cuban independence. Working from exile in New York, he founded the Cuban Revolutionary Party in 1892 and in 1895 landed on the island with a liberation force of overseas Cubans and sympathisers, to join up with the local guerrillas. Unfortunately, his pen was mightier than his sword and he was killed in his very first battle against the Spanish. So the man who deserved to be the first president of an independent Cuban republic sadly missed his opportunity.

If size were all, Martí's amazing twenty-storey ziggurat with its dainty little Gothic crown, all in white marble – not to mention the seventeen-metre high statue of the hero himself in the pose of Rodin's *Thinker* – should by rights dominate the Plaza de la Revolución. But it is knocked completely out of the running by a striking steel frieze, which looms at the far end of the square.

The Memorial Ernesto 'Che' Guevara is a giant copy of his iconic image. Based on the famous photograph taken by Alberto 'Korda' Gutierrez in Havana in 1960, the frieze portrays El Che in his fighter's beret adorned with the Cuban star. His long tangled hair pokes out wildly in all directions, his moustache droops, but his gaze is nothing short of messianic. Inscribed underneath is '*Hasta la victoria siempre*' (Forever, until victory). It is possibly the most famous photograph of our era, the emblem par excellence of the rebellious young of all nations, and lately even a style statement of the retro chic. It has made the fortunes of generations of T-shirt and poster manufacturers, and it is the image which every visitor to Havana, Cuban or tourist, comes to La Plaza de la Revolución to see. It's ironic that Che Guevara, who disapproved of the cult of personality, should himself end up as one of the icons of the age.

In the Museo de la Revolución, I boggled at the larger-than-life wax model of El Che, striding out of the jungle in camouflage, along with countless photographs of his campaigns with Castro in the mountainous centre of the island. Roadsides throughout Cuba sported propaganda posters glorifying the Revolution, and El Che in his trademark beret was always one of the central figures. Every large hotel in Havana had its exhibition of revolutionary photographs, with El Che prominently displayed, sometimes as a guerrilla, sometimes as a government minister in a business suit. Even small provincial towns had their memorials or museums, full of the same photos. Second only to Fidel Castro, Che Guevara was the dominating presence in Cuba.

The longer I stayed in Havana, and the more I learned from the Cubans themselves of the triumphs and disappointments of the Revolution, the more curious I became about the role of this enigmatic figure, Che Guevara. (Even his nickname is an enigma, as no one seems sure what it means. Is it Argentine slang for 'pal'? Or does it allude to a strange habit of speech? Did he and his fellow Argentines sprinkle their sentences with meaningless 'ches', as English-speakers add meaningless 'likes', 'whats' or 'yeahs'?) How did this aristocratic Argentine, a qualified doctor and a chronic asthmatic, evolve into Cuba's jungle fighter and the author of a book on guerrilla warfare? What Damascene conversion transformed him into Fidel Castro's right-hand man and the propounder, in *Man and Socialism in Cuba*, published in 1965, of the official ideology underpinning the Cuban brand of communism?

Two books had recently been published in English: Alberto Granado's *Travelling with Che Guevara: The Making of a Revolutionary* and Che Guevara's own *Motorcycle Diaries*. Both books described the same motorcycle tour of South America, which the larky pair, on holiday from medical school, undertook in 1952 on La Ponderosa II (The Powerful One), Alberto's ramshackle 500cc. Norton. I read the books in Havana and decided to cycle in their wheel tracks, to see if I could get under the skin of Ernesto Guevara de la Serna and understand his extraordinary conversion into 'El Che'. Perhaps I would find the spark to the conflagration somewhere in his writings or in the wilds of his beautiful, contradictory continent.

But in case you get the wrong impression, I should like to point out that I was in Cuba in the winter of 2002–3 and it was during my stay there that I conceived the idea of this cycle ride. Two years later, before I had even got round to making the journey, let alone writing this book, Walter Salles brought out his delightful film, *The Motorcycle Diaries*. So I was pipped to the post, but I was not a copycat! Following Che was my own original idea.

My cycle ride in their tyre tracks would take me from Buenos Aires across Argentina, over the Andes and into Chile. But when they reached the Atacama Desert, in the north of Chile, the two friends hitched lifts into Peru, where they visited Cuzco and Machu Picchu, then made their way down to the Amazon. Alberto Granado had a special interest in leprosy and they wanted to study the disease and give some practical medical help in the colonies of the Amazon Basin. I had already, years ago, visited both Cuzco and Machu Picchu, and didn't particularly want to go there again; nor did I have any expertise to offer the leper colonies. So I didn't plan to follow them beyond the Atacama Desert. I had to find an alternative route back to Buenos Aires, without retracing my tracks, which I always hate doing. And in line with my usual interests, it had to be a historical route.

I found it in the Spanish Silver Route, which ran from Potosí on Bolivia's Altiplano (High Plains) to the Atlantic ports on the estuary of the Rio de la Plata (the Silver River), of which Buenos Aires was the greatest. The fabulous treasure of Potosí was transported by the Spanish conquistadors from its solid silver mountain, El Cerro Rico, high up in the Andes, down to the sea along the only practicable path – a route which was pre-Inca, then an Inca highway, then the Spanish Post Road, then the line of the British and North American railways, built in the nineteenth century. And the link between the two routes, Che Guevara's and the Spanish Silver Route, was another railway, the British-built FCAB (Ferrocaril Antofagasta a Bolivia), which I could ride from Calama in the Atacama Desert to Uyuni on the Bolivian Altiplano.

As things turned out, I rode my bicycle more or less up to the point where the ramshackle motorbike, La Ponderosa II, juddered and gave up the ghost in Chile, after which I travelled, like my two revolutionaries, by whatever means of transport happened to be available. They hitch-hiked in lorries, while I tried to complete my journey by train. The original nineteenth-century rolling stock still steams on (literally) in some places. Under-resourced and neglected, the South American railways are potent symbols of the pioneering spirit and commercial confidence that conquered one of the world's loftiest mountain ranges and laid railway tracks across burning desert and scrubland scoured by southern gales to open up the continent to European settlement and development. They represent the triumph of nineteenth-century capitalism, while Che Guevara has come to symbolise the twentieth century's struggle against capitalism's inequalities. I thought how appropriate it would be to ride those trains, before twenty-first-century progress leaves them to crumble and die.

It was altogether a fascinating journey – and the Silver Route – the part of it which started off in my mind as simply an addendum, a device to get me back from the north of Chile to my starting point in Buenos Aires – turned out to be just as interesting, and certainly as broad in scope, as the Che Guevara ride.

When I came to do my research, I realised how abysmally ignorant I was about South America's colonial and pre-colonial past. No English school syllabus, to my knowledge, even so much as touches on the great epic of the exploration and settlement of this huge, multifaceted continent. My own steep learning curve is reflected in one or two of the background chapters, where I try to summarise the exciting discoveries I myself have made. Those chapters are easily identified and readers with little taste for historical fact and speculation can, I suppose, skim over them and still make sense of my actual journey.

In this book, I ride my bicycle across the windswept pampas and over the Andes, travel slowly in groaning, rickety trains, or speed along the highways in the comfort of air-conditioned Chilean and Argentine coaches. For perfect freedom, travel on two wheels, or two feet, is always the best. But long journeys on trains and buses are wonderfully sociable experiences and I was delighted to find that my Cuban Spanish, learned in Che Guevara's Havana, enabled me to get to know so many interesting South Americans as I travelled through the southern half of their great continent.

1. RAIN ON JACARANDAS

*It is not, one feels, for nothing that it was named Buenos Aires,
since the airs are admirable and every air a tango.*

(Philip Guedalla, *Argentine Tango*)

I flew into Buenos Aires on a Tuesday morning, early in November, 2004. My cycling companion, Katherine, had arrived on a slightly earlier flight and was waiting for me by the baggage carousel. She had already pumped up her own tyres, straightened her handlebars and hooked on her panniers, so she was free to give me a hand with Condor. When all was in order, we wheeled our bikes across Arrivals to join the queue at the information desk.

'Is that your bike?' asked the Englishman behind me. He was peering at my name, which Condor Cycles had painted on the down-tube.

'That's a very famous Condor,' he said. 'Fancy meeting it at Buenos Aires airport! I hope you're taking it for a ride – and writing another book about it. I've read all your others.' What a flattering start to a journey!

According to the girl at the desk, the 40 km from the airport to the city centre was mainly motorway, on which we were not allowed to cycle, so she directed us to the airport bus, where the driver was happy to accommodate our machines. We were deposited on the outskirts of the capital and, as the streets are laid on a regular grid, we map-read our way with ease to the Hotel Chile for our meeting with Julian. It was a smooth and utterly painless introduction to Argentina.

In fact, my stepson Julian ensured that our entire stay in Buenos Aires was smooth and painless. He was furbishing a second-hand Argentine racing yacht in the marina at San Isidro, preparing it for higher things than the occasional regatta. He was making it oceanworthy, to voyage in the wake of Darwin's *Beagle*, and had already spent eight months on the task. He was renting a room with a charming Argentine family, working in the boat shed all day and taking lessons in Spanish. By the time we met him, he was almost a *porteño*, as the citizens of Buenos Aires call themselves.

The next day, Katherine and I took the local train from Retiro Station, passing gardens, tennis courts, swimming pools and villas, which grew grander as our journey progressed along the estuary of the Rio de la Plata. There was little evidence of Argentina's current financial crisis in these opulent suburbs. We met Julian for lunch in a smart café beside San Isidro Station, then strolled with him down flights of steps with white balustrades, through clouds of jasmine, rose and bougainvillea, to Lower San Isidro and the boat shed. After the greyness of a London November, the riot of colours and scents was over-whelmingly exotic.

I'm no sailor and have no knowledge of the finer points of boats, but I was relieved to see that Julian's acquisition looked seaworthy, if rather on the small side for coping with the wild seas around Tierra del Fuego, the Chilean fjords and the Pacific Ocean.

'Don't worry about the size!' he said cheerfully. 'Think of a light bulb. Nothing in the world floats better, except perhaps a cork.'

There is a saying in South America: 'An Argentine is an Italian, who speaks Spanish and wants to be English.' Buenos

Aires has always felt itself to be a European city, marooned in the uninhabited vastness of its countryside, and the *portenõs*, who constitute about one-third of Argentina's total population of 40 million, have consequently looked to Europe for their inspiration. 'Our entire country is imported,' said the great Argentine writer Borges. 'Everyone here is really from somewhere else.' 'I'm Italian,' they will say, or 'I'm Welsh,' or 'I'm English too. My name is Pablo Parsons.'

These mingled races have built a grand capital, on a sensible grid system, with wide boulevards and squares, but few buildings predate the nineteenth century and most are an eclectic mix of European styles. Even the cathedral, which houses the mausoleum of The Liberator, General Jose de San Martín, is a recent mongrel fusion of neoclassical columns and gloomy baroque vaulting. We were able to do the whole of our sightseeing in one drizzly morning. The purple jacaranda blossoms, like clusters of harebells, and the pink-flowering Judas trees were in their full spring glory along the boulevards, and they remain my most vivid memory of that pleasant, but architecturally undistinguished, city.

Julian gave a luncheon party one day, so that we could meet his Argentine friends, all of whom he had picked up directly or indirectly as a result of his boat purchase and his days in the marina. They were cultivated and well heeled, which made me realise how useful it is to be a sailor. The richest, classiest people hang around in marinas and share a passion for sailing. They are the perfect bunch of contacts. By contrast, those welcoming a woman on a bike are always friendly, but not necessarily the sharpest string-pullers in town. One of Julian's sailing friends, the leading Argentine oceanographer, was even descended from a president of Argentina. He was kind and affable, if a bit on the grand side, as one might expect. 'This restaurant is fairly horrible,' he said airily, 'but Julian seems to love it.'

It was a cosy, family-run establishment down by the docks. We arrived in pouring rain, but were soon cheered by the convivial company, the free-flowing wine and the flavour of our delicious, freshly caught fish. We were a large party. Julian's landlords, Eduardo and Adriana, with their son and pretty undergraduate daughter, were joined by his solicitor, boat-builder, shipping broker and a raft of friends from the marina. I was surprised to be kissed by them all, but realised later that this is the normal greeting in Argentina, even on first meeting. I was struck by their gentle good manners, their excellent English and their illusion that everything in England was perfect. Adriana talked to me about Argentina's rocketing inflation and all the destitute people who had 'fallen out of the bottom of the system'. She was amazed to hear that the British too were having problems with the shortfall in their pension funds. How could such a well-run paradise as England possibly have the same kind of difficulties as the bankrupt Argentina?

We had little to do in Buenos Aires, which was as well, because we needed to make our preparations for the ride – following Che Guevara across South America.

Our hero's parents were *porteños* and Ernesto Guevara de la Serna should have been born in the capital, but he arrived prematurely in Rosario in 1928, the first son of the splendidly named couple Ernesto Guevara Lynch and Celia de la Serna y Llosa. His father's family, a mixture of Spanish and Irish stock, had lived in Argentina for twelve generations, making them aristocrats in a country of immigrants. On his wealthy mother's side, he was descended from General Jose de la Serna e Hinojosa, the last Spanish Viceroy of Peru. Both parents were left-wing intellectuals. In fact, they were card-carrying members of the Argentine Communist Party for some fourteen years.

He was born at a time of great prosperity, when Argentina was one of the wealthiest countries in the world and the French coined the phrase, '*riche comme un argentin*'. His parents had travelled up the Paraná River shortly after their marriage to look into the cultivation of *maté*, the Argentine version of tea, and were in Rosario, checking out a *maté* mill, when Ernesto suddenly arrived. The maté scheme came to nothing and the family returned to Buenos Aires where his father, who seemed to make a speciality of failing enterprises, became involved in a struggling shipbuilding company. By coincidence, its yards were in San Isidro, where Julian was working on his boat.

There followed a period of roaming around Argentina, partly in pursuit of his father's business dreams and partly in search of a beneficial climate. Ernesto suffered from severe attacks of asthma throughout his life, which was undoubtedly one of the main reasons for his enrolment at the Buenos Aires medical school in 1948. His interest lay in research into allergies rather than in clinical practice.

Perhaps because of his vagrant childhood, or perhaps by nature, Ernesto Che Guevara was a wanderer, insatiably curious about the world. In 1949, he made a solo 4000-mile trip around North Argentina on a sort of motorised bicycle, which he had designed and built himself. But that only served to sharpen his restlessness. So in December 1950, in the university long vacation, he signed on with the Ministry of Public Health as a nurse in Argentina's merchant marine and sailed to Brazil, Venezuela and Trinidad. It was a frustrating experience. He complained in his letters that he was spending far too long at sea, with too little time in port for exploration. Bored at sea, and even more bored with the middle-class comforts of home life in Buenos Aires, he longed for a real adventure.

In 1952, two years before he qualified as a doctor, he embarked on his first extended trip beyond Argentina. He set off with his friend, Alberto Granado, a slightly older leprosy specialist, on Alberto's temperamental motorbike, La Ponderosa II, to cross South America into Chile, then travel north to Venezuela. His family were concerned.

'Alberto, you're the elder,' said Ernesto's influential mother, 'so try to get him to come back and finish his studies. A degree never hurts.'

Setting out from Buenos Aires, the intrepid pair headed south, to follow the great curved shoulder of Atlantic coastline through a succession of seaside resorts. But first, Che stopped in Palermo Park, where the dog sellers gathered. He fell in love with a young Alsatian, which he bought for his fiancée, Maria del Carmen Ferreyra, known as Chichina. He named the puppy 'Comeback' (in English), as a promise of his return. So they had an extra passenger on La Ponderosa as far as Miramar, where Chichina was on holiday with her family.

'Comeback' was a great worry to them both, being seriously accident prone. He travelled in a little bag on the back of the motorbike, his snout poking out and sniffing the breeze. Every time they had a spill – which was often – he shot up into the air, keeping up what Che called 'his affinity for aviation'. In addition, the poor little thing was trodden underfoot by a horse and had persistent diarrhoea. But they got him in one piece to Miramar, where Che handed him over to Chichina, who gave Che her bracelet in return, as a keepsake.

What should have been a stay of two days turned into eight, as Guevara kept postponing their departure, torn between his longing for adventure and his reluctance to leave the girl he loved. Alberto stalked impatiently up and down beside the ocean, which he was seeing for the first time in his life, and feared that he would find himself travelling alone to Venezuela. But Che finally pulled himself away and they continued their journey, staying every night with convenient friends and relations of the Guevaras all the way down the Atlantic coast to Bahía Blanca.

It is fascinating to compare the two accounts of that stay in Miramar. Che Guevara's diary was written at the time, as they travelled along. He may have polished it up later, as most writers do, but it still conveys his mood and feelings on the actual journey. Interestingly, he displays little or no interest in politics, even though he was writing in the turbulent days of Peron's first presidency. He writes lyrically of his love for Chichina and the agony of parting. Alberto, on the other hand, wrote his diary of the trip, *Travelling with Che*, in 1978, 27 years after the journey and 10 years after Che's death in Bolivia, when he was already a legendary figure. With the wisdom of hindsight, Alberto gives a different slant to the visit.

He scarcely mentions Chichina and says nothing of Che's dilemma. Instead, as a man of humbler origins, he is highly critical of the conceit and frivolity of Che's social class, and marvels that their views did not corrupt his friend. He tells of Che's quarrels with his hosts – how he defended the national-isation of healthcare, denounced the abuse of medicine for profit, and generally demolished his opponents with his brilliant arguments in defence of social equality. He concluded by grabbing Comeback's collar and saying to Alberto, 'Come on. Let's shake off these toffs and give the dog a bath.' Alberto knew what the future held in store for Che Guevara and shone the torch of his future fame on his unremarkable past. Alberto's Che is not just a rather untidy, lovelorn student on a motorbike, but a political visionary in the making.

If Katherine and I had followed the motorbikers down the coast, it would have taken us the best part of a fortnight on our bicycles to cover the 1000 km from Buenos Aires to Bahía Blanca, a fortnight of popular seaside resorts, each one similar to the last, and none of particular interest. When I first cycled round the world, I cast off all my responsibilities and time was immaterial. But since those carefree days, my life has become extremely busy again. I no longer have the luxury of getting on my bike and riding away, with no thought of schedules or timetables. The coastal route to Bahía Blanca would take too long, while the more direct inland route would involve us in 630 km of fume-laden highway across unchanging *pampa humeda* (damp prairie, as distinct from the arid prairie scrubland further south). Neither route seemed worth the effort, so I opted to save time by taking the train. But easier said than done.

On our first morning in Buenos Aires, before our trip to Julian's boat yard, we took a taxi to Constitution Station to book our sleepers. It was a marvel of Victorian engineering, twice the size of London's Paddington. Light flickered through the acres of dusty glass and tramps slept peacefully behind the cast-iron pillars of the huge vaulted concourse. We pushed through the crowds, past a bewildering array of ticket counters, until we eventually found the right one and bought first-class singles to Bahía Blanca for the amazingly low price of £3.20 for a thirteen-hour journey! But we couldn't book our sleepers. They had to be booked on Friday, the day we were due to travel. So we went next to the goods shed to enquire about the transport of our bikes. It was an even more gigantic building, ramshackle in the extreme, with rain pouring down through holes in the roof. Our footsteps echoed in the vastness, which was deserted except for three totally relaxed Indian employees, a few stray dogs and a black cat. We noted that the manhole covers were made in Birmingham and the great cast-iron scales came from Sheffield – appropriately enough, as the Argentine railways were mostly built by the British. The young man who seemed to be in charge of the shed was wonderfully handsome. Dressed in a scarlet puffa jacket and neatly pressed jeans, he had oiled his long black locks and screwed them up into very fetching ringlets. He assured us that there would be no problem with the despatch, provided we got the bikes to the shed by 4 p.m. on Friday.

Once we had settled all that, we could concentrate on the only real imperative in Buenos Aires: the tango! Originating in the 1880s in the squalid southern barrios of La Boca, Pompeya and Barracas, where poor immigrants from Spain and the south of Italy mingled with Africans and gauchos from the pampas, tango expressed the nostalgia and loneliness of the world's uprooted and dispossessed. Its ritualised fancy foot-work was the peacock display of desperate men, who had only their machismo to cling to. Though tango gradually moved up the social scale and acquired international respectability through the mournful lyrics of Carlos Gardel in the 1920s and later musicians from the conservatoires, its aching melancholy, heart-felt longings and laments for lost love are still firmly rooted in the docks and bars of its birth. It is the soul of Buenos Aires.

I'd warned Julian well in advance that Katherine and I wanted to be taken to the tango – the real thing, not a floor-show for tourists. He was much dismayed, because he is not a dancing man, but he made dutiful enquiries of his Argentine friends. It turned out that his landlord, Eduardo, was something of an expert on the history of tango and was able to recommend an authentic *milonga*.

Julian turned up at our hotel to escort us. He was looking quite svelte, as he had put himself into the hands of a local dietitian and managed to shed about 12 kilos.

'If you pay for professional advice,' he said, 'you tend to keep it. Otherwise, it's a waste of good money.'

He was wearing a pair of outsize suede shoes, beige, with a strange raised seam up the front and thick crepe soles. He was most proud of them.

'These are excellent shoes,' he said. 'They will take me anywhere.'

'Except onto the floor of a dance hall, I thought, though I made no comment.

The *milonga* is a dance and also the place where it happens. The dance is a more modern form of tango, with less intricate steps. The place is any large hall that happens to be free. The evenings usually begin at 8 o'clock with lessons in both tango and *milonga*, and the dancing proper begins about two hours later. *Milongas* are cool and trendy, the equivalent of 'clubbing' for the bright young things of Buenos Aires.

Our *milonga* took place in a large parish hall. Entrance tickets cost £1.50 and the place was bursting at the seams. There were dancers of every age, in every kind of dress, from schoolchildren and students in jeans through to the really venerable in formal suits and dance dresses; and some were extremely skilful exponents of the art. We found a table near the edge and ordered a bottle of wine and a snack, though we noticed that the serious tango dancers stuck to water. The atmosphere was very sedate, somehow 1930s. Even the music came from an old-fashioned record player. We watched in awe as a young man at the next table escorted his partner onto the dance floor. They looked the perfect part. He was as sleek as an otter in an elegant dark-grey suit, slightly waisted, with a white shirt, a red and black diagonally striped tie and shiny black patent-leather shoes. His white teeth gleamed, as did his dark, oiled, sleeked-back hair. He could have stepped straight out of an old advertisement for Brilliantine. He danced like a dream and all the ladies were desperate to be swept across the floor in his arms. But the partner he chose most often was his perfect complement. A small, slight girl with black hair cut in a neat bob surrounded by kiss curls, she wore hectic scarlet lipstick, the shortest, skimpiest little black lace dress and incredibly high heels. They danced with taut, sensual elegance, in 'the vertical expression of a horizontal desire', as some wag has described tango. The music and spectacle were so bewitching that even Julian was carried away and almost missed the last train back to San Isidro.

It was the rainy season and it had rained steadily on us most of the time we were in Buenos Aires. On our last day there, it was still drizzling on the jacarandas. We cycled to Constitution Station, where our bikes and emergency tent were weighed on the Sheffield scales and loaded into a baggage van, which 'Ringlets' assured us would be shunted out of the yard in the early evening and attached to our train. Not being risk-takers, we watched the loading operation very closely, then climbed into the van and locked our two precious machines together. Then we went off to reserve our sleepers.

After a long search and many enquiries, we found the sleeper ticket office, which was due to open at 1.30. We arrived at 1.00, by which time there were eight people ahead of us in the queue. The window was duly opened at 1.30 and the first five people were issued with tickets. The rest of us were turned away and the window was closed with a bang. No one knew why. In fact, it turned out that there was to be no sleeping car on the train!

Not counting the short run out to San Isidro on a local train, our journey on the *Expreso del Atlántico* was our first experience of the Argentine State Railways, the Ferrobaires, or ENABIEF (Ente Nacional de Administración de Bienes Ferroviarios), to call it by its full title. This railway was built by the British as the Buenos Ayres Great Southern Railway and in its heyday it ran five daytime express trains and five night expresses every day and night of the week between Buenos Aires and Bahía Blanca. Before it was nationalised by General Peron in 1947, its issued capital on the London Stock Exchange was over £72 million. Now there is sometimes one train and sometimes, in the high season, three trains a week, but Julian's friends in Buenos Aires were astonished to learn that even this sparse service existed. The smart people fly.

'There aren't any trains,' they declared with great conviction – until I showed them my ticket. 'Well, even if these trains exist, you mustn't travel on them. It's not safe. They'll be filthy, and you'll be robbed.'

If I had a pound for every time I've been given those dire warnings on my travels, I should be a millionaire by now. 'You can't go up the Amazon on a cargo boat! You can't take a bus across Brazil! You can't cycle across Pakistan! You can't take a night train to Budapest! You can't cycle on your own in Syria! It's dangerous!' I've always ignored these doom-laden cries and always been perfectly safe.

Despite the lack of the sleeping and restaurant cars that the internet had promised, we spent a fairly comfortable night. The first-class seats were huge wing armchairs with leg rests, all made of real leather, and there was ample space to spread out. They dated back to the great days of steam, when the Argentine Railways made fortunes for their British share-holders, and the Argentine cattle barons sat back in luxury, smoking their cigars and being waited on by uniformed attendants. Little maintenance had been done since those heady days, as the wealthy now travelled to their estancias by private plane and the train was packed with the urban poor, but the once luxurious compartments still had a certain dilapidated grandeur. And at least the train left Buenos Aires and arrived in Bahía Blanca on the dot.

We were still plagued by the rain. As we pushed our cycles over the railway tracks and began to pedal into the centre of Bahía Blanca, the prevailing drizzle turned into a downpour.

But after our busy time in Buenos Aires and our night sitting up in the train, a hot shower, a pizza and a siesta in a comfortable hotel seemed as good a way as any to spend a wet day. We dined that evening in a traditional German restaurant, founded in 1962, so very old by Argentine standards, where we ate the best steak we had ever eaten in our lives. Not only was it delicious in flavour and so tender it cut like butter, but it was so huge that it made our English restaurant steaks look no bigger than Oxo cubes! One steak, one salad and one helping of chips would have been enough for four. I don't know if it's the grazing, the butchering or the hanging that does it, but Argentine steak is unbeatable. It's quite simply the best steak in the world.

2. ON THE ROAD TO BARILOCHE

You won't get where you want to go, if you only travel on the sunny days.

(Fridge magnet)

Bahía Blanca was a big city like any other, with shops and supermarkets where we could stock up on snacks for the road. What distinguished it, and made it essentially Argentine, was its grandiose architecture in every style under the sun. The Italianate town hall (1904) and the French-style Banco de la Nacíon (1927) were just two of a crowd of impressive structures around the spacious lawns of the be-statued Plaza Rivadavia, while Classical theatres and fin de siècle mansions lurked down every side street. But what appealed to me more than the city itself was its port of Ingeniero White.

Originally called 'Nueva Liverpool', it was built by the same Buenos Ayres Great Southern Railway which had brought us down to Bahía Blanca. It was a port for new arrivals, at a time when immigration from Europe was actively encouraged.

WORKERS REQUIRED: IF ENGLISH, FRENCH OR GERMAN, GOOD.
NO WEAKLINGS, SICK OR ANARCHISTS ACCEPTED.

So reads a contemporary notice in the delightfully eccentric Port Museum. There you can see barbers' shops, of which each immigrant community for some reason had its own, reconstructed bars, schoolrooms, shops and fascinating displays of photographs of the early settler families. Sited in the old Customs House, it describes itself as 'a museum of local lifestyles', even serving meals based on early twentieth-century immigrant cooking. The port's name was changed in 1901 by President Roca, in honour of its Anglo-Argentine engineer.

Ingeniero White is no longer home to the European immigrant communities who once settled there. Grass grows between the paving stones and the crenellated factories, petro-chemical plants and grain silos tower forbiddingly over empty streets. The port still flourishes, exporting almost half the country's grain. Yet although it maintains its position as second in Argentina only to the port of Buenos Aires, its workers have fled to more agreeable suburbs around Bahía Blanca. Ingeniero White is no more than a ghost town, but its museum is great fun and well worth the bus ride out to see it.

The torrential rain showed no signs of abating and we resigned ourselves to a long stay in Bahía Blanca, waiting for tolerable cycling weather. But we woke to a brilliant morning, with delicate feathers of cirrus cloud swirling across a pale-blue sky. It was our sixth day in Argentina and the first time we had seen real sunshine. We loaded our bikes and pedalled south down Avenida Colón into a time warp. Just beside the railway tracks, in the English quarter of the city, stood Brickman Street, a perfect terrace of late-Victorian houses. Built in red brick, with roses and hollyhocks in their neat little cottage gardens, they were visions of home for the English foremen and technicians working on the port and the Buenos Ayres Great Southern Railway. They were a little bit of picture-postcard England in a far country.

When we left the shelter of Avenida Colón, the force of the wind struck us like a punch on the nose. We joined Ruta 3, the main north–south artery, which runs all the way from Buenos Aires down to the Straits of Magellan. It is Argentina's busiest highway, but on that Sunday morning, with a public holiday due the next day, traffic was very light. And when we branched off to the right along Ruta 22, there was scarcely any traffic at all. This was the road that would lead us westwards across the southern edge of the pampa to the Argentine lakes and the Andes. The map showed a few small towns dotted along it, but they were too insignificant to feature in the guidebooks. From now on, we were on our own. Our adventure had begun.

There was marsh and swampy grassland as far as the eye could see. To a motorist flashing through, it would all look the same, and it would all seem flat, but there was plenty of colour and variety for the slow cyclist to see: yellow broom, eucalyptus, poplars, amazingly tall purple thistles and the occasional field of purple flax. At first we had seagulls for company, with peewits in the marshes. Then the seabirds left us and the sky was filled with kestrels and heron, birds of prey wheeling on the strong thermals. There were even one or two small rises to add interest to the pedalling. It would all have been so beautiful, had it not been for the wind. Although it dropped slightly through the morning, it remained fickle. Sometimes the air was completely still. Then a sudden buffeting would almost throw us off balance, or give us a harsh slap in the face.

'Why are we cycling from east to west?' groaned Katherine, when she saw a pair of cyclists rushing towards us, winging along with the wind behind them, scarcely turning their pedals.

'Because that would be the sensible, easy direction – not the one that Che Guevara took. We are recreating a historical ride.'

Compared with Alberto and Ernesto, we were travelling quite comfortably. The prevailing wind may have been against us, but at least we had smooth tarmac to ride on, whereas they had to cope with unmetalled tracks over sand dunes. According to its owner, La Ponderosa looked like 'a huge prehistoric animal. On either side were waterproof canvas bags and on the back a rack loaded with everything from a grill for barbecuing meat to a tent and camp beds.' As all this gear was behind the centre of gravity, the front wheel had a nasty tendency to rise up and hurl them off, even in the best of conditions. On the dunes of Medanos, they found themselves sitting in the sand on six occasions before they skidded out of control on a corner and Che's foot was badly bruised, trapped under the cylinder.

Medanos was the first cluster of buildings along our route. We were pulled up at a 'zoological check', and had to shelter from the wind in the lee of the shed while we polished off our big bag of apricots. We were not allowed to take them over into the next district. The two chirpy young men on duty were happy to help us eat up, and the officer in charge brought us glasses of chilled mineral water. The inspection turned into a merry social occasion, as it so often does when on a bicycle.

Argentina and Chile both impose very strict border controls on agricultural produce. They are jealous guardians of their crops and fruit, and especially of their vines. Their vine stock was imported by French immigrants before the disastrous outbreak of phylloxera, which wiped out huge swathes of vineyard in France. The vine stock in South America was safely rooted, protected from infection by the vastness of the Atlantic Ocean, so the vintners there are exceedingly proud of their wines. They are not just fine on the palate. Many of them are produced from ancient vine stocks, which no longer exist in Europe.

Although Medanos was only 50 km from Bahía Blanca, we were both exhausted by the wind. We had done no training and were not in good shape. A little motel stood behind the petrol station. It looked seedy, but it was a port in a storm. The proprietor eyed us suspiciously and told us he was full, which I doubted, as it was only just past noon. I think we were not his usual type of customer and he just didn't want us. However, he directed us to a beautiful hotel, which we had not noticed because it stood back from the road and was screened by trees. There were lawns, a swimming pool, table-tennis tables and even a few exercise bicycles. The shapely blonde owner interrupted her sunbathing to show us round, accompanied by a friendly English sheepdog and a rather less friendly Rottweiler.

As always, at the start of a ride, there was a lot of sorting out to be done. We had finished our first day's cycling, so we had a much clearer idea of what we needed on the road. I'd been comfortable early that morning in a vest, long-sleeved shirt and windproof jacket. By 10 o'clock, I was warm enough to take off the windproof. So the thick jersey I'd kept handy on my rear carrier was obviously surplus to requirements and could safely be packed away. It was, after all, the Argentine summer, even though the weather to date had been less than dazzling. We spent a happy afternoon in our room unpacking and repacking our panniers, to the music of rustling plastic bags. A bird in the trees outside provided the accompaniment, singing 'Three Blind Mice' repeatedly. That evening, as we were the only guests in the hotel and there was no dinner on offer, we went back to the filling station, joining the truckies and their travelling girlfriends for a dish of pasta. We were expecting mince in our spaghetti bolognese, but the pasta arrived with something like half a kilo of prime stewing steak perched on top. Argentina is no country for vegetarians!

The next morning, our hostess recommended a hotel in Algorrobo and rang up to book us a room. We should not have found the place ourselves, because it lay about 5 km off our Ruta 22. By contrast to the first day's torment, the second was one of those days when cycling is sheer bliss. The sun up above, no wind, no hills to climb. Our bicycles seemed to pedal themselves, as we sped along past fields of beautifully groomed horses, fat cattle and tall, thick barley. Argentina is so fertile, it could feed the world. Its topsoil is so rich that it never needs to be rotated, and its meat is superb. We stopped for a drink of water at the fence of a smallholding, and a little white ewe and a brown ram came trotting over to us, hoping for tidbits. We passed a few shacks selling garlic and smoked hams, but there were no other buildings along the road, and very little traffic.

The idyll ended at tea time, when it clouded over and the heavens opened again. There was a petrol station at the Algorrobo junction, with a café behind it, where the burly proprietor was grilling sausages in his vest over an open fire, the traditional Argentine *parrilla* (barbecue). He was surrounded by crawling babies and two little children, old enough to feel important, were laying tables and helping to serve. Katherine and I enjoyed a bottle of beer and some welcome bread and cheese, while we waited in hope for the rain to stop. But it persisted, and night fell as we cycled down a long, dark avenue of trees to Algorrobo village and our beds for the night. Our dinner of parma ham and pasta was provided by a neighbour called Ana in her front room, as our simple hotel didn't do meals.

The next place with accommodation was Rio Colorado on the river of that name. It was 90 km along our road – quite a manageable distance in decent weather conditions. But the notorious Patagonian wind was blowing a westerly gale into our faces and it took us five hours to struggle the first 30 km to Montes de Oca (Goose Mountains). It was marked on the map as a place, but perhaps the name was meant to be a joke, as there was nothing to be seen there. There were no buildings, no signs of human habitation, and not even the smallest pimple of a hill, let alone a range of mountains. The land was basically a continuation of the flat, coastal salt marshes. There were violent showers, which were over as soon as they began. We kept stopping to put on our waterproofs, only to have the sun come out again before we had zipped the last zip. And the sun was so strong that cycling under it in rainproofs was like cycling in a sauna. So off they came again. We were carrying a tent, but the ground was too soggy to contemplate camping, and there was nowhere to buy food. We had no alternative but to turn back. And how we flew! Scarcely needing to turn our pedals, we were blown back all the way to Algorrobo inside an hour. I began to agree with Katherine, that crossing South America from east to west was a strategic error!

29

We couldn't face any more nights in the gloomy Algorrobo hotel, and the weather forecast for the next few days was dire. We decided to move on as fast as we could, but the bus refused to take our bikes and the pick-up trucks we thumbed swept by in the rain. We retreated to the friendly petrol station *parrilla*, to console ourselves with cheese sandwiches and beer, and the boss there suggested the driver of the Bahía Blanca minibus. We tracked him down at his home and persuaded him to make a special journey to Rio Colorado when he'd finished his dinner. The poor man had already done a normal day's work, and now he faced a 90 km drive each way, with the strain of a dazzling pampas sunset in his eyes all the way to Rio Colorado. Wisely, he took a friend for company, as a precaution against dropping asleep on the straight, unlit road home. It also spared both him and us the effort of making conversation at the end of a weary day. In Rio Colorado, he recommended a good hotel, drove us there and waited outside to make sure that there was a room for us. We collapsed onto our comfortable beds with a whisky and the remains of the *parrilla*'s cheese sandwiches, while our friend drove away, highly delighted with his 100 pesos (about £20). He had certainly earned them.

We explored Rio Colorado, pursued by a man in a white van bristling with aerials. He was a reporter, who was trying to persuade us to appear on local television. When we pleaded the inadequacy of our Spanish, he was so insistent that he offered us an interpreter. Then Katherine had a bright idea.

'It's not safe,' she declared. 'If we were to appear on the television, advertising to all and sundry that we were two ladies cycling alone across the pampas, we should be asking for trouble. Anyone could waylay us in the middle of nowhere and rob us. We have to be very cautious.'

The reporter accepted that argument and drove off. We were to use it on a number of occasions later, when we were harassed by the media. Little happens in the sparsely populated centre of Argentina, and Katherine and I, two English ladies of uncertain age arriving in small towns on our bicycles, were a big event. Perhaps it was mean of us to resist. There are, after all, some 150 daily papers and over 40 television stations dotted around the country, so we ought perhaps to have helped them fill their acres of empty column and hours of broadcasting time. But I knew from my experience in Spain, where I had recently done a lecture tour, that being interviewed on television in Spanish, with or without an interpreter, is an exhausting business – and one interview always leads to another. I wanted to save my energies for my cycling. And from a purely materialistic point of view, I doubted if a broadcast on local radio or television in the middle of Argentina would sell a single copy of any of my books. So, selfish or not, we refused all interviews.

Rio Colorado was a spacious town, a holiday resort with parks and lovely hotels, whose lawns stretched down to the river. I cycled in the sunshine to the tourist office, to enquire about our onward route. There was a modern highway running straight as an arrow for 149 km to the next town, Choele Choel. My map showed no settlements along the way and the weather was still too uncertain for rough roadside camping. So my hopes were pinned on the old road, which looped out of town beside the Colorado River, along with the railway line. It was quite a bit longer than the modern highway, but there looked to be five decent-sized villages along it, presumably at railway stations. If we set out along that old road, the ride would take us two or three days, depending on the strength of the wind, but we would have the railway to support us. Failing a guest house, we could probably sleep in the station buildings, and we could pick up food in the villages. We could even jump on a train to Choele Choel, if things went drastically wrong.

But my hopes were dashed. According to the staff in the tourist office, who knew the road well, its tarmac was patchy and poorly maintained, full of potholes and totally unsuited to touring bikes. Not being masochists, we had no choice but to take the bus. In fact, it was quite a relief to be spared that stretch of endless, uninhabited pampa.

Argentina reminded me in many ways of Australia. Both are sparsely populated countries, where elegant cities suddenly turn into wilderness. You walk down a perfectly normal suburban street, with flowers in the gardens and family cars parked by the kerb. The street ends, and you find yourself, without warning, standing in silent emptiness. Hundreds of miles of outback or pampa, unpunctured by a single building, stretch before you to the limit of visibility in three directions. Towns are pinpoints, fragile constructions in the middle of pitiless scrub, vulnerable to the erosion of the elements and the fickleness of history.

There were no towns along the modern cross-country highway to Choele Choel, but at least we were able to speed through the emptiness in the comfort of a coach. Our motorbiking heroes were not so lucky. They had to take the only road in existence at the time, the rough track beside the railway line. They got as far as Pichi Mahuida, the third village shown on my map, where they barbecued some slabs of meat for lunch and rested their jolted limbs in a pine copse beside the river. Then they had carburettor trouble and ran out of petrol. But worse was to come. They spent the night in a grain store at Benjamín Zorrilla railway station, and Che Guevara woke up shivering and vomiting. His first serious attack of asthma on the journey had flared up. The quinine tablets, which usually helped, did nothing for him. His condition worsened, keeping them prisoners all day in the shed. By evening, they realised that Ernesto desperately needed medical help in Choele Choel. Alberto packed up the motorbike and drove it slowly, so as not to rattle his friend, who had a migraine with flashing colours on top of nausea, fever and difficulty in breathing. The nurse at the hospital at first turned them away, telling them they must go and apply to the director for admission. When Alberto pointed out that they were not a couple of tramps – they were a doctor and an 'almost-doctor' – the situation miraculously changed and they were accommodated, like the gentlemen they were, in a comfortable room with a private bath. 'As if having a degree,' adds Alberto piously in his diary, 'made us more sensitive to cold or comforts than two humble workers would have been.' He can never resist the temptation to moralise and air his socialist principles.

Despite all their problems, the two friends were buoyed up by their adventure. When Ernesto's fever broke and he fell into a peaceful sleep, aided by what he referred to as 'a little-known drug: penicillin', Alberto went for a stroll along the Rio Negro.

'I felt happy,' he wrote, 'for nothing makes a person happier than to see his dreams come true. I thought of all those to whom I had confided my plans when they were still fantasies – especially the girls, for whom the trip was their most dreaded rival . . . who were still leading dull lives, but happy to do so. My life had been no different, but I always considered I was marking time. My new life has now begun, and I have no regrets about the old one.'

Che Guevara, younger than his friend, was in more rhapsodic mood: 'We seemed to breathe more freely, a lighter air, an air of adventure. Faraway countries, heroic deeds, beautiful women whirled round and round in our turbulent imaginations. But in tired eyes which nevertheless refused sleep, a pair of green dots representing the world I'd left mocked the freedom I sought, hitching their image to my fantasy flight across the lands and seas of the world.' Chichina was still very much on his mind.

So far, their journey had been more continuous and more eventful than ours, but we hoped for better things beyond Choele Choel. The 250 km of road along the Rio Negro to the provincial capital, Neuquén, was dotted with conurbations large and small, where we guessed there would be plenty of places to stay.

Cyclists' luck! The day we spent sitting in the coach to Choele Choel was cool and utterly still. Not a leaf stirred. But at dawn the next day, a harsh wind from the north-west attacked us like flying knives, while the merciless sun decided that summer had finally arrived. We were still pedalling across the pampa, but we were reaching its outer limits. The grassland was broken now by rows of poplars protecting the occasional vineyard. The local wine was a Tempranillo, which we had sampled the night before in Choele Choel and found to be every bit as delicious as our steaks.

Thinking of Julian and his Darwin project, I had to make the first stop of the morning in the village of that name. In the great days of steam, when both passenger and goods traffic was heavy along its branch line from Bahía Blanca to Neuquén, the Buenos Ayres Great Southern Railway founded Darwin to provide homes for its train drivers and conductors. It was almost exactly halfway between the two cities and was the place where they changed shifts. Once a bustling centre, it stood quiet and forlorn that morning. A handful of grey cement-faced cottages, their windows tightly shuttered, were grouped around the still smart, but deserted, station buildings, where rusty bogeys and bits of old engines cluttered up the sidings. The only sign that the village had once been home to so many people was the hedges and stands of trees, grown tall over the years. It was the cypresses that I first noticed as we pedalled towards Darwin along the highway, sentinels of a past life on the edge of the featureless pampa.

At a roadside stall, we stopped for a chat and a kilo bag of shelled walnuts, which cost next to nothing. The aged vendor lurked behind his pyramid of honey jars.

'Churchill passed through here on his way to Chile, when he was young,' he announced. Then he added proudly, 'Chimpay is a famous place, you know. It's the "Cradle of Cerefino". Millions come here on pilgrimage. He helped the poor Indians and died in Rome, but they brought his remains back home and they work miracles.'

Pictures of Cerefino were plastered all over the place, on roadside hoardings and café walls. A South American Indian, he looked more like an accountant or a village schoolmaster than my idea of a saint, in his neat suit, tie and spectacles. But I suppose modern saints have to wear modern clothes. The recently canonised can hardly go around dressed like St Francis of Assisi.

The day became sultry and oppressive, with distant thunder. The one motel in Chimpay was locked up and deserted, but we managed to get into the garden and took refuge from the heat in the cool, tiled arcade. The owner came back late in the afternoon, as the filling station attendants had assured us she would. She was a welcoming, talkative woman, so we soon knew her life history.

'My parents migrated from Chile to Argentina, two years before I was born. You've no idea how rich Argentina was then! It was a magnet, and people came flocking from all over South America and Europe to find work here. Now it's the other way round. People queue at the visa offices to leave. But I was born here and my life's in Chimpay. I'm an Argentinian. I shall stay here. I shan't go back to Chile, though I still have family there. I just hope that better times are round the corner.'

In the local café that evening, a rheumy old man came over to join us and rhapsodised about Cerefino, regaling us with astonishing tales of his miracles. Then, as a parting shot, he smiled sadly and said, 'When you get back to London, tell them to give us the Malvinas.'

The Argentines were still smarting over their defeat in the Falklands, and every town and village had its war memorial, often with '*Volveremos!*' (We shall return!) carved below the list of the fallen. But no one ever showed us any personal animosity. The war was viewed rather as an unfortunate conflict between friends.

Part of the fun of cycle travel is that you never know where you will be sleeping from one night to the next. In Chimpay, we had a lovely room in a modern motel. The next night, we found ourselves in a roadside *hospedaje*, which was a totally different experience.

Hospedajes (lodgings) are the bottom rung of the accommodation ladder. Ours was a truck-drivers hangout with such dire, ant-infested facilities, that I preferred the privacy of the nearby bushes. Our bedroom was a black hole, with a yellow frosted-glass window and one pathetic little wall light. The earth floor had a sheen, like the floors of polished cow dung in rural India, and there was one single bed and two pairs of bunks. The only decoration on the dingy distempered walls was a pair of bull's horns, sticking out above one of the top bunks, at just the right height for poking an eye out.

But the front of the *hospedaje* was a well-patronised restaurant, with a vine-covered verandah, where Katherine and I spent a peaceful afternoon. Katherine embroidered, while I caught up on my notes and read. The restaurant was the social centre of the village and the only stop on the road between Chimpay and Villa Regina, so there was plenty of interesting activity to watch. An all-purpose tub of water stood out at the front for general use. First, a perspiring lorry driver submerged his greasy head in it. Then a puppy was lifted up to drink out of it. A shirt was rinsed in it. And then passing motorists filled their drinking bottles from it!

The owners of the *hospedaje* were obese to the point of danger. I thought of the French restaurant notice: '*LE PATRON MANGE ICI.*' The fattest was the young girl who seemed to be in charge. She worked with tremendous energy for one her size, bossing her two huge brothers around. One did his best, but found many jobs beyond him, as he had a withered arm. The other poor young man seemed mentally challenged. He tried hard, but his sister had to explain everything to him twenty times over, even simple tasks like wiping the table and setting out clean cutlery. But the food was excellent.

We slept surprisingly well in our hovel, perhaps helped by rather too much rough, local red wine at dinner, and tackled the long ascent from the *hospedaje* with vigour. We climbed to a high plateau, where raindrops the size of penny pieces began to stain the asphalt. The early morning blue with wisps of feathery cloud was behind us, and forked lightning tore the bruise-black sky ahead. A fierce wind whipped up the storm, but we were lucky. Once we had freewheeled down to Chinchales, the landscape changed. Apple orchards, sheltered by rows of poplars, lined the road and shielded us from the worst of the weather. On the outskirts of Villa Regina, the Sunday streets were deserted and we had no plan of the town, so we hailed a man in a passing pick-up truck. He guided us through the rain to an old-fashioned hotel, where my first hot bath for a fortnight (as distinct from showers) made a new woman of me. My only memories of that unmemorable stopping place are that bath and a most fantastic bitter cherry and almond ice cream. The Italian immigrants brought their skill and their recipes with them, so the ice creams of Argentina are a serious temptation, even to a non-ice-cream-eater like myself.

We had finally finished with the pampa and entered a smiling landscape of vineyards and orchards. For two days, we bowled along in the shelter of the apple trees, cycling easily in top gear for the first time on the ride. The contrary winds had strengthened our legs and we had found our form. Just before Cipoletti, we met cycle paths that were quite separate from the road and provided a welcome refuge from the convoys of thundering fruit trucks. We entered Neuquén in style, looking forward to our first rest day since Buenos Aires and our first real opportunity for people-watching.

I had decided that Argentina was just about the world's most macho country, where men saw themselves as gauchos, independent spirits herding a million head of cattle across the wind-swept pampas in their baggy *bombachas*. Breakfast in the hotel did nothing to change my view. The fruit salad and yogurt were kept in a glass-fronted refrigerator. The businessmen helped themselves, then swaggered back to their tables, mobile phones stuck in their belts, without bothering to close the fridge door. That was a job for the maids. Then a family came into the restaurant. The husband and teenaged son immediately sat down, while the wife rushed back and forth like a waitress, serving them both from the buffet table. The South American writer, Isabel Allende, says that, despite progress in education and enhanced career prospects for women, daughters are still brought up to serve and sons to be served. Girls may be modern, but the minute they fall in love, they repeat the age-old pattern, waiting on their boyfriends 'as if they were invalids'.

Compared with much of South America, Argentina is an advanced country, where women work hard, making a valuable contribution to the economy. Yet though they may be lawyers, teachers, architects and computer experts, I noticed that they were still represented on television as feather-brains, interested only in shopping, hairdressers and spending their husbands' money. Both sexes live in a sort of dream society, which touches on reality only tangentially. I read some remarks by the owner of a matrimonial agency, whose business thrives on South America's highest divorce rate. 'Argentines don't know how to form proper relationships. The men always want someone young and beautiful. The women all want money. Nobody's realistic.' But an obsession with money, either earned or provided by a husband, seems to me to be a perfectly realistic response to the country's financial collapse. The women of Argentina may perhaps be more astute than she gives them credit for.

Katherine and I travel well together, because we go out separately some of the time, to give each other space – essential on a long journey. I spent a pleasant solitary morning in Neuquén, sending emails, doing my laundry and visiting the cathedral, a modern building of rough, mellow brick both inside and out. The mortar was so deeply recessed in the walls that the bricks stood out proud like knobbly knitting, in a sort of moss stitch. Even the nave columns were built of brick, laid in an interesting cruciform pattern. In the afternoon I went rather reluctantly, out of a sense of duty, to the local museum. The European paintings were as dull as I had feared, but the local Argentine work, though of no particular artistic merit, did give a fascinating insight into the country's great pioneering days. And the brutal portrait of Charles II of Spain, with his great chin, bulbous lips and pop eyes, showed quite clearly why the inbred House of Habsburg had to fall. He died prematurely senile and childless, embroiling Europe in the War of Spanish Succession between France and Austria. The French were victorious and a grandson of the Bourbon Louis XIV ascended the throne of Spain as Philip V in 1700.

West of Neuquén and Plottier, there were great sandstone cliffs to our right, and we were back in scrubby country, though there were meadows sheltered by lines of poplar trees where the Rio Negro neared the road. Estancias offering equitation, fishing and tennis took over from fruit orchards and we lost the juggernauts which had terrified us on the way into Neuquén. We surprised a flock of black vultures feasting on a run-over fox. They glared at us, daring us to disturb them, but gave in at the last moment and hopped clumsily out of the way, dragging scraps of entrail in their greedy beaks. Scavengers are an essential part of nature, but they do lack charm.

As the morning heated up, we spotted a wooden shack, half hidden in bushes. It was a basic shop, where we bought a two-litre bottle of warmish local cola (less fizzy than Coke or Pepsi) and collapsed into two of the chairs set out under protective fly netting. We had been served in the shop by a young woman. Now an old man came bustling out, hugged us and kissed us on both cheeks, to our great surprise. He then produced a small kettle, cups and saucers, sugar and a new, unopened jar of Virginia Suelto, smooth instant coffee. It tasted of nothing, but it was welcome all the same. We were joined by his wife and small granddaughter.

'We used to live in Bahía Blanca, but we came out here fourteen years ago.'

'Why did you move?'

'Because it's so beautiful here,' he replied. 'Just look at it!'

He gazed around in fond admiration, beaming at his rickety shack and the muddy, clogged-up stream which trickled through his bushes. It could have been a really attractive site, given a bit of clearing up and landscaping. A retired English couple would be out there, busily pruning and planting, and in no time at all there would be lawn running down to a sparkling stream, flowers in profusion and goldfish in a pond. But the two old Argentines were delighted with it, just as it was, in all its dusty, litter-strewn tangle. For them, peace and quiet, and the hospitality they were able to offer us, were pleasure enough. So why struggle? They would take no money for the coffee and they both kissed us warmly when we left and came up to the road to wave us off. We ended a perfect morning in Arroyito, in a garden motel shaded with vines.

In the evening, another terrific storm broke. Our small motel and petrol station stood isolated in the vast surrounding emptiness, the only target for the forked lightning which tore across the wide skies; and a tornado from the south-west, sweeping the rain horizontally in its path, shook the doors and windows with such force that I thought they would cave in. The poor Alsatian guard dog was locked outside and barked in terror, while cicadas, clattering like demented castanets, took refuge in our bedroom. We had to run around catching them in a tooth mug and evicting them onto the verandah before we could go to sleep.

By morning, the rain had cleared, the sky was blue and cloudless, but it was still blowing a gale. At Arroyito, Route 22, which we had followed almost the whole way from Bahía Blanca, forked off to the right towards Zapala, while we turned left down Route 237 to San Carlos de Bariloche – south-west into the very teeth of the wind. The road ahead seemed to stretch to infinity, a single strip of black tarmac with a rough gravel hard shoulder. It ran straight as an arrow through red mountainous desert, where there was not a single tree to give shade. The sun beat down, and the wind whipped burning sand into our eyes and mouths. On our first descent, we managed just 7 kph, and that was pedalling!

There were 400 km of this barren moonscape before we reached Bariloche, and we knew that the road would soon begin to climb into the foothills of the Andes. The first time I cycled round the world, I was determined to cycle every inch of the way, just to prove that I could do it. In this kind of situation, I would have persevered against all the odds, even if it killed me. Then, on my second circuit of the globe, when I crossed the Gobi Desert where the winds are notorious, I learned how stupid it is to fight them. If I waited a few days, I could cover the distance to the next oasis in a quarter of the time, with one tenth of the effort. Had I been alone in

Argentina, I would probably have waited. I would have gone back to the motel and spent a profitable few days tidying up my notes. But forcing a companion, who needed to be home by Christmas, to hang around indefinitely with little to do was not really an option. So 10 km along Route 237, I decided that the bus to Bariloche was the only way forward. In terms of endurance, I had nothing left to prove, not even to myself. I knew that I could manage the 400 km ordeal, if I put my mind to it. But life is short, so why punish myself and Katherine? Having agreed the decision, we turned our bikes with relief and flew back along the road to the bus station in Plottier, just short of Neuquén.

We were hauling a tent around Argentina and seemed destined never to use it – which was just as well, because there was nowhere to hide a camp in the treeless, bushless aridity of the road to Bariloche. But what fun it would be to cycle that route the other way, down the mountains, with the wind behind me! I could whizz from one *hospedaje* to the next, free of the tent and all its discomforts. It would be real cycle-sailing, with no need even to turn the pedals. A trip to be savoured in the future?

Travelling with our bicycles in Argentina had been wonderfully hassle free to date, so we were surprised to meet problems in Plottier. The station officials insisted on removing the wheels and strapping them to the frames before they would load the bikes in the baggage hold of the Bariloche bus. Then there were seating problems. Katherine and I had booked late, so we had to sit separately. I had been allocated a window seat and was looking forward to a good view of the passing landscape, but there was a young man sitting in my place. I summoned the conductor to complain. 'But he has to have the window seat,' said the conductor, 'because he's blind.' It was difficult to make any retort, when the poor young man was sitting within earshot, but I did wonder by what reversal of logic it could be necessary for a blind man to sit next to a window! However, I made no fuss and sat down obediently in my aisle seat.

I was rather sorry not to be cycling that challenging route. The bleakest stretch was the bit we had attempted, at the Arroyito end. After that, we skirted the stunning blue expanse of the Ezequiel Ramos Mexia dam, through an area rich in dinosaur fossils. My guidebook described the amazingly well-preserved dinosaur footprints near the water's edge and the virtually complete skeleton of a *Giganotosaurus Carolinii* in the museum at Villa El Chocon. This was the world's most gigantic carnivore, at 14 m long and 4.7 m tall, even huger than the fearsome North American *Tyrannosaurus rex*. Unfortunately, the nearest we came to these marvels in the bus was a large wooden cut-out of a dinosaur beside the road with CUIDADO DINOSAURS! (Beware of dinosaurs!) written on it.

Picún Leufú, at the end of the great dam, had a *hospedaje*. After that, the red, rocky landscape was empty again, with climbs that became longer and far more serious. The highway followed the course of the Rio Limay, which provided glimpses of green in the far distance, but along the road itself, trees were such rarities that I made a note of every single one of them as we passed, for future reference. 'Km 1410. Clump of trees behind rickety fence. Km 1416. Poplars on both sides of road. Km 1478. Roadside shrine with one poplar.'

Shortly after Piedra del Aguila, we had our first view of the Andean snowcaps, before the bus swept us down to another vivid blue dam. There were two or three small areas of mountainside where attempts had been made at afforestation, and we actually passed a trout farm shaded by trees on the Rio Limay Chico. But the overwhelming impression of the landscape was one of mountainous desolation. Near Confluencia, which seemed to be a holiday resort, there were weird rock formations, like jagged chimneys rising from the red desert sand. Then the road entered the Nahuel Huapi National Park, which surrounds Bariloche, and we were out of the desert and into dappled shade. We had arrived in Hansel and Gretel country.

3. OVER THE ANDES

Up in the mountains, at a place called Casa Pangue, is a vantage point from which you get a panoramic view over Chile. It's a sort of crossroads; at least it was for me at that particular moment. I was looking to the future, up the narrow strip of Chile and what lay beyond.

(Ernesto Che Guevara)

Bariloche, Argentina's ritziest resort, owes its present size and importance to the Germanic settlers, who crossed the Andes from Chile in the early twentieth century. They brought with them the folksy architecture of German fairy tales – gingerbread houses and hotels with fretted timber gables straight out of the Tyrol or the Black Forest. They brought their partiality for solid German food, for wild boar, venison and pork, all served with lots of potatoes, and their sumptuous cakes, which are still known locally by their German name of *Kuchen*. They even brought, and continue to use to this day, the Gothic script which was abandoned in their German homeland years ago. The city's hotels may refer to themselves as *hosterias* and have Spanish names, but their signs are up in Gothic and they are essentially German establishments, with scrubbed pine, big breakfasts of ham, cheese and cake, and a general air of *gemütlichkeit*. It would be no surprise at all to see the Seven Dwarfs emerging from their fancy fretwork porches, or Little Red Riding Hood setting out for her grandmother's cottage, tripping through the ranks of garden gnomes with her basket of provisions over her arm.

The superbly situated civic centre, on a mountain-ringed hillside overlooking Lake Nahuel Huapi, continues the Germanic theme. The grey-green stone of this engaging ensemble of buildings is local, but the wooden balconies and shutters and the steeply pitched gables are pure Alpine. The only truly Argentine feature is the equestrian statue of General Julio Roca, whose army swept through the country's southern territories in 1879, killing thousands of Mapuche and Tehuelche and subjugating the rest. This 'Campaign of the Desert' opened up Patagonia to European settlement, for which the grateful Argentines elected General Roca president in 1880. It also resulted in a nation that is predominantly of white European stock. In most other parts of South America, there has been an intermingling of the races, so that the *mestizo* (person of mixed race) is in the majority. But the violence of Argentina's early days left few of the indigenous people alive and created a tension between the races which has never been resolved. They are oil and water, moving through the same landscape with little interaction.

Like the European Alpine resorts, Bariloche prospers on two distinct tourist seasons. There is winter skiing on Cerro Catedral; while in the summer, when we were there, the town was seething with climbers, trekkers and fishermen, setting off into the wild beauty of the cordillera and the national forests. Outdoor shops dominated the main streets, rivalled in number only by megastores with fantastic displays of chocolate, for this little piece of Central Europe set down in the Argentine Andes is the chocolate capital of South America, if not of the world. Chocoholics are in paradise here, dreaming their chocolate dreams in front of the windows of Fenoglio's, Mamuschka or La Mexicana. Dark, milk, white and orange chocolate in bars, logs, eggs and rabbits, pralines, fudges, hazlenuts, creams and liqueurs, whole supermarkets bursting with chocolate temptations.

Che Guevara and Alberto Granado passed through Bariloche on their way to Chile, but, having their own transport, they reached it by the Seven Lakes Route, which is far more picturesque than the highway Katherine and I travelled in our bus. They followed the same route from Nequén as we did through Piedra del Aguila as far as the Rio Collon Cura. What was then a swiftly flowing stream, which they had to cross on a cable ferry, is now the main feeder to the Piedra del Aguila dam, which we crossed by a spectacular road bridge. At this point, they turned right and began to climb steeply up to Junín de los Andes and San Martín de los Andes, now a popular holiday resort on the sky-blue tongue of water which is Lake Lacar. Here they sat on the lake side, drinking *maté* and dreaming of founding a medical research institute. Remote from civilisation, they would live in the densely wooded mountains, fishing to their hearts' content and solving their supply problems with a helicopter.

The Seven Lakes Route runs from San Martín through the Nahuel Huapi National Park to Villa la Angostura on the northern edge of Lake Nahuel Huapi itself, which it then skirts to reach Bariloche. To see where the motorbikers had travelled, Katherine and I took a Sunday excursion. It was a day of constantly changing mountain weather, one moment blazing hot, the next drizzly, and the next overcast with a chill wind; each lake was a different colour under the variable sky. We caught Lago Escondido (Hidden Lake) in its startling emerald green glory, but the other six lakes were disappointingly grey, ruffled by sudden squalls. We stopped in San Martín for lunch, and found another Hansel and Gretel village, full of timber-gabled nick-nack shops selling witches, gonks and hand-crafted wooden jigsaw puzzles, all so Tyrolean that it was almost a parody of itself. Then on through banks of yellow broom, orange calafate, pink and purple lupins and red bottlebrush shrubs, to the Valle Encantando (Enchanting

Valley) with its strange basalt columns. Then back to Bariloche.

We felt justified in taking the bus, rather than following that route on our bicycles, because La Ponderosa II was beginning to give serious trouble, necessitating lifts and side trips. As far back as Bahía Blanca, the rear brake had failed and the bikers were facing the prospect of crossing the mighty Andes, relying on gear change alone to slow them down. Then, on the approach to Piedra del Aguila, the handlebars snapped off from the frame and they had to fasten them on with wire before pushing the bike 20 km into town to get the frame welded. Compared with these major problems, the broken chain and the spate of punctures on the sand and gravel roads to Bariloche were mere trifles.

The ferocious Patagonian winds and the lack of accommodation along the road had deterred Katherine and me from cycling to Bariloche. It was an easier route on a motorbike, because an engine can cover the ground faster, but it was no pleasure trip. Some nights there was such a hurricane blowing that it was impossible to pitch the tent, and our heroes had to tie their motorbike to a telegraph pole, cover it with the tent canvas and shelter behind it. Of course, being men in a macho society and Argentines with good Spanish, they could do what two ladies would find difficult – march up to a labourer's hut or a police station and beg beds inside. They used their 'broken headlamp trick' to give them an excuse as night fell. In fact, they were mean cadgers, and proud of it. As Che Guevara boasted, 'We aren't all that broke, but explorers of our stature would rather die than pay for the bourgeois comfort of a hotel.'

Despite the concern for the poor which they both express in their diaries, they had no compunction at all about spongeing on labourers and helping to eat their meagre rations. Their worst night was the night of the broken handlebars, when they had to sleep in the garage grease pit. But they sometimes slept in style and fished for rainbow trout on the estancias of Che Guevara's family friends, such as the Von Putnamers. Alberto calls them the Von Puttkamers and says they were Nazis, living in 'an imitation Black Forest structure', who escaped to Patagonia after the Second World War – which the family denies, claiming that they settled long ago. Ernesto was not at all interested in their background. He cared far more for the hospitality they might offer and for his medicine. He simply wrote to his mother that they were 'friends of Jorge's, especially the Peronist one who's always drunk and the best of the three. I diagnosed a tumour in the occipital zone probably of hydatic origin.' He looked at the world as a kind-hearted young doctor would, sympathetic in a general way towards the sick and the poor. Colonel Juan Peron was the all-powerful nationalist president, who bestrode Argentina from 1946–55. The Guevara family of left-wing intellectuals were bitterly opposed to his style of authoritarian rule. Yet a slight tangential remark is the only mention in Ernesto's diary of this towering figure. While Alberto fumes about the exploited underclass, the victims of an unjust socio-economic system, Ernesto, the future revolutionary, seems as yet politically unaware.

In a letter to his father, he tries to put his philosophy of travel into words. 'I do not cultivate the same tastes as tourists – the Altar of the Fatherland, the cathedral, the gem of a pulpit, the miraculous little Virgin, the Hall of the Revolution. This is no way to learn about a people, its manner of living or interpretation of life . . . its soul is reflected in the hospital-bound sick, the prison inmates, the anxious pedestrian one talks with, watching the Rio Grande's turbulent flow at one's feet.'

Nor is he much concerned with landscape. His descriptions are rare and perfunctory. Of the Seven Lakes Route, he writes simply: 'We set off again along lakes of different sizes surrounded by ancient forests, the scents of nature caressing our nostrils. But strangely enough, the sight of a lake, wood, lone house with neat garden soon begins to pall.' Ernesto's diary is crammed with adventures, the people he meets, their health problems, the meals he enjoyed (or lack of them), the places he spent the night. It is the compassionate young backpacker's approach to travel, but viewed in his case through the lens of the medic.

Being a town mouse myself, I sympathise with his lack of rapture over landscape. When the magnificent Andean lakes have been described so lyrically, so often, and painted with such artistry, what is there to add? Countryside that is 'unspoilt' in the view of the Romantics, is to me just raw material, like clay waiting to be formed by the potter's art. I like to see the hand of man – his ordering of the landscape into fields and orchards, his gardens and his buildings. It is not the land which moves me, but the human beings who have shaped it against the odds, struggling across deserts and mountain ranges in bitter weather to awaken the land out of its unproductive disorder and establish better lives for themselves and their children. Unlike Che, I love prowling round churches and museums. But it is the courage and skill of the pioneers that stirs me the most. Men, women and their works are a greater inspiration to me than any number of snow-capped peaks or turquoise lakes.

Alberto tried harder with landscape, but food was more often on his mind. One entry in his diary particularly amuses me: 'We met a couple from New Jersey in their sixties who have driven here from the United States in a station wagon. Although the vehicle is well kitted out, it's still admirable that they should have the spirit and energy to undertake such a journey at their age.' How times and the perceptions of pensioners have changed! Unfortunately, the Americans failed to turn up that evening, so 'Pelao and I returned sad and hungry to the police station, where the prisoners were just being fed.' Another free meal.

('Pelao', I'm told, is slang for 'skint'.)

After a few days' rest and relaxation in Bariloche, we were ready to cycle across the Andes, which fortunately get lower as they curve south. The Perez Rosales Pass into Chile is a mere 1022 m (3350 ft) – and most of the journey is by catamaran.

We were taking the spectacular Three Lakes Crossing, which involved cruises across Lago Nahuel Huapi, Lago Frias and Lago Todos Los Santos (also known as Lago Esmeralda), with stretches of unpaved road between. As it was national parkland, no cars were allowed, but for travellers without bikes, there was one daily series of connecting buses in each direction. A profitable monopoly for Catedral Turismo, who organised the package!

The whereabouts of the Perez Rosales Pass was kept secret for centuries by the Poya, Vuriloche, Puelche and Pehuelche, Bariloche's indigenous peoples. Their livelihood was the lakes, and they used the pass to trade with the Mapuche in the west. The Spaniards reached southern Chile long before they gained access to southern Argentina, and the quest for routes through the Andes became an obsession with them, especially as they believed that the fabled wealth of the City of the Caesars lay somewhere to the east of the mountains. Search parties were massacred and tentative Jesuit missions sacked before the Three Lakes Crossing, which is known to trekkers by the alternative name of The Route of the Jesuits, was finally discovered, mapped and cleared of hostile locals. By the beginning of the twentieth century, the way was safe for all those Germans to cross from southern Chile into Bariloche and build their Black Forest houses.

We bought our tickets in advance for Wednesday, but cycled out of Bariloche on Tuesday, as the catamaran across Lago Nahuel Huapi was due to sail out of Puerto Panuelo at 9 a.m., and Puerto Panuelo was 25 km along the lakeside. We hate early starts with no breakfast!

As soon as we left the shelter of Bariloche's buildings, the wind struck us a deadly blow. Then it began to rain, which intensified to torrents, and cloud crept down to swathe the mountains in coats of grey wool. We were thinking of treating ourselves to a night in the Llao Llao, Argentina's most famous hotel, but when visibility was nil, it seemed a waste to pay a fortune for a view, so we gave up the struggle just short of the port and scuttled into the shelter of the brand-new Gran

Panamericano. It was a huge hotel, largely empty, so the staff were delighted to have two drowning guests to cosset. They were all sophisticates from Buenos Aires, Bahía Blanca and Mar del Plato, and all spoke excellent English, including Sergio, the hall porter, who was particularly keen to ensure our comfort. His sister had married an Englishman who had a job in Barcelona and he was saving up to visit them.

I have done the Three Lakes Crossing twice. The first time, I did it by boat and bus – and it was a perfect day. When Katherine and I did it on our bikes, the weather was, of course, abysmal. Cyclists' luck again! It was not actually raining when we sailed out of Puerto Panuelo, but Lake Nahuel Huapi, which the guidebooks describe as deep blue, was grey and frothy in the wind, while the lakeside mountains were virtually lost in the rain clouds. Peering through the mist, we just managed to catch a glimpse of the tomb of Vicente Perez Rosales, the founder of the national park, on a lakeside cliff. The captain turned off the engine and sounded the catamaran's horn in homage as we drifted slowly by.

We were all decanted in tiny Puerto Blest. While the other passengers scrambled around the boat, searching frantically for their luggage to transfer it to the waiting coach, Katherine and I pedalled off in a leisurely fashion to cover the 6 km to Puerto Alegre. It was a beautiful traffic-free ride through the woods and we arrived at the jetty on Lago Frias long before the bus passengers. The sun came out briefly while we waited for them, and the waters of the lake gleamed a perfect peppermint green. To add to the pleasure of the moment, our next catamaran was named *El Condor*, just like my bicycle.

Lago Frias is a pocket-sized lake and it took *El Condor* only twenty minutes to steam across to Puerto Frias, scarcely time for us to relax and brace ourselves for the toughest part of the journey, the 27 km track over the Paso de Perez Rosales into Chile. But twenty minutes was long enough for the weather to turn sour on us again. Thick clouds dropped down from nowhere and hid the majestic snow-capped peak of the giant Mount Tronador, which I had seen standing magnificent against the cloudless blue sky on my previous crossing. I was sorry that Katherine was missing so much natural beauty.

We set off along the unpaved road at around 2.30. Our ascent was short and steep, just 5 km to climb from Lago Frias at 762 m up to the Pass at 1022 m. We managed to cycle about a quarter of the distance, but then we had to get off and push, which was scarcely any easier. It wasn't actually raining, but recent downpours had turned the track into a sea of mud – really sticky going for bicycles weighed down with heavy panniers. Our wheels sank at times almost to the height of the pedals, as we squelched and slid along in our trainers. Truckfuls of stones had been chucked down on bends in the road and into the deep tyre ruts. They were no doubt of some assistance to the bus drivers on skiddy corners, but the stones were so big and jagged, so painful to the feet, that even the mud was preferable.

At the summit, we entered Chile, thinking that the way down from the pass would be easier than the way up. We were mistaken. It was a fiendish descent, as the stones and mud would have challenged hardened mountain bikers, which we were not. Except for short distances, we found it impossible to cycle on our tourers; and when we walked, we struggled to control our heavily panniered machines, which wanted to scamper down like runaway colts. I took one nasty tumble, when I was cycling along what looked like a reasonable bit of track and the stones skidded out from under my wheels down the steep camber. A particularly sharp piece of rock gouged a long furrow in my left leg, a patch of gravel did for my left elbow, and I knew that both legs would be badly bruised. Dripping blood, I persevered on foot down the precipitous path, as did Katherine, who has a dodgy knee at the best of times. We had to go on, as there was no alternative, but we were utterly exhausted when we finally arrived in Peulla. It had taken us six hours to cover the 27 km between Lago Frias and Lago Todos Los Santos. Given a decent strip of tarmac, the sharp drop down from the 1022 m Perez Rosales Pass to Peulla at 150 m would have been a breeze, a glorious swoop through the forest trees to the glistening lake below. But in wretched weather, on a rocky, muddy track, it was a nightmare. 'Unspoilt' landscape? You can keep it!

I'm not usually an advance booker, preferring to take pot luck when I reach my destination. Women travelling alone are always looked after and, failing a hotel, the locals will always find you some sort of accommodation. In fact, the more difficult the situation, the more enriching the experience often is. With efficient forward planning, I would never have found myself spending the night in old ladies' spare rooms, seven-in-a-bed with Tajik nomads, in Chinese army barracks, pilgrim dormitories, or sleeping on a waiting-room table with Indian railway passengers for company. Yet these are the stuff of real travel. Leaving things to chance and trusting people is the way to find out what life in a country is really like. But I knew Peulla would be different, as the spot on the map was basically a landing stage and one hotel, which was usually full of bus and boat passengers. Little prospect of serendipitous encounters there. So guessing that we would be arriving late, I had telephoned from Bariloche and made a provident booking for once.

But before we could sample the delights of our monopolistically expensive hotel, we had to clear Chilean customs and immigration. The first hut we came to on the path into Peulla housed the Chilean customs. They had closed down for the night, but an official came yawning out when we knocked and shouted, and simply waved us through into Chile. Then we pushed our bikes along to the police block. This too had shut down, but I tapped on the back window, where there was a light. A man in shirtsleeves and slacks opened the window and told us to go round to the front of the building and wait. Five minutes later, the same man opened the front door, dressed this time in immaculate police uniform, cap, boots and all, with a '*Detectivo*' badge on his breast pocket. It was like a scene from a Feydeau farce, with the same characters popping in and out of different doors in different outfits. He was a bit fazed because customs had let us through without an official declaration form, and he wanted to send us back there. I explained that this would be a waste of time, as the officer had let us through, then firmly shut up his shop. In any case, we were carrying nothing edible (the Chileans are quite obsessive about this and ban the importation of any foodstuff whatsoever, even a wrapped, unopened bar of chocolate) and we were poor lady cyclists, who could not conceivably be into contraband or illicit piles of money. The detective hesitated, as the Chileans are efficient people who like to work by the book. But we looked so bedraggled that compassion finally conquered. He stamped our passports and let us through, officially, into Chile.

We were almost too tired to eat our dinner, but the hot bath afterwards was paradise, soothing my grazed and weary limbs. Just after breakfast, a young forest ranger came to the hotel, looking for the two lady cyclists he had heard about. He had found a rear reflector on the mountain pass and guessed it belonged to one of us. It was mine and he helped me to fix it back on again. It must have been knocked off when I took my tumble.

We had a day's leisure in Peulla, waiting for that morning's bus from Bariloche to catch up with us. It was a welcome rest after Wednesday's ordeal on the pass. In the morning sunshine, we saw Lago Todos Los Santos, or Lago Esmeralda, in all its gorgeous greenery, though it didn't look particularly emerald to me. It seemed to be almost the same milky peppermint green as Lago Frias, but not quite. The lakes of southern Argentina and Chile, when they are not a uniform grey under storm clouds, are amazing in colour – indigo, cobalt, sky blue, turquoise, emerald and peppermint – each one a slightly different tone, depending on the glacial sediment or algae in their waters.

The sun was still shining when we sailed out of Peulla at 4 p.m., but the lake clouded over almost immediately, obscuring the famous view of Volcán Osorno, the most perfect volcanic cone in Chile, possibly in the world. Only Mount Fuji in Japan comes anywhere near it in graceful snow-capped symmetry.

By the time we reached Petrohue, two hours later, it was raining cats and dogs. The road out of the village was surfaced in fine black grit, the same volcanic ash as the lake shores. Despite the stone bed underneath, we skidded precariously on our narrow tyres, just managing to stay upright and in the saddle. There were 7 km of this anguish before we reached tarmac near the Petrohue waterfalls, which we were too wet and fed up to contemplate visiting. In Ensenada on the eastern shore of Lago Llanquihue, we found a blissful wood-burning stove in the hotel dining room, where we crouched over the blaze, reviving whiskies in hand. Things could have been worse. We were soaked to the skin ourselves, but the plastic bags in our panniers had kept the contents dry, so we had warm changes of clothing. And the receptionist brought an oil heater and some extra chairs and coathangers up to our bedroom, so that we could spread our dripping outer garments over the furniture and dry them off. It was a quaint hotel, full of domestic and sporting antiques like old blackleaded stoves, collections of irons, sewing machines and ski boots. They had even planted an old aircraft propeller and a ship's funnel as garden features on the front lawn. It had not been an easy journey, but we had chanced on a warm and interesting shelter from the storm.

Our crossing into Chile may have been uncomfortable, but Che and Alberto had an even worse time of it. Che, in particular, was in a desolate state of mind. He had just received a letter from Chichina, breaking off their engagement. 'We were in the kitchen of the police station, sheltering from the storm unleashing its fury outside. I read and re-read the incredible letter. Suddenly all my dreams of home, bound up with the eyes that saw me off in Miramar, were shattered, apparently for no good reason. An enormous weariness came over me . . .' Chichina's parents had never approved of Ernesto Guevara and it seems that Chichina had finally yielded to family pressure and given him up.

Heaving La Ponderosa II onto the launch across Lago Nahuel Huapi and off again in Puerto Blest was extremely hard work, and was followed by similar titanic struggles for the short crossing of Lago Frias, which Ernesto describes as 'a dirty green'. But their ride over the pass was uneventful and by the time they reached Peulla, Che felt that he had reached a sort of crossroads, both physical and psychological. He was beginning to come to terms with being jilted and starting to look forward to the future again, 'up the narrow strip of Chile and what lay beyond'. He was also picking up medical contacts. There was no leprosy, Alberto's special interest, in Chile, so the Chilean doctors they met on their journey were fascinated by their experience of the disease. They gave them introductions to specialists connected with leper colonies on Easter Island and up the Amazon, which they were to find extremely useful later.

Alberto, who had no romantic problems to contend with, was as usual concentrating on socio-political matters. He contrasts the beauty of the landscape and the kindness of the people with the sordidness of the exploitation to which they were subjected by the company owning the hotel, the coaches and the launches, the only source of jobs in the area and the only provision for tourists. Determined not to add revenue to such a sinfully capitalist concern, he and Ernesto chatted up the watchman on Peulla quay and persuaded him to let them sleep in a shed full of sails and tar-covered ropes. Then, 'in line with our policy of not paying for anything if we can help it', they managed to get a job on a boat crossing the lake with a cargo of timber and a car.

It was a rickety contraption, towed along by the steamer *Esmeralda*, which was carrying the tourists. They were scarcely under way before it started to dip at the bow, and they had to redistribute the cargo and transfer some of it to the steamer. Even so, water still came pouring in. The pump was ineffective, so, stripped to the waist and covered in oil, they spent the crossing baling out the bilge with buckets.

But Lago Todos Los Santos was warm enough to bathe in, so they spruced themselves up in Petrohue and picked up a bevy of Brazilian girls. Che is possibly still too upset over

Chichina to take advantage of the situation – or perhaps he is just more reticent about his conquests than his friend. But Alberto found a fellow-scientist among them and, after discussing biochemistry for a time, he says coyly that they went on to 'topographical anatomy'. He concludes with a typical young medic's joke: 'I hope I didn't get as far as embryology.'

4. THE CHILEAN LAKE DISTRICT

You have to be thin to be a Chileno. Otherwise you fall off.

(John Gunther, *Inside South America*)

'Don't be such a wimp! You're an intelligent woman and you've got two good legs, so why don't you just go?'

I was sitting under an awning outside a café on the waterfront of Lake Llanquihue in Puerto Varas, when Alan and Valerie strolled by. I had met them on one of the boats across the Three Lakes and now they joined me for a snack lunch. Alan had taken early retirement and they had become wanderers, like me, escaping the British winter in the southern hemisphere, and travelling round Europe in the summer in their camper van. They had not been particularly adventurous in their youth, but one of their sons had started them off.

This son had found Valerie looking at a brochure of package holidays in Malaysia and Borneo. An experienced backpacker himself, that was when he'd called her a wimp. Valerie had smarted at the insult and had brooded over it long and hard.

Here Alan took up the story. 'So when I asked her one day what she wanted for her sixtieth birthday, she said "A rucksack and a ticket to Malaysia." I stood in the kitchen doorway gobsmacked. If I hadn't had the doorpost to lean on, I'd have fallen over with the shock. We'd been married for nearly forty years and I thought I knew her, but that came as a total surprise. I thought about it for a minute, then I said, "OK, if you get me a rucksack and a ticket too." It was the start of the best years of our lives. We've never looked back. I can't understand why more people don't do it. We love the travelling, and it's less expensive than staying at home if you organise it yourselves. Once you've paid the air fare, life in these countries is remarkably cheap.'

I was on my own now. Katherine and I had cycled out of Ensenada thinking, in our innocence, that the road along the lakeside would be flat. But it was a pretty steep switchback and there were two heavy downpours on the way. We reached Puerto Varas in bucketing rain, which continued on and off for days. The air was too damp for our clothes to dry off and we crouched in front of the fan heater in our hotel bedroom, trying to keep warm. The beautiful Volcán Osorno was still hidden in cloud and Katherine was getting seriously fed up with the weather and the lack of cycling. She decided to go home early.

On the day she left, I took a minibus down to Puerto Montt, the busy little port where the mainland stretch of the Pan-American Highway from Alaska ends and the Chilean fjords begin. South of the port, the map of Chile turns into a myriad tiny islands, like a scattering of snowflakes. A navigational nightmare of 1000 or more nautical miles, through the narrowest of straits and the most convoluted of channels, leads down to Tierra del Fuego, a parrot-shaped island perched on the southern edge of the inhabited world. Beyond it lies only Antarctica. I thought of Julian, who was planning to sail single-handed from Ushuaia, the most southerly city on the planet, through the Beagle Channel and up through those dangerous fjords. Puerto Montt would be his haven after anything from six weeks to four months of intensive, painstaking solo navigation. In a sailing boat, everything would depend on the wind and weather. He's a brilliant yachtsman, but there are still times when I worry.

Puerto Montt was thoroughly dismal in the rain. The cathedral's exterior was stained dark with damp, in pitiful contrast to the gleaming white marble of the Parthenon, which the tourist leaflets claimed was its inspiration. It was built of alerce wood and looked more like those models made out of matchsticks than the temple of Athena. The alerce (*Fitzroya cupressoides*), like the monkey puzzle, is one of Chile's rarities. It grows for 200 years before it seeds and can live for up to 4000. As happens all too frequently with hard woods, after years of ruthless logging, it has been replaced in its southern habitats by swift-growing commercial pines, and is now no more than a scattered survivor in national parks.

The great earthquake of 1960 destroyed most of Puerto Montt's early German architecture and the town centre is now a dreary conglomeration of concrete structures, hurriedly thrown up in the brutalist fashion of the time. I went to the John Paul II Museum, where there were said to be riveting memorabilia of the Pontiff's visit to Chile in 1987, like the spoon with which His Holiness ate his morning egg on a LanChile flight, but the building was boarded up and dilapidated, so I took a photograph of an old black steam engine on the seafront and caught the next minibus back to Puerto Varas.

The citizens of southern Chile, like their cousins over the Andes in Bariloche, are mostly Spanish-speaking Germans and Swiss, with cross-over names like Juan Schmidt and Pablo Weingartner. Tall, buxom blonde women with rosy cheeks and dirndl skirts stalk through the streets with their friends, and it's always a bit of a culture shock to hear them conversing in animated Spanish. On my own now, with no one to share accommodation costs, I had to economise, so I left the hotel where Katherine and I had been staying and transferred to a B & B run by one of these ladies. Her name was Gerda and she lived in a rickety old house, faced and roofed with wooden shingles, on a hill above the lake. My room was plain, but clinically clean with a comfortable bed.

Because I speak German, I was immediately given preferential treatment above all the other lodgers. While they took their breakfasts in the chilly dining room, crammed with gloomy Teutonic furniture in dark wood, I was invited to join Gerda at the kitchen table, in the warmth of the stove. Between nipping in and out of the dining room to serve breakfasts, she told me her family history.

'My grandparents were the first generation to settle in Chile. They spoke nothing but German. My parents were bilingual, and so was I, as we went to Spanish-speaking schools here in Puerto Varas and spoke German at home. My own children have a smattering of German; but my grandchildren have none at all. They speak Spanish all the time, and they're taught English as their second language.'

Over our mugs of coffee and stacks of generously buttered toast, Gerda and I had German conversations, which some-times turned hilarious when I couldn't remember a German word and she couldn't come up with it either. After struggling to find the German for 'suitcase' or 'raspberry', we would both simultaneously come out with the Spanish *maleta* or *fram-buesa*, then revert in shared amusement to German. We were both rusty through lack of practice, but Gerda was delighted to have the opportunity to converse in the language of her childhood. We spent many happy hours together in her cosy kitchen.

Meanwhile, outside, the weather had cleared. Families were bathing and children were building sandcastles on the grey-black beaches of Lake Llanquihue. Elegant Volcán Osorno and the jagged, exploded cone of Volcán Calbuco rose in snow-capped majesty out of the sparkling waters. Puerto Varas was transformed – and poor Katherine had missed it all. I luxuriated like a cat in the sunshine and did some leisurely exploration of this pleasant tourist resort.

The town centre was modern, smart and undistinguished, with the usual assortment of cafés and expensive outdoor equipment shops, including a branch of the American firm, Orvis, for all the local trout fishermen. But the surrounding slopes were showpieces of pre-war German domestic architec-ture, Gothic script and all. Dominating the town from a hilltop was the Church of the Sacred Heart, built for the German Jesuits between 1915–18. A copy of the famous Gothic Marienkirche in the Black Forest, albeit in corrugated iron, its interior was cool and airy, with a pale polished wood floor, smelling of beeswax, cream walls with grey trim and a lovely deep-blue ceiling. A Catholic church, its plainness owed more to the Lutherans than the Jesuits. Just as I came out, the carillon started to play the German carol, 'O *Tannenbaum*'.

That being the sum total of the sightseeing I had to do in Puerto Varas, I took a day trip on the local minibuses to Frutillar, another German settlement on the lake, where the Museo Colonial Alemán has a watermill in its grounds and fully furnished recreations of German colonial houses and barns. The neat, folksy shops and cheerfully painted wooden houses reminded me of New England, of the Pennsylvania 'Dutch'. We British exported neo-Georgian to our colonies; the Germans took their white clapboard and shingle houses to the Americas. Frutillar stands on the lakeside, surrounded by rich, rolling pastures, where brown and white cattle graze in the shadow of the volcanoes. It is an idyllic spot.

Apart from its stunningly beautiful location on Lake Llanquihue, a few quirky little things make me smile whenever I think of Puerto Varas. One is typical of the straightforward, 'no beating about the bush' mentality of the German race. There were handwritten lists Blu-tacked to the insides of shop windows, giving the names of the people who owed the traders money and the exact size of their debt. When they were shamed in this way into paying up, their names were heavily blacked out.

I visited one of these shops, an old-fashioned draper's, and it was like going back half a century to my childhood. The shelves around three walls were stacked to the ceiling with cardboard boxes of men's shirts and underpants, women's blouses and knickers and children's school uniform. In the middle of this vast selection of sensible items of apparel, behind a glass display counter full of handkerchiefs and gloves, stood an elderly gentleman in a brown overall. I had left my one and only travel nightdress behind in a hotel in Argentina and needed to replace it.

'A T-shirt?' he asked brightly, as I walked in.

'No. A nightdress.'

He pulled out his steps and reached for a carton at the top of one of the precarious stacks. It contained thick brushed-cotton nightdresses, which buttoned up to the neck, reached to the floor and had long sleeves. They came in two colours – baby blue and sugar pink

'These are very nice,' I said tactfully. 'But I was looking for something a bit lighter, a bit more summery.'

At this, he reached up for another carton and produced exactly the same nightdresses, except that they were calf length with short sleeves. I had no choice but to take one.

'Do you like the blue or the pink? PINK PANTHER!' he added triumphantly, in English, his little moustache quivering with delight at his joke. I chose the blue, which I shall have to wear to my dying day, as it's too sensible ever to wear out and I'm too economical to throw it away.

I walked out of the shop with my purchase wrapped in a brown-paper parcel, averting my eyes from the display in the shop window. The Y-fronts clothing the mannequins' nether regions had so much paper stuffed down the front of them that they looked positively obscene. I realised later that this kind of display was a feature of most drapers' shops in Chile – which is surprising in an otherwise very modest, almost prudish society.

Another small amusement concerns the *gasfiters*. All tradesmen in Chile are called *gasfiters*, a term which was obviously borrowed from the English, but they are *gasfiters* whether they fit gas, do carpentry or repair electrical appliances. Unlike the situation in England, where skilled technicians are as rare as gold dust, Chile has so many of them that they sit in a row in well-frequented spots, such as the exit to the supermarket, with their toolboxes at the ready and placards indicating their specialities. *GASFITER ELECTRÓNICO*, for example. Potential customers patrol the rank and select the likeliest looking candidate. It's so much simpler than riffling through Yellow Pages and telephoning a list of heaven knows whom. At least, under the Chilean system, you can see what sort of a man you're inviting into your home.

In 1952, Puerto Varas and Puerto Montt were as far south as you could get overland in Chile, as General Pinochet's ambitious Carretera Austral (Southern Highway) down to Villa O'Higgins had not even been imagined as yet. Reckoned today to be one of the world's greatest mountain bike adventures, this 1240 km of mostly unpaved road winds its way through mountains, dense forest, lush vegetation and interminable mist and rain, using ferries to cross lakes and circumnavigate glaciers. It links a few small fishing villages, which were previously cut off from the world except by sea, and would stretch right down to Puerto Natales and Tierra del Fuego, were it not for the inconvenience of the Southern Icefield in between. As Villa O'Higgins is almost on the Argentine border, it would be relatively easy for the Carretera Austral to cross over and link up with the Argentine roads running south, but in the present political stand-off between the two countries, that simple solution would be unacceptable.

Further north, the Andes form a natural and (since a treaty in 1881) undisputed boundary between the two countries. But when they reach the far south, the mountains of this turbulent volcanic zone have more or less tumbled down into the Pacific, and the boundary has become no more than a man-drawn line on the map, jealously guarded by both countries, with occasional rows and skirmishes. The situation has become even more sensitive since the Falklands War, when it is rumoured that the recapture of the islands by the British was co-ordinated from an old English sheep farmer's outpost near Punta Arenas, with considerable veiled support from Chile.

But these were not considerations to tax our friends. Their only option at the time was to turn north, towards Santiago. By chance, Ernesto picked up a commission to drive an estate car to Osorno. He had never driven a car before, but Alberto showed him how to operate the clutch and brakes, and he managed to judder and jerk his way along the highway behind La Ponderosa. His only victim was a little pig, which had the misfortune to run in front of the car before he had quite got the hang of the mechanics.

La Ponderosa's state of health was now becoming a real worry. In fact, her problems had moved up a notch, into the terminal. Just out of Osorno, she lost the screw which held the chain guard on. Then there were two punctures in her elderly tyres and, shortly afterwards, both riders were catapulted to the ground. The front fork had come loose and, worse still, the aluminium casing that protected the gearbox hit the road and split into four. Getting the pieces welded together in Lautaro took the remainder of their cash, but they set out again in high spirits, until they rounded a bend, saw a herd of cows ahead of them down a steep slope and their brakes failed. Ernesto, who was driving at the time, had the presence of mind to work down through the gears, so they lost speed and crashed into the roadside bank uninjured. Using cadged wing nuts and pieces of wire, they managed to get La Ponderosa going again – but then her chain snapped. By this time, according to Alberto, 'La Ponderosa was begging for mercy.' They got a lift with her in a furniture lorry from Los Angeles to Santiago, in return for help with a removal. And there, with great sadness, they abandoned their ramshackle, but much loved Norton 500cc. They had coaxed her over the Andes, but mechanical failure had forced them to end the serious motorbiking phase of their journey and resort to hitch-hiking.

I too had coaxed my bike over the Andes and I suddenly thought, 'If they can accept lifts up the length of Chile, so can I. I'm following in their wheeltracks, and I don't need to cycle where they didn't ride La Ponderosa.' That was a happy thought.

Having cycled along it in California and Peru, I was familiar with the Pan-American Highway, which stretches 27,000 km from Circle, just outside Fairbanks, Alaska, down the entire length of the west coast of the Americas to Quellon at the southern end of Chile's Chiloe Island – or would stretch the entire length, were it not for that 92 km of impenetrable rainforest on the borders of Panama and Colombia, known as the Darien Gap. Described as 'a laboratory of bio-diversity', it is one of the world's protected regions and has been at the heart of disputes between politicians, economists, ecologists and biologists for more than eighty years, since the Fifth International Conference of American States first planned the Highway in 1923. So far, the ecologists have won the battle to keep the Darien Gap in its pristine state.

Anyway, the Pan-American Highway runs down through Chile from the Peruvian border as Ruta 5, and from what I'd seen of it in the past, I was not enchanted at the prospect of riding my bicycle along it. It is Chile's main artery, crowded day and night with speeding buses and trucks. Much of it is dual-carriageway, which is bad enough, but the narrower sections are even more harrowing. Through the larger towns, there are parallel streets, and sometimes parallel service roads in villages. But Chile is such a narrow, mountainous ribbon of a country (4500 km long and less than 300 km wide at its very broadest point), that the Pan-American is forced to take what is virtually the only practicable route from north to south, through the gap between the Andes and the coastal ranges. There are no alternative roads. I was scared to death at the very thought of cycling it – and then La Ponderosa's break-down offered me the perfect escape. I would continue to follow Ernesto and Alberto northwards, but I would do it, as they did, cruising along on alternative transport.

So the next day found me on a coach going north from Puerto Varas, with my bicycle tucked away snugly in the baggage hold. We drove through a perfect green and yellow landscape, which seemed a miracle after the brown, scrubby tussocks of the pampas and the mountainous steppes of southern Argentina. Lush green grass dotted with buttercups and dandelions, yellow gorse and broom and a profusion of wild yellow lupins lined the roadside. Framing the picture, towered the forested mountains, dark with evergreens – firs, cypresses, evergreen beeches and even the occasional monkey puzzle (*Araucaria araucana*). This is Chile's national tree, but it has been decimated by logging over the centuries and now, like the native alerce, is found chiefly in national parks.

I sat next to a copper miner, who was going back north to work after attending a family wedding. There was the usual conversational opening.

'You're not from Chile, are you? Where do you come from?

'England. I live in London.'

'Ah, England. Mrs Thatcher. The Iron Lady. She was a great friend of our General Pinochet, you know. In fact, they were so friendly, we thought they might get married!'

'Well, there was just one slight snag to that idea. They were both married already.'

'Oh, that wouldn't have worried our General. He was very good at getting rid of people who were in the way.'

I was astonished at this openness. It was the first and only time anyone mentioned General Pinochet in conversation. Chile was a country where no one was prepared to talk about politics. The Pinochet era was still a raw wound. Supporters of the General, who had done well under his rule and profited from the country's economic development, kept quiet about it. The General was in disfavour and was to face trial for human rights abuses, so it was expedient not to confess one's former allegiance. The victims of the regime were also silent. They were waiting quietly for justice. As in Argentina, the only demonstrators were the Mothers of the Disappeared, who marched weekly, in silence, round the main squares, holding up photographs of their missing children.

Isabelle Allende, the Chilean writer, who is a niece of President Salvador Allende, fled the country after the military coup of 1973 and now lives in California. In her book, *My Invented Country*, she tells how the Chileans, in the first three minutes of conversation, feel the need to establish whether the person they're speaking to was for or against Pinochet's dictatorship before they express any views of their own. But they do it in a veiled way. If they fled the country, 'When did you leave?' elicits the required answer. If they left before 1973, they were right-wingers, fleeing Allende's brand of socialism. After 1973, they were leftists, fleeing the Pinochet regime. Those who stayed in the country are more difficult to situate, because they have learned the hard way to keep their opinions to themselves.

I suppose the majority of my fellow passengers had passed through the smiling landscape of southern Chile so often that they had lost interest in it. Apart from my copper-mining friend, who was eager to chat, the rest of the passengers tilted back their seats as soon as they got into the coach, drew their curtains and went to sleep. No one read, talked or looked out of the window. I squinted at the scenery, as best I could, through the gaps in the curtains and people's heads, until I reached *OSORNO. LA PATRIA DE LA LECHE.* (Osorno. The homeland of milk.) The homeland of a million contented cows grazing on rich green pastures.

Another major destination for nineteenth-century German settlers, Osorno lost most of its old buildings in the 1960 earthquake and is now a comfortable, but undistinguished town. None of the waiters in the Club Alemán spoke German, but German kitsch was alive and well. The house next door to my hotel sported a wooden storks' nest on the chimney stack, complete with a family of wooden storks and storklets.

In the evening, there was a free concert in the rebuilt Catedral de San Mateo. A tenor singing operatic lollipops and popular South American songs preceded the main work, the *Misa Criolla* of Ariel Ramirez. The choir was accompanied by an interesting band of guitars, mandolins, maracas, drums, a double bass and a honky-tonk electronic keyboard. There was not a spot of Indian blood in the packed audience, though one or two of the tenors and basses looked to be *mestizos*. Statistically, *mestizos* may constitute the majority of the population in Chile, but the urban elite, who go to concerts and dine out in restaurants, are predominantly of white European descent, and more North European than Latin. The main indigenous minority, the Mapuche (People of the Earth) of south-central Chile, gave the invading Spaniards a particularly hard time and it was not until the Pacification of Araucania in 1881 that settlement in the south became safe. Osorno was founded in 1558, but was so besieged and terrified by the warlike Mapuche that it was abandoned, and not resettled until the Germans arrived.

I slept in a hotel in Osorno, but Ernesto states cheerfully that they 'freeloaded' again there. 'The Chileans, exceedingly friendly people, welcomed us wherever we went,' he enthused. Alberto, as usual, engaged in political argument with everyone who entertained them, from the administrator of the hospital in Osorno to the poor tenant farmer who took them in after another 'broken headlight' story. With their South American penchant for autocrats, the Chileans all infuriated him by praising General Ibañez, their elected president, but a dictator in style. 'What the country needs is a strong ruler to set right its wrongs,' they told him. 'And Ibañez is a man who doesn't even have Peron's intelligence!' adds Alberto with great scorn.

There were two other English guests in the hotel, a retired couple like myself, who had taken up independent travel. We got into conversation over breakfast.

'Whenever things get a bit difficult, I always ask myself "What would Anne Mustoe do?"'

'Oh, you and Anne Mustoe!' said her husband.

'Well, she's such a help. Her books tell you everything you need to know. Have you ever read any of them?' she asked.

Another flattering encounter!

In Valdivia, my next stop, Ernesto caused a stir in the streets by appearing in a pair of calf-length trousers, 'not some fashion of mine, but inherited from a generous but short friend'. My coach climbed the forested coastal range, then swooped down to the riverfront resort on the estuary of the Calle Calle. Here I explored the great fish market, one long row of stalls lining the jetties and making a fine display under their striped awnings. I finally learned the local names for all the fish, which had puzzled me on restaurant menus – the red spider crabs, the *maltones* (giant mussels) and *choritos* (normal mussels), the huge oysters, salmon, trout and *congrios*, which I had assumed were conger eels, but were in fact members of the cod family, with long tapering bodies and white flesh. It was still German territory, so I visited the German museum, an old clapboard family home, filled with its original nineteenth-century furniture.

'It's just like my grandparents' home,' said an elderly gentleman from Hamburg. 'It brings it all back. This heavy furniture. Exactly the same.' Some of the furniture was locally made, but the oak pieces were obviously imported direct from Germany and were a sign of the family's prosperity. They were evidently a musical lot too, as they had a square piano and a small pipe organ, as well as a type of piano I had never seen before. It was the size of a concert grand, but rectangular, and it had keyboards at both ends, for playing duets. My Hamburg acquaintance said that such pianos were well known in Germany.

There were five of us touring the house that morning – the old couple from Hamburg, a young Australian couple and myself – and we discovered, as often happens to travellers, that we were all in a way connected. The Australian girl said that her grandparents were Germans, who had migrated to Sydney; and I have a grandson who works as a translator in Hamburg. We clung to one another, talking nineteen to the dozen, in a mixture of German and English, so delighted to have met in the midst of a sea of monoglot Chileans. Outside the tourist industry, the south of the country seemed to speak nothing but Spanish and the Mapuche language, Mapudungun (the language of the earth).

I was still in pastoral country, but the temper was toughening as I travelled north. I saw my first graffiti in Valdivia 'Yanquis out of Iraq' and the stalls in the covered market were awash with punk leather collars and belts, spiked bracelets, Hell's Angels badges and posters of Che Guevara.

I was looking for a South American poster to hang in my newly decorated kitchen, but the ones I had seen so far had been severely limited in scope. Apart from the inevitable Che Guevaras, the only subjects were a stout baby with a toothless grin, wild white horses galloping across a green field with snow-capped volcanoes in the background, a Harley-Davidson motorbike with an easy rider on board, the Madonna dressed in blue, and Christ tearing open His breast to display His fiery Sacred Heart. But in Valdivia market, I saw just the thing, a black and white portrait of the great Argentine writer, Borges, above the text of one of his poems. He wrote it when he was already old and blind, to express his regret at his faint-heartedness and concern for convention. He wished he could relive his life, but more dangerously and less dutifully. He would go barefoot from spring to autumn, eat more ice cream and fewer healthy beans, watch more sunsets, swim more rivers, climb more mountains and go for more rides on merry-go-rounds. I suppose the poster made me feel a bit smug. Unlike Borges, I had sloughed off duty and convention years ago, and was actually doing most of the things that he could only dream of. It was my poster and I wanted it. But the stall was shut. I was just turning disconsolately away, when neighbouring stallholders cried, '*Llega! Llega!*' (He's coming), and a vision appeared in a gaucho hat, check shirt, jeans and cowboy boots. He had a ponytail and a long droopy moustache, like a bandit out of an old Western. His stall was chaotic, but he somehow managed to produce a pristine Borges poster out of the jumble of dusty tat and Mapuche handwork, and even found me a cardboard tube to put it in.

On the way back to my hotel, I stood on the riverbank and watched a single scull cutting swiftly and cleanly through the water. The motion was so graceful that it seemed effortless, like a hawk gliding along on a thermal. As the boat swept past me, I was surprised to see that the rower was a girl. South American women are generally more decorative than sporty. But perhaps Chile was the exception? I had certainly seen Chilean women on mountain bikes in the national parks; and among the rural Mapuche, the women rode horses as well as the men.

When Che Guevara reached Temuco, he had the bright idea of visiting the local offices of *El Diario Austral* and spinning the editor a yarn about the two distinguished Argentine leprosy specialists, who had treated over three thousand patients, and were now passing through the town on their motorcycle tour of South America. The publicity worked well. The two 'experts' were recognised for days to come and offered hospitality on the strength of the article. Alberto, as usual, was happy to accept it, but not without a bit of moralising. 'The press really is the fourth power in a bourgeois republic and a lot of people believe more in the printed word than in what they see with their own eyes. How dangerous such power can be in unscrupulous hands!'

Temuco's most famous son is the Chilean Nobel Prize-winner, Pablo Neruda, a poet I find exceedingly opaque. I always get lost in his maze of words, and end up wondering what the poem was really about. But Temuco is very proud of him. He moved there in 1906, at the age of two, when it was still a frontier village. A peace pact had been signed with the fierce Araucanian Indians and his father got a job down there, helping to lay the railway tracks which would open up the region to Western civilisation. The dark, rainy forests of his childhood would haunt Neruda's poetry throughout his life.

Thanks to the unpredictable surrounding volcanoes, which have flattened most of the older buildings, the city is now a modern commercial conurbation and an important military base. Even its new cathedral is more like a shiny glass office block, with a skyscraper tower. Its purpose would be unrecognisable, were it not for its huge neon cross. The capital of Araucania, Chile's Region IX, the city stands in the heartland of the Mapuche people, though they live for the most part out in the country and come into town only to sell their produce, their pots and their baskets.

Although Neruda moved further north, to Santiago and Valparaíso, served abroad in the Diplomatic Service and spent some years in Spain, escaping arrest as a prominent member of the banned Chilean Communist Party, he often went back for inspiration to his roots in Temuco. And when he did, he stayed in the historic Continental Hotel. I found it little changed since the days of his visits. An old man in a brown overall sat behind the reception desk, tapping away at an ancient Remington typewriter. The floors were of polished wood and there were long hospital-like corridors, their wood-plank walls painted grey and cream. But the sitting areas downstairs were remarkably spacious, with great squashy 1920s leather armchairs and framed press cuttings from the hotel's glory days. The vast, echoing restaurant gleamed with white linen, polished cutlery and glasses. I dined there alone, and I could see why the people of Temuco didn't come flocking. The food was a major disappointment – packet vegetable soup, an escalope with no meat, just ham and cheese fried in breadcrumbs, a fresh peach on a side plate and a cup of Nescafé. The staff consisted of one old retainer of each sex in an overall.

But my big excitement was that I was allocated Room 9, the favourite bedroom of Pablo Neruda. Gabriella Mistral, the other Chilean Nobel Prize-winning poet, preferred Room 10 and President Allende Room 11. I stood on the bare polished floor, where Neruda had stood so many times, surrounded by the same heavy furniture with its white linen runners and antimacassars. There was a notice on the wall, framed in dark wood, with a border of hand-painted flowers. It was a quotation from the local paper: 'Here, in Room 9 of the Continental Hotel, Pablo Neruda spent the night every time he came back to steep himself in the countryside of Temuco, his homeland. 1940–1970. *El Diario Austral.*' Printed over the flowers of the lower border, were his dates: 1904–1973; Nobel Prize 1971.

At this point, I parted company with my motorbiking friends. They continued by fits and starts up the Pan-American Highway, stopping at a garage in Lautaro to get the casing of the gearbox welded back together again. There Ernesto made a pass at the mechanic's wife, which went dangerously wrong, and they had to flee the town. La Ponderosa II was fortunately by then in a fit state to bear them speedily away, but that was just before her chain snapped and she had to be stowed away in a Los Angeles furniture lorry for her final journey to Santiago.

I was hoping to travel north to Concepción on one of Chile's only two remaining passenger trains, the nightly sleeper from Temuco to Santiago, run by the national Empresa de los Ferrocarriles del Estado. Despite being short of passengers, the station staff were totally unbending about my bicycle. It had to be dismantled and boxed before they would take it. When the Chilean coaches were so accommodating, and accepted Condor with a smile – wheels, handlebars and all – I decided the train was just too much hassle. I rode away from the station disappointed. Since then, I understand the train service between Temuco and Santiago has come to an end (in September 2006) and I'm not surprised!

Failing to catch the train gave me wider options and I chose to travel north along the charmingly named Costa del Carbon, the Coal Coast. I wanted to visit Cañete, because I was intrigued by the story of Pedro de Valdivia's death there on Christmas Day, 1553.

In the second half of the fifteenth century, the Inca Empire spread south into Chile but, for all their power, they could get no further than the Rio Maule, some 250 km south of what is now Santiago. They were held in check by the ferocity and fighting efficiency of the Mapuche. The Spanish conquistadors had experienced few problems with the northern peoples, even the blood-thirsty Aztecs and the sophisticated, well-organised Inca, but they too met their match as they pushed south from Peru into Chile. And their troubles increased when the Mapuche warriors abandoned their llama-drawn sleds in favour of horses captured from the Spaniards.

In January 1540, Pedro de Valdivia set out from Cuzco, the Inca capital, with an army of conquest. Despite some determined resistence in the Coquimbo and Aconcagua Valleys, his troops reached the Rio Mapocho, where Valdivia raised the Spanish flag on 12 February 1541, and founded a new city which he named Santiago de la Nueva Extremadura (St James of the New Extremadura), in honour of the patron saint of Spain. The usual Spanish grid of streets around the Plaza de Armas had hardly been laid out before the Picunche burned it all down. So Valdivia rebuilt the town as a strongly guarded fort, before pressing further south down the coast.

The Spaniards were always avid for gold and silver. They chased one legend after another in search of fabled cities, where the streets were said to be paved in gold and the citizens were decked out in rubies and emeralds. However much gold they found among the Incas and Aztecs, it was never enough. They scoured the Americas for more, for the limitless wealth of the legendary El Dorado, which they never discovered. Their obsession with gold and silver was a puzzle to the Pre-Colombians, who prized the metals simply for their malleability and shine, not as the means of exchange. They used them to produce exquisite bowls, goblets and jewellery. But these artefacts were often plated, just to give a glittering finish. They were not always fashioned in solid gold and silver – which came as a great disappointment to the Spaniards, when they smelted them down.

Chile too was a disappointment. Not only did the Spaniards fail to find El Dorado there, but the local peoples, who burned and pillaged, were a constant bar to settlement. In 1553, in a concerted Mapuche uprising, Pedro de Valdivia was captured on the Carbon Coast, just north of Cañete. There are conflicting accounts of the way in which he met his death, but my favourite is the most appropriate for a gold-greedy Spaniard. With black humour, the Mapuche made him drink a draught of molten gold, which they poured down his throat straight from the furnace.

I love visiting small places where no one ever goes, unless they happen to live there. Cañete is just such a place. I arrived at one of the few hotels during siesta time. The front door was ajar, but the señora was fast asleep in her bed. I roused her and she gave me a tour of the bedrooms, so that I could pick the one I wanted. I chose a light, airy pine-clad room with a cheerful modern feel, then went out to explore the town. As the lady didn't seem to believe in keys, I had to trust to luck and leave all my possessions in an unlocked room in a wide open hotel.

Cañete has a sort of 'Wild West' look, like a makeshift settlement for pioneers. The buildings are mostly single-storey, built of brightly painted wood with roofs of tin sheeting, or what looked suspiciously like asbestos tiling. Yet the backwoods appearance is deceptive, as the place is clearly thriving. There was not much motorised traffic, but teenagers of both sexes were milling around the centre on bikes. It was a busy market for cheese and local vegetables, plus a few stalls for the usual cheap clothing, shoes and watches. Surprisingly, the regular shops in the main street seemed to be mostly hairdressers' salons and boutiques for the latest Cañete fashions. I bought a new pocket calculator in a well-stocked stationer's shop from a boy who had spent a year in Oregon, learning English.

I was the only guest in the hotel. Next morning, over breakfast, the señora tried to engage me in conversation, but her accent was so unfamiliar that I could understand scarcely a word she said. After all my efforts to learn Spanish, I felt quite deflated, but I cheered up when I entered the Mapuche Museum and could understand everything the ticket-seller said to me. He was pure Mapuche, dressed in a gorgeous multicoloured slipover, which he told me his wife had knitted for his birthday, basing the pattern on a traditional Mapuche textile design.

The museum had a beautiful display of pottery, textiles, weapons, musical instruments and silverware, the whole cultural life of a people carefully laid out in its spacious modern building with illuminating explanatory material. I was particularly fascinated to read about the afterlife, according to traditional Mapuche beliefs. There were three destinations. The chieftains either became volcanoes, or inhabited them. The warriors went up into the sky, where they became clouds and continued to watch over and protect their people. The ordinary folk came to a miserable end. They went to a cold, wet place across the sea, where they farmed, mostly black potatoes. The firewood there was damp, like everything else, so a fire was kept burning on their graves for a whole year. They could take that with them into the other world, to get their damp kindling ablaze. When the options were so unattractive, it was no wonder that the Catholics, who promised good people a joyful life among the angels in a Christian heaven, had such high conversion rates!

In the grounds of the museum, there were traditional *ruca*, reed-built roundhouses. By this time, the ticket seller and I were chatting away like old friends, so he gave me the conducted tour. He showed me the beds and cradles inside, which had tree stumps for legs, and pliable branches and liana for webbing. There was an open hearth for cooking, but no other furniture. What was really surprising was the range of musical instruments, all of which my companion could play. He started off with a kind of alpenhorn, which he called a *ñolkin*, a bamboo pipe about two metres long and very thin, ending in a small deer horn, not much bigger than a Meerschaum pipe. Then he demonstrated some flutes and pan pipes, and had a go on a little twangy Jew's harp. He was very proud of this, as he had made it himself, and had also carved the grooved wooden holder in which it nested. He sang me a song in Mapudungun too, which was somewhat tuneless to my Western ears. Somehow, it seems far less embarrassing to listen to someone playing an instrument than it does to stand solemnly in front of a solo singer. I was relieved when the dirge ended and my attention was drawn to a hockey stick and balls. He dribbled enthusiastically round the garden. Hockey was the traditional Mapuche sport.

I ended the morning with a walk from the museum to the Fuerte Tucapel, the stockade where Valdivia got more gold than he'd bargained for. Cañete itself was a town which could be explored thoroughly in twenty minutes, every nook and cranny of it, so there was nothing else to do but wait for the bus which would carry me to Concepción.

It was a long, slow ride. The steep slopes of what used to be a coal-mining region were now thickly forested with commercially planted conifers and the one narrow road was choked with logging trucks and their trailers. But I enjoyed South Chile's typical green and yellow landscape, the broom, dandelions and buttercups, the emerald pastures and the dark green of the pines – or I would have enjoyed it, had it not been for my fellow-passenger.

When I boarded the bus, this Passenger from Hell was sitting in the window seat that I'd booked and no amount of polite requesting could get him to move to the aisle. At the first bus stop, he leaned out of the window and bought two huge, greasy empanadas (heavy meat pasties), full of foul-smelling meat, which he gobbled noisily. Then he picked his nose for a while and spent the next half-hour shouting loudly into his mobile phone. Finally, he went to sleep, overflowing his own half of the seat and sprawling over mine, totally oblivious to the view from the window, which he'd so rudely appropriated.

Not that the view was much to shout about by this stage. We were driving along the Costa del Carbon, through a string of old pit towns, like Lota and Coronel, which were gamely trying to lighten the burden of unemployment by turning themselves into seaside resorts and the inevitable 'mining heritage centres'. Then our bus crossed the Bio-Bio River by the John Paul II Bridge, Chile's longest at 2450 m, and I finally left the dark forests and unpredictable weather of the southern lakes behind. From now on, it would be sunshine all the way.

5. THE HEROES

No great man lives in vain. The history of the world is but the biography of great men.

(Thomas Carlyle)

Enter any town or village in Chile, and the most important streets will bear the same selection of names. The main thoroughfare, the tree-lined Spanish *alameda*, will almost certainly be called the Avenida O'Higgins, after Bernardo O'Higgins, the first Head of State of the newly independent Chile. He was an illegitimate son of Ambrosio O'Higgins, an Irishman who entered the service of Spain in South America, became Captain-General of Chile and then climbed to the dizzy height of Viceroy of Peru, one of the most powerful posts in the Spanish Empire. In 1817, Bernardo O'Higgins rose on a South American revolutionary tide and joined forces with the Argentine General Jose de San Martín, the Liberator, who led an army over the Andes into Chile. Together, they defeated the Spanish royalists in the battles of Chacabuco and Maipú (more street names) and on 1 January 1818 Bernardo O'Higgins stood in the Plaza de Armas, the main square of Concepción, and declared the independence of Chile from the Spanish Crown.

Never the main street, but in a most honourable central position, there is invariably a Calle Cochrane. Admiral Lord Cochrane, the tenth Earl of Dundonald, was one of the British navy's most colourful characters. 'The Wolf of the Sea', he struck terror into the hearts of Napoleon's sailors and in 1809 was awarded the Order of the Bath for his daring fireship attack on the French fleet in the Aix roads. He subsequently became a bit too colourful. In 1814, he got involved in a plot to make money on the London Stock Exchange by spreading false rumours of Napoleon's abdication. He was sentenced to a term of imprisonment, expelled from Parliament and deprived of his Order of the Bath. Providentially, during this period of disgrace, Bernardo O'Higgins came to the rescue, inviting him to Chile in 1817 to take command of what was at that time Chile's small naval squadron. Within a year, Cochrane had transformed the squadron into a powerful navy, defeated the Spaniards at sea and won control of the Pacific. Rebellion obviously suited him. Having sorted out the Chilean navy, he went on to Brazil to join their struggle against Portugal, and later to Greece to engage in their war of independence from the Turks. His adventurous life ended happily. In 1832, he was reinstated in the British navy, promoted to command of the important American and West Indies station, and finally given a splendid burial in Westminster Abbey. (Cochrane is, incidentally, the model for the daring naval commander, Jack Aubrey, in the popular series of novels by Patrick O'Brian.)

The third national hero rises like a seaborne Don Quixote from the War of the Pacific, not from the independence struggle. He rejoices in the name of Arturo Prat and he sometimes takes pride of place, even above Bernardo O'Higgins, in the north of Chile. For example, the main street in the port of Antofagasta is Calle Prat, while in Iquique he commands the main square, Plaza Prat. But he has a strong connection with Concepción too, so more of him later.

O'Higgins, Cochrane and Prat. What Spanish-speaking country, other than Chile, could have three national heroes with such delightfully improbable names? Perhaps their very Englishness and Irishness is the reason I always feel so much at home there. Add to the street names department stores such as Ripley's and Johnson's, the Banco Edwards and MacKay's Biscuits ('*Galletas* MacKay. *Mas ricas no hay*', as the jingle goes. 'Mackay's Biscuits. There are none more delicious') and I am almost back in England. Except in the German south, cakes in Chile are known as *queques;* they take *onces* (English 'elevenses'), albeit at five o'clock in the afternoon; and they even play cricket at *El Club Principe de Gales* (The Prince of Wales Club) in Santiago!

Arriving in Concepción, I cycled from the bus station to the Avenida O'Higgins and found a hotel just by the central Plaza de Armas. Away from the obvious tourist centres like the Lake District, where modern hotels cater for the foreign visitors, the middle range of Chilean hotels, where I usually stay, are old fashioned in the extreme. In Concepción, my room was typically gloomy (they like to keep out the sun). The décor was dark green, maroon and cream. There were quilted maroon covers on the two beds, my circular mirror was framed in maroon satin with white lace edging, and the lavatory cistern was encased in a beautifully fitted jacket of quilted maroon satin with ecru lace trim. Breakfast was the usual Chilean disappointment – two individual packets of Nescafé, a glass of luminous powdered orange juice, which tasted of nothing but aspartamate, two dreary rolls and two pre-packed portions of butter and tasteless mauve jelly, masquerading as grape jam. As a coffee lover, I find Chile's obsession with Nescafé hard to take. In Argentina, where they serve excellent coffee, the hotels keep a tin of Nescafé handy, especially for their Chilean visitors, who insist on it. There are a few smart bars in downtown Santiago, where the longing for a strong espresso or cappuccino can be satisfied, but otherwise, Chile is a coffee desert. By way of compensation, Chilean wines are superb.

On my first morning in Concepción, I caught one of the white buses marked 'Base Naval' and rode out past the racecourse and steelworks to the port of Talcahuano. There I surrendered my passport at the gates of Chile's main naval base and made my way past various cannon, through a plaza with a statue of Lieutenant Arturo Prat, to a wooden jetty. Not being good at heights, I didn't at all care for the steep steps and gangways overhanging the water, but the Chilean sailors were most attentive and handed me down safely. Thanks to Admiral Cochrane and a number of British successors, their uniform was identical to that of the British ordinary seaman, except that they wore 'Armada de Chile' on the ribbon around their caps. They helped me onto a raft with a fixed rope, which two of them then pulled across the port to the *Huascar*, a magnificently restored 1865 ironclad from Lairds' shipyard in Birkenhead. A notice at the top of the gangway asked for respectful behaviour, as the ship was the shrine of heroes.

The *Huascar* was built for the Peruvian navy. In the War of the Pacific between Peru and Bolivia on the one hand and Chile on the other, she blockaded Iquique harbour in May 1879, and attacked an old and rather rickety Chilean frigate, the *Esmeralda*, under the command of Lieutenant Arturo Prat. The wooden *Esmeralda* with its 40 lb guns was no match at all for the ironclad *Huascar*, whose guns weighed in at 300 lb. She splintered like matchwood when she was rammed. With the courage of desperation, Arturo Prat leaped from his sinking ship, boarded the *Huascar* and, armed only with his ceremonial sword, laid into the Peruvian crew. He was shot down almost immediately, as were two of his men who leaped on board after him, inspired by his doomed heroics. Five months later, the *Huascar* was ambushed and captured just outside Antofagasta by two more modern Chilean ironclads, the *Cochrane* and the *Blanco Encalada*. The Peruvian Admiral Grau was killed onboard along with a third of his crew, while the *Huascar* was hastily repaired and put into service on the Chilean side under Commander Manuel Thomson.

Their navy's subsequent dominance of the sea was the key factor in Chile's victory over the combined forces of Peru and Bolivia. They went on to launch a land offensive and marched into Lima, the Peruvian capital. This was simply a proud gesture, in response to populist demand. What was far more significant was the capture of the southern provinces of Peru and the entire Bolivian littoral – a conquest which gave the Chileans control of the rich mineral resources of the Atacama Desert, including the nitrate fields, the source of enormous wealth. The landlocked Bolivians are still petitioning to regain their access to the Pacific Ocean.

The *Huascar* was lovingly preserved. On that summer morning, her brasses gleamed so brightly that I was too dazzled at first to notice the small memorial on the deck, marking the spot where Arturo Prat died. Below decks, the mahogany table in the officers' dining room gleamed, and the leather, mahogany and brass in the salon and chapel smelled of beeswax and elbow grease. I boarded the ship with a party of Mapuche, families with parents, grannies, children and babies, all on a day's coach trip. The Mapuche fought fiercely against the settlement of their lands by the Europeans, so I was interested to note their obvious pride in Chile's victory, as they studied the plans of naval battles and the rows of portraits in the *Huascar*'s displays. I suppose we all like to be on the winning side.

As well as the memorial to Lieutenant Arturo Prat, there was one to the Peruvian Admiral Grau, who died on board the *Huascar* when it was captured. And perhaps most touching of all, there was a notice in one of the cabins about a less-sung hero, Second Lieutenant Ignacio Serrano. He was one of the two Chileans who leaped on board the *Huascar* after Prat. Although he was mortally wounded, with his dying strength he seized the oil lamp beside his bunk and tried to set fire to the ship by hurling it against the cabin's wooden partition.

My other stop in Concepción was the History Museum, which is more like an arcade in a fairground than a serious exhibition. I had great fun doing the rounds of the beautifully made tableaux in glass cases, which came alive with lights and dramatic soundtrack at the touch of a button. I suppose the triumphs of history are my escape from the bleakness of the present. CNN, which I always think of as 'the disaster channel', featured an Iranian earthquake, gas poisoning in China, a Californian mudslide, an air crash in Benin, a suicide bomb in Tel Aviv, the latest Iraqi casualties, SARS in Guandong Province and one mad cow discovered in the USA – all in the same bulletin that evening!

I escaped the news into the last rays of the sun on the Plaza, where an ice-cream man cycled round with his cart, children played, lovers embraced and parents pushed their babies along in prams with cloths over the hoods, like parrots in cages, blacking them out to keep them quiet. There was a nice fresh sea-breeziness in the air and, as Ernesto remarked, people were most friendly and welcoming. I had a string of visitors to my park bench, offering assistance and chatting about everything from wages and the cost of living to a father's funeral. And the waiter in my restaurant was delighted to have a customer from London, as he was doing an external degree in business studies from the University of Westminster. I liked Concepción and was sorry to leave.

Christmas was fast approaching and I had an invitation to spend it in Santiago, so I bypassed Chillán, the birthplace of Bernardo O'Higgins (and also of Chile's most famous concert pianist, Claudio Arrau), and Lautaro, where Che Guevara was chased out of town by a jealous husband. I pressed on north to San Fernando, in the heart of Chile's wine-growing region.

The muzak in my lunch-time café there was 'The Holly and the Ivy', 'Greensleeves', 'Jingle Bells', 'Rudolf the Red-Nosed Reindeer', and delightful old popular songs, such as 'I'm Putting All my Eggs in One Basket', which I remembered from my childhood. The shops were buzzing and festive fever was in the air. The manageress of my hotel had tears in her eyes when she found out I was travelling on my own at Christmas. I told her that it didn't worry me.

'But aren't you Catholic?' she asked.

'No. I'm Protestant.'

'Ah, that explains it then. Perhaps New Year is more important for you. Me, I love Christmas!'

I don't usually confess to being a writer, because that often inhibits the people I meet. They talk less freely, afraid of an unflattering appearance in one of my books. I tell everyone that I'm a retired teacher, which seems harmless enough. But the kind-hearted woman in the hotel was so sad on my behalf that I resolved to tell her my true profession later that day. I would explain that it was better for writers to travel alone, as they talked to more people and were more open to experience. I would assure her that I was travelling alone from choice, not because I was some pathetic, friendless loser. My Spanish being far from fluent, this speech would take some preparation and I would need to work on it during the afternoon.

Meanwhile, I took a minibus out to La Hacienda Los Lingues, to see a large working estate, which had been in the same family since 1599. I entered the gates unchallenged, strolled around the dazzlingly prolific flowering courtyards and peered inside the gloomy family chapel. The clatter of knives and forks and loud American voices from secluded tables in the shrubbery told me that the hacienda was now an expensive hotel, catering for the top end of the package market. (It is in fact only one of four hotels in the whole of South America which qualifies for membership of the exclusive Relais & Chateaux Group.) I was eventually spotted by one of the hordes of waiters and waitresses, all sporting Black Watch tartan waistcoats. He led me to Reception, where an elegant young man in jeans offered to take me on a conducted tour of the hotel for the outrageous sum, in Chilean terms, of $15 US – as much as I usually paid for a night in a hotel room with private bath and breakfast. I declined, as the last *micro* of the day was due to leave for San Fernando in fifteen minutes' time. So I was told that I could walk around the park and stables for free. The family are well known as breeders of pure Chilean Aculeo horses (whatever they are!) and there were at least forty of these magnificent creatures in the stables, with more galloping round in an adjacent field. The stable walls were plastered with prize certificates and photographs of the owner receiving trophies.

I hung about at the main gates waiting for the *micro* until well past 3 o'clock. I was a long way from the Panamerican Highway, where there was always ample transport, and I was beginning to get rather worried. But then a red pick-up truck came out of the hacienda, driven by one of the young men in a Black Watch waistcoat. The one passenger seat was occupied by an older woman, similarly waistcoated, but he was driving to San Fernando, which was all that interested me, so I scrambled up into the back of the truck and settled down as comfortably as I could in the middle of the spare tyre. A mile or so down the road, we stopped to pick up two teenage boys, dressed to kill for an evening on the town in their smartest casuals and shades. They were clearly amused to find a *gringa* travelling in the back of a pick-up truck like themselves and kept collapsing into fits of giggles. The unmetalled road was very dusty, but fortunately the woman soon got out at her house and I was able to take her seat in the cab. Just in time, for the evening irrigation of the crops was beginning and the rotating hoses gave the two boys in the back a thorough soaking. The driver was a friendly young man and we chatted all the way into town. Like most Chileans, he valued his country's ties with Britain.

'Just north of Santiago,' he said, 'there's a replica of Buckingham Palace. The lady of the house is related to your Queen Elizabeth.'

He insisted on driving me right up to my hotel door, so I insisted on giving him 2000 pesos (about £2) 'for Christmas'. Compared with the 120 pesos I paid on the minibus out to the hacienda, it was a generous tip, but I didn't know how I should have managed without the lift – and he was so pro-British that I suppose I wanted to create a good impression. We are all ambassadors of our country, whether we realise it or not.

When I walked into Reception, the manageress and her son were waiting for me, all agog.

Two people had arrived from Cambridge ('You know Cambridge?' she asked) and had seen my name in the hotel register. 'They say you're a famous writer! You never told me.

They're so excited to find you in the same hotel that they've gone out to get wine for a celebration.' I assured her that I was not at all famous, but I was pleased to be spared the effort of my carefully rehearsed explanation.

Dot and Tim from Cambridge, who were keen cyclists, had been out shopping for Christmas cake and wine, so that we could all have a little party after dinner. We were joined by the manageress, her son and her man friend, with me acting as interpreter. She was delighted that I had found some congenial company, for she still didn't believe that I could travel alone, especially so near to Christmas, without feeling desperately lonely.

6. A SANTIAGO CHRISTMAS

*We reached the capital on Saturday. My first impression was that I was
back in Córdoba, though the mountains here are higher and closer.*

(Alberto Granado)

The two temporary furniture removers carried out their
part of the bargain – help with the shifting of the furniture
in return for a cheap ride in the van from Los Angeles to
Santiago for themselves and La Ponderosa. Alberto, ever the
hero-worshipper, gives an admiring account of one of Ernesto's feats. They were being teased by the Chilean removal
men, who were calling them Buenos Aires weaklings and
slackers. There was an extremely heavy item of furniture in the
van, a wardrobe so huge that it could scarcely be manoeuvred
along the corridor. Losing patience with the ribbing, Ernesto
ordered everyone to stand back and leave the job to him. He
put his arms around the great cumbersome object, lifted it with
ease and carried it single-handed into the bedroom. After that,
he went and sat on the kerb outside and took no further part
in the unloading. The Chileans said no more.

Apart from a perfunctory visit to the zoo and the Museum
of Fine Arts, they spent their few days in Santiago getting a visa

for Peru and trying in vain to find spare parts for La Ponderosa. In the end, they had to abandon her in an Austin garage, run by an Argentine mechanic. 'As we wrapped her in the tent, I felt as though we were putting a shroud on the corpse of a loyal friend,' wrote Alberto. But the two travellers cheered up when they bumped into a water-polo team from Córdoba, and joined them in their celebrations after the match. Ernesto, who always enjoys his food, writes lovingly of all the ham, cheese and wine they consumed at the party, not to mention the four kilos of grapes which came their way during the removal.

Not having visited Córdoba myself, I had no way of telling if Santiago was nothing but a busier version of Alberto's home town. I was just delighted to be back in one of the cities I love best in the whole world.

The Plaza de Armas that evening was bursting with Christmas crowds. There was a great multicoloured Santa's castle, complete with toiling elves, reindeer and sacks of toys, a brightly decorated civic Christmas tree, bands of drummers, a children's entertainment with singers and dancers dressed as giraffes, balloons, face painting, white-faced clowns, funny walkers who stalked unwary pedestrians and mimicked their every move, stand-up comedians, evangelists, and the opportunity to be photographed with Father Christmas on his sled. Straw from the manger had been strewn on the flagstones, with a sprinkling of mock snow, a phenomenon never seen for real in Santiago; and robins in the snow were just as popular on the Christmas cards of sunny Chile as they are in England. As background to all this seasonal activity, the crystal voices of the choristers of King's College Chapel, Cambridge, echoed through the main thoroughfares, treating the shoppers to the Festival of Nine Lessons and Carols. It was, of course, midsummer there, so it was amazing to a northerner to see people mopping their brows and sucking iced lollies as they struggled out of Ripley's under their mountains of Christmas presents.

In the restaurant, where the television was exhorting people to 'Give a Bed for Christmas' to poor families whose children had to sleep on the floor, my cyclist's eye spotted a young man wearing a T-shirt with the words 'The Bike Shop' boldly displayed. I walked over to his table.

'*Donde es* The Bike Shop?' I asked. Blank incomprehension. 'Where's The Bike Shop?'

'Tennessee.'

Glinn was a nice lad, who had spent the last month riding the buses from city to city, mostly in Argentina, and hiring mountain bikes when he got there. I joined him for dinner and we compared the kind of notes that fascinate two cyclists. Then I bought a cone of my favourite Chilean ice cream, a strong green peppermint with the bitterest, darkest chocolate chips, from the best ice-cream parlour in Santiago and strolled back licking it to the Plaza de Armas. In the cathedral, the Symphony Orchestra of Chile and the Choir of the University of Chile in Santiago were performing Beethoven's Symphony No. 9. The great west doors were wide open, the chandeliers in the nave were brilliantly lit and the concert was free. It was all wonderfully welcoming and whole families wandered in, clutching parcels and dressed in casual summer clothes. At the opening bars, the pews filled up and people had to perch on the tombs or sit in the confessionals. They listened until the children got bored and fidgety, or the babies started to howl, and then they wandered out again. It was so relaxed and informal that there were even a few Indian faces in the audience. Beethoven bangs about rather too much for my taste and it was years since I had last sat through the whole of one of his symphonies. But I had to admit that 'The Ode to Joy' was splendidly performed that night and wonderfully exhilarating.

The next evening, I got into conversation with an elegantly dressed man, who was sitting alone on the next table in my restaurant. He turned out to be an off-duty colonel in the Chilean army.

'Where will you be spending Christmas?' he asked.

'In a nunnery.'

Juan laughed, thinking I was joking. When he realised I was serious, he said, 'That won't be much fun! Why don't you come to Christmas dinner with us? I'll just check with my mother and give you a ring at your hotel tomorrow to confirm. We live in Providencia, very near to the Metro station, so you'll be able to reach us quite easily.'

I'd arranged to go out to the nunnery on 23 December and spend the whole of the Christmas season there. One of my friends from my days as a headmistress was at one time head of a school in the Roman Catholic Society of the Holy Child Jesus. It was Sister Jean who had arranged for me to go and stay in the Society's House in Santiago. It was out in La Cisterna, one of the city's poorer districts, too far out for me to cycle, according to the tourist office. So I left Condor reclining at his ease in my hotel and travelled out on the Metro.

'We're not very easy to find,' said Sister Elizabeth Mary, when I phoned. 'But just outside La Cisterna station, there's a big McDonald's. You can't miss it. I'll meet you there at five o'clock, in the doorway.'

There was no mistaking her. Sister Elizabeth Mary was North American, taller and leaner than most Chilean women, and dressed in the sort of pink trousers and flowery blue and white T-shirt that no middle-aged, middle-class Chilean woman would dream of wearing. And the recognition was mutual.

'You must be Anne. I'm Elizabeth,' she said, with a firm handshake. 'I knew it was you, as soon as you came out of the Metro. No Chilean woman ever strides along the street like that!'

We took a taxi to the Centro C. Connelly, named after the Society's foundress, and I was introduced to the other two Sisters, both North Americans. Edwina was a large, elegant lady, who drifted around in beautifully cool flowing dresses. Peggy, always in cotton trousers, was small, neat and slim. The only other resident was Nancy, the Chilean novice, a young woman in her thirties.

It was the start of a delightful few days. The Centro C. Connelly was a large old house, where the three nuns inhabited the original single-storey building. Behind it lay a court-yard luxuriant with lemon trees, fuchsias and the kinds of tropical plants that struggle to survive as weedy dwarves in our centrally heated rooms. In Santiago they flourished amaz-ingly out of doors, sprouting leaves as large as dinner plates in the shade of the overhanging vines. Across this dappled green space, where we took our meals, lay the chapel, the shower and laundry block, Nancy's room and the guest quarters.

My room was just about the best appointed room I have ever stayed in anywhere, on all my travels. There was a comfortable armchair for reading in. My desk was equipped with writing paper, envelopes, pens and pencils, stamps, a card of welcome, a vase of wild flowers and even a tiny Christmas tree with miniature decorations. There was a kettle, coffee, tea and biscuits on a side table and a small packet of beautifully wrapped and beribboned sweets beside my bed. There was even that rarity for travellers: an abundance of coathangers in the wardrobe. And as the place was American run, everything worked: the electricals, the washing machine, the lavatory flush and the hot water.

We all sat down in the courtyard to *onces*, our 'elevenses' cups of afternoon tea, then I went shopping with the Sisters in Montecarlo, the local supermarket, to make up Christmas food packets for the poor. Elizabeth also bought our own Christmas turkey and I contributed the wine to go with it.

I felt a bit embarrassed about my invitation to go to Colonel Juan's for Christmas dinner. I was afraid it might offend the Sisters if I abandoned them for the main celebration, when they had most kindly invited me to spend the whole of the festive season with them. And I had other doubts too. I had, after all, allowed myself to be picked up by a strange man in a restaurant in downtown Santiago, and I had only his word for it that he was an army colonel and a respectable family man. For all I knew, he could be the mad rapist of Santiago. I screwed up my courage later that evening to lay my quandary before the Sisters.

'Oh, what fun!' cried Elizabeth immediately. 'What a wonderful opportunity! We've never been invited into that sort of household. They're probably Pinochetistas to a man. You must go, and tell us all about it afterwards.'

'Are you sure he means Christmas Day?' asked Nancy. 'In Chile, we usually have our Christmas dinner on Christmas Eve.' Peggy rang to check and, to my relief, spoke to Juan's mother. So he really did have a mother and a family; and I was indeed invited for Christmas Eve. This meant that I could share the colonel's Christmas dinner on the 24th, then join the Sisters for theirs on the 25th. It was all working out beautifully.

Juan telephoned later. 'I thought I should warn you. We shall all be going to Christmas Mass at eight o'clock. If you'd like to come with us, you'd be very welcome. Otherwise, you can stay here in the flat and read or watch television or something. Whichever you choose to do, make sure you get here by seven-thirty. It's not safe to be out on your own in Santiago much later than that.'

I smiled to myself. As a lone traveller, I'd been out on my own every evening and felt perfectly safe wandering round the streets of Santiago, but urbanites the world over give dire warnings about the dangers lurking in their cities. The Sisters agreed with him and added, 'If you come back late, don't just take any old taxi. Ring us up and we'll send one of our known taxi drivers out from La Cisterna to collect you. There are criminals out there, and some people who have taken so-called taxis have never been seen again.'

I spent Christmas Eve informing myself about Cornelia Connelly, whose biography Elizabeth had written in Spanish, chiefly for the Society's Associates in South America. Then I dolled myself up in my silk jacket and black silk palazzo pants, bought a bunch of flowers for Juan's mother and travelled across Santiago to the Pedro de Valdivia Metro station. I was met there by Juan's teenage son, Francisco.

'You speak excellent English,' I said. 'Do you go to a bilingual school?'

'No. I just have the talent for it,' he replied modestly. 'I'm concentrating on my English, because I so want to go to London. I want to see the Changing of the Guard and Nelson's Column. But most of all, I want to go to Westminster Abbey, to pay my respects at the tomb of Admiral Cochrane. How many people in England know about Admiral Cochrane?'

'Very few. The South American independence struggle is not taught in English schools, so no one knows much about its heroes.'

'I was so inspired by Admiral Cochrane that I used to want to go into the navy. But I've changed my mind now. I think I'll go into the army instead.'

Francisco was greatly impressed to hear that I'd visited the *Huascar* and seen the spot where Arturo Prat so nobly fought and died. He had never been to Concepción himself, so I told him about that other hero, Second Lieutenant Ignacio Serrano, the one who, with his dying breath, had seized the oil lamp beside his bunk and tried to set fire to the ship.

'And after all that heroism and all that the ship means to us, the Peruvians want the *Huascar* back. It's disgusting!' he said.

Francisco escorted me to Juan's flat. He and Maria de los Angeles lived with their father, while their mother, who was separated, lived somewhere else in Santiago. Juan's own mother lived in another flat in the same block and it was she who came over to be our hostess for the evening, along with an old friend of hers. We all walked together to the enormous Church of our Lady of Divine Providence, Francisco telling me with pride that it was built on the very site of the farm where Arturo Prat had spent most of his childhood. Juan was a lay reader there, but we still had to scramble for seats, as the church was absolutely jam-packed with the prosperous of Providencia.

The Mass was unlike any church service I'd ever attended. It began with Santa Claus in a Christmas play for the children, compered by a kind of woman MC, who described the proceedings over a microphone. Then a vigorous male voice choir, accompanied by electric guitars, bawled out a selection of carols and Christmas songs, including very secular items such as 'Jingle Bells'. Suddenly, the church went dark and a spotlit doll was carried aloft down the shadowy aisle by two priests and laid in an elaborate crib with a lit-up model of Bethlehem town behind it. This aroused a storm of clapping from the congregation (a new practice of which Juan's mother disapproved).

Then we began the Festival of Nine Lessons and Carols, with nervous little children stumbling their way through most of the readings. By the time we all stood up for the Gospel according to St John – 'In the beginning was the Word, and the Word was with God, and the Word was God. The same was in the beginning with God' – we had been sitting in our pews for almost two hours and I thought we might be nearing the end of the service. But not a bit of it. The vicar, who had so far played only a minor role, now began to prance up and down the aisle with a microphone, picking out children and asking them what they were giving to Jesus for Christmas. Santa joined in, and together they made the point that Christmas was a celebration of the birth of Christ. It was a time for Christian re-dedication, not just a time to receive lots of presents. Finally, we got to the sacrament. The Host was served by seven priests in seven different parts of the church, but even so, the size of the congregation made it an extremely lengthy Communion. As we left the church, we were all given a Christmas card and a caramel. By this time, it was 11 o'clock, and we had been sitting there for more than three hours! But that vicar certainly knew how to pack them in, and how to keep them there.

We walked back to Juan's flat and *colo de mono* was produced. This is a traditional Christmas drink, made of aguardiente with chilled milk, coffee and cinnamon. I opted for a glass of Juan's fine Chilean wine instead. The family were all very thoughtful towards me, even producing a Christmas present, a handsome maroon leather wallet, so that I wouldn't feel out of it when they were all exchanging their gifts – which were surprisingly few and modest for people who were obviously pretty well off.

Juan rang the convent, to tell the Sisters that I would be staying the night with his family, and at about 2 a.m. we at last sat down to our Christmas dinner. I was absolutely starving by that time, and not a little light-headed after a few glasses of wine on an empty stomach. We began with thinly sliced cold roast beef on a bed of lettuce, followed by a joint of roast pork, roast potatoes, sweetcorn and tomato salad, and ended with bowls of strawberries and cherries. Somehow, the conversation over dinner got round to the differences between Protestantism and Roman Catholicism. Despite their obvious involvement with their church, Juan and his mother seemed to be rather weak on Catholic dogma and I found myself, in my semi-inebriated state, having to explain the doctrine of transubstantiation to them, in Spanish. It was also news to them that the Cardinal Archbishop of Santiago was *papabile*, i.e. in the running to be the next Pope. They got very excited about that. 'Just imagine! A Chilean Pope!' Juan's mother returned to the flat to produce breakfast later that morning. Then I took the Metro and a taxi back to the convent, arriving just in time to join the Sisters for *their* Christmas dinner.

Their table was spread in the shade of the vines and, instead of the usual grace, we sang the Gloria together before tucking into our turkey with cranberry sauce; Peggy conducted a short Christmas service during the pause between the turkey and the pudding.

'How was the Mass last night?' asked Elizabeth.

'Long. It went on for about three and a half hours.'

'You should have stayed here. Ours was only an hour.'

They were highly amused that I, a Protestant, had spent my Christmas dinner explaining the doctrine of transubstantiation to a devout Catholic family and discussing papal infallibility with them. But they were disappointed that I had nothing to report on the political front. The conversation never got round to General Pinochet. Juan's only political remark concerned Pablo Neruda, the Chilean Nobel Prize-winner.

'I don't like Neruda,' he said.

'Why not?'

'He was a communist.'

To which my response was, 'I don't like Neruda either, because I'm not moved by his poetry.' Not a profound remark, but my Spanish doesn't rise to literary criticism.

After two substantial Christmas dinners with plenty of wine in the space of twelve hours, I really needed my siesta that afternoon. I retired to bed with the book of Elizabeth Jennings' poetry which Elizabeth had given me for Christmas, and a history of the Papacy by Eamon Duffy of Magdalene College, Cambridge. For lighter reading, I savoured my Christmas emails, especially one from my friend Hugh, which began with the throwaway line, 'The last time I spent Christmas in a nunnery was in 1945 . . .' He always likes to be one up!

I was interested in the casualness of the Sisters' dress, their jeans and pink trousers.

'Is it because it's Christmas and you're off duty that you're dressed like this? Sister Jean says that members of the Society should dress like young widows.'

'So?' said Elizabeth.

'Well, she usually wears a sort of neutral skirt and tweed jacket with a white blouse.'

They all looked amazed. 'You Brits!' was the reaction. 'Of course we always dress like this.'

As Cornelia Connelly had been inspired by the Jesuits to found her Society of the Holy Child Jesus, there were many similarities between the two Orders, including one which Sister Jean had told me was now an embarrassment. The title of the Society's Head was 'Superior General', a title which was no longer acceptable in these egalitarian days, when the Church is no longer militant. It was felt that neither 'Superior' nor 'General' could be used, and some other title must be found. After long deliberation, Jean told me they had decided on the simple title 'Leader', but that had upset the German Sisters, for whom its translation '*Führer*' had unfortunate connotations. I was chatting about this with Elizabeth after supper on my last evening, when it just slipped out in the course of conversation that she herself had been the Superior General in Rome when all this was being debated! She had served her six years in Rome, which was the customary tenure of the office, but had managed to get it reduced to four years for her successors. Six years of Vatican politics was, in her view, too long to be away from the real work of the Society.

The three Sisters left at crack of dawn on the 27th to attend a conference and I spent my last day in the Centro C. Connelly talking to Nancy. The Sisters and I had carried on our conversations in English, a language which was still a struggle for her, so she had been rather out of things. Now was my chance to practise my Spanish and listen to her story.

She told me that she came from a family of twelve children in Concepción (which I thought was an appropriate place name!). Before she decided to 'take the veil', she had a small dressmaking business.

'I was drawn to this particular Society, but I hesitated for a long time before applying to join,' she told me. 'You see, the Sisters' main role is educational. They run schools for girls, and work amongst poor women, running literacy classes and self-help groups to give them confidence in themselves and teach them their rights. I didn't go to university, or even high school, so I didn't feel that I was qualified to do that sort of work. But they took me on and I've found my place now. I've found things I can do that are really useful. The Society runs crèches and kindergartens, to enable women to go out to work and earn some money of their own. Here in Santiago, I work in a kindergarten, helping with the child-minding, and I visit patients with AIDS on a regular basis. At the same time, I'm studying to improve my English and learn more about Christianity. In March, they're sending me to California, to work among the poor Mexican immigrants there.'

'Will it be your first time out of Chile?' I asked.

'No. I've worked in a hospital in Philadelphia. I wasn't much use, because my English was so poor at the time. But I had one great day, when I helped a young woman who'd been shot in the neck and was paralysed. She couldn't move or speak, but I managed to get her into a wheelchair and I took her outside for a walk in the grounds. It was the first time she'd been out of doors since her injury, and you could see from her eyes that she thought it was wonderful. It was such a small thing, yet no one had thought of doing it for her.'

She wanted to know all about my travels. 'I can use a computer now,' she said. 'I shall improve my English by studying your website. And in San Diego, when my English gets really good, I shall read all your books.' That was music to my ears. She was a lovely girl and I hope she does well in a Society where novices are scarce.

The work of the Sisters among the poor women of Cisterna chimed well with Chilean Government schemes, run by the National Society for Women. Posters around the towns carried slogans encouraging their empowerment and their entry into paid occupation: *CHILE NECESSITA FUERZA DE MUJER* (Chile needs the strength of women) and *CREA FUTURO CON MANOS DE MUJER* (Create the future with the hands of women).

In a country so ravaged by earthquakes, there are few buildings of any antiquity left standing in Chile. One of the few exceptions in Santiago is the Church of San Francisco, which dates back to 1586. Legend has it that Pedro de Valdivia, the founder of Santiago, travelled down from Peru with a carved image of the Virgen del Socorro (the Virgin of Help) riding before him on his saddle, to protect him from harm. He gave the statuette to the Franciscans, who placed it on the high altar, and it is this image of the Virgin which is believed to have protected the Church of San Francisco on the many occasions when other churches in the city have been flattened by seismic disasters.

I stood in front of the high altar in some mystification. Rising from a sea of white chrysanthemums was a large, romantic statue of the Virgin, dressed in silks and lace and encircled by lights. She didn't at all resemble my idea of Valdivia's simple wooden Virgen del Socorro. Had the original been hidden away behind this opulent successor? There was no one around whom I could ask.

Unlike the elaborate Virgin before the high altar, the church itself was a model of Franciscan simplicity, with powerful rough-hewn stone arches reaching up to a pink and grey-green coffered ceiling, each wooden coffer decorated with a delicate little flower. And the altar to Saint Francis himself, who was known to preach to the birds and beasts, was plastered all over with photographs of pet dogs, cats, rabbits and parrots, with prayers for their recovery from illness, or touching little notes of gratitude for their survival.

It was my fourth visit to Santiago, so I had already done the rounds of the museums and watched the Changing of the Guard at La Moneda, all khaki breeches and gleaming riding boots, with the classically named Orfeon National blasting out stirring marches on their trumpets and euphoniums. The one bit of sightseeing I still had to do was the Postal Museum. I'm not a keen philatelist, but I wanted an excuse to explore the Correo Central, a flamboyant French fin de siècle building, because it stands on the site of Pedro de Valdivia's original house in the Plaza de Armas. Appropriately enough for a post office, it's the site where he penned his first letter to the Emperor Charles V of Spain, describing his foundation of Santiago de la Nueva Extremadura in 1541.

When I think of Santiago, which I often do in England on dreary winter days, I remember the first time I arrived there. I was on my second circuit of the globe and I'd just cycled over the Andes in Peru and struggled down through Nazca and the Atacama Desert. Then, miraculously, after weeks of dust, potholes, basic accommodation and even more basic fare, I found myself in a sophisticated city, where I could put on my silk suit and step out for an evening at the ballet. There were delicatessens, stacked with flavoursome dishes, like tables laid in paradise, and noble Chilean wines. The air was balmy and in the distance there loomed the snow-covered peaks of the Andes, the city's majestic guardians. It was town-mouse heaven. I walked around in a daze of delight, marvelling at the almost Swiss cleanliness and efficiency of the city. I could have been in Geneva or Lausanne, except that the colour and vitality of the street life could only be South American.

I have read in the guidebooks that there is smog in the winter; and the city, like any capital, has its share of slums. I've visited Santiago myself only in delightful summer weather and, being a woman travelling alone, I have more sense than to poke around in city slums, so I accept that my view may be skewed and romantic. But I can only describe things as I see them.

Recently, at one of my talks about my travels, a woman in the audience asked me a question I'd never had before: 'If you could be transported by magic, this very minute, to anywhere in the world, where would you choose?'

Without a moment's hesitation, I said, 'Santiago de Chile.'

7. A SANTIAGO FUNERAL

Pallida Mors aequo pulsat pede pauperum tabernas
  Regumque turris.

(Pale Death with impartial foot knocks on the doors of poor men's huts and kings' castles.)

(Horace)

I guessed that something significant had happened when I flew into Santiago airport on 11 December 2006 and saw the queue at Immigration. It was notable for the number of photographers weighed down with really serious equipment and reporters carrying those furry-looking microphones, which they push into the faces of reluctant interviewees in the streets. One glance at the local newspaper headlines and all was explained. General Pinochet had just died and the world's press was descending on Santiago to cover the funeral.

His body lay in state in the chapel of Santiago's military academy, where his supporters kept up a vigil. They lit candles and carried banners, emblazoned with GRACIAS, PINOCHET! (Thank you, Pinochet!) Thousands filed past his coffin, including some Neo-Nazi youths, who managed to give Hitler salutes before they were ejected. His opponents occupied the Plaza de la Constitución, burning his portraits, brandishing pictures of devils with pitchforks and singing and dancing into the early hours. Overnight, graffiti appeared on the walls: *PINOCHET BIENVENIDO AL INFERNO!* (Pinochet, welcome to Hell!)

General Augusto Pinochet Ugarte was the powerful figure who had dominated Chilean politics for over thirty years. Even in retirement, he was still, as the world knows, the subject of bitter controversy. Should he be hailed as the strong president who had put Chile on the road to economic prosperity and be granted immunity from prosecution? Or should he stand trial for crimes against humanity and be brought to account for the thousands who 'disappeared' in the aftermath of his 1973 coup?

When he died, the decision had already been taken to bring him to trial in Chile. This raised a particularly tricky problem for the newly elected socialist President, Michelle Bachelet, and her Cabinet. Should they, as his supporters were demanding, give General Pinochet the funeral of a former head of state? Or should he be buried in obscurity as a man under trial for human rights abuses? Passions in the country were running high and the new government was being put to a dangerous test.

In the end, a brilliant compromise was reached. General Pinochet had been a professional soldier and, as president, had been commander-in-chief of the armed forces. Even after he was voted out as president in 1990, he still retained this military rank until 1998. So the government decided to hand over the arrangements to the army. They would be allowed to give him a grand funeral, as befitted a former commander-in-chief of the armed forces, but no member of the government would attend, except the Minister of Defence, Vivianne Blanlot, in her official capacity as the Cabinet member responsible for the army.

On the morning of the funeral, I took my seat in the Marco Polo Café on the Plaza de Armas, where there was a large television screen. The café was doing a brisk trade, but most of the customers were chatting away with typical South

American animation over their coffees and soft drinks. Apart from myself, only two elderly gentlemen and an ancient waiter were taking any notice at all of the ceremony which was unfolding on the screen.

The funeral mass in the chapel of the military academy lasted for almost three hours. There were eight addresses, some by family members, some by former colleagues and finally the address of the Commander in Chief of the Army, General Oscar Izurieta Ferrer. It had been agreed that the speakers should avoid all reference to politics and that Pinochet should be referred to throughout as 'General Pinochet', not 'President'. The concluding speech of General Izurieta was a fine piece of diplomacy. Having given a strictly factual résumé of Pinochet's career, he went on to say that he hoped the general's death would calm the passions which he had aroused during his lifetime. 'Let us leave the fair and objective judgement of his role to history.'

There were two casualties of the occasion, men whose 'words cost them dear', according to the national newspaper *El Mercurio*. One was the general's grandson, Captain Augusto Pinochet Molina, who jumped up uninvited and praised his grandfather as the president who had defeated the Marxist menace. The army rushed to issue an official statement, distancing themselves from these remarks and emphasising that the army was at the service of everyone in Chile, irrespective of their politics. Captain Pinochet was reprimanded for his breach of military discipline and expected to be demoted.

The other casualty was General Ricardo Hargreaves, the general commanding the south of Chile. He gave an interview to a leading southern newspaper, *La Prensa Austral*, in support of General Pinochet. He told the journalist that he had assisted him willingly in the coup of 1973 and had served him wholeheartedly in its aftermath. General Hargreaves had recently been approved for promotion to the post of General Commanding the Santiago Region, but he was asked by General Izurieta for his resignation. The minister of defence was quoted as saying, 'We are not talking here about Pinochet. We are simply saying that the military should not express political opinions, or associate themselves in any way with those who are expressing them.'

After the funeral mass, the army took over and performed the rest of the ceremony with great dignity and precision. We're quite conceited in England about the perfect military discipline of our Brigade of Guards on State occasions, but I have to admit that they could have put on no finer display than the Chilean army. Two soldiers folded the national flag, which was draped over the coffin, and General Izurieta presented the immaculately neat bundle to General Pinochet's widow. Then the coffin was placed on a gun carriage and did a ceremonial lap of honour round the parade ground in front of the military academy, to the great acclamation of the thousands of Pinochet supporters assembled there. The gun carriage was followed, in traditional fashion, by the general's riderless horse – though I suspect it was a long time since the portly ninety year old had last gone out for a ride on it. Finally, the body of the general, accompanied by his family and General Izurieta, was whisked off in an army helicopter to Concón, on the coast north of Valparaíso, to be cremated. It is thought that his ashes were scattered in the grounds of the family seaside home in Santo Domingo.

It may seem strange that a devout Roman Catholic in a Roman Catholic country should be cremated, not buried. But Pinochet was a controversial figure, in death as in life. There may have been fears that a tomb or monument would be desecrated, or might turn into an embarrassing place of pilgrimage.

While the official solemn rites were being performed, an alternative ceremony was taking place in the Plaza de la Constitución in front of La Moneda, the presidential palace. It was in honour of 'the victims of repression' and of President Salvador Allende, who died in the bombing of the palace during Pinochet's coup of 1973. The ceremony drew a miscellaneous crowd of about six thousand people – socialists, communists waving red flags, human rights activists and the Mothers of the Disappeared, carrying photographs of their lost sons and daughters. *ADIOS, CRIMINAL Y LADRÓN'* (Goodbye, Criminal and Robber) read the banners. Chile being a well-ordered country, permission had been granted to hold this rally, but the police were in obvious attendance.

I was just tucking into my lunch of a tortilla with a glass of wine in the Marco Polo, when pandemonium erupted in the Plaza de Armas. Their rally over, the anti-Pinochetistas had dispersed and hundreds of them were now running through the square, shouting and waving banners. The normally laid-back waiters feared the worst and flew out in a body to bring in the café chairs and furl the umbrellas. But the mob was noisy rather than destructive. They rushed in at one end of the square, ran across it and rushed straight out again at the other end. The mounted police had no quelling to do, and the café's chairs and umbrellas were soon restored to their usual places outside.

In fact, considering the political passions which General Pinochet aroused, the days surrounding his death and funeral passed by with remarkable tranquillity. It was a happy chance – or perhaps it was discreetly engineered – that his supporters congregated on the outskirts, outside the military academy, while his opponents gathered in the city centre. The two factions were far away from each other, well out of fighting range. There were only thirty arrests.

That evening, everything was back to normal. I strolled around the Plaza de Armas, licking my customary chocolate-chip mint ice cream and watching the street entertainers, the chess players and the evangelists, who were all carrying on as usual. The only incident was totally unrelated to the week's events. A man with a bleeding head and face came running through the square, pursued by his aggressor, who was being pursued in his turn by two other men. The carabinieri were on the scene in a flash. They bundled the attacker into their van and summoned an ambulance. The square settled down again. Chile is a safe, orderly, well-mannered country.

It is also a country with a sense of humour. That weekend one of the satirical magazines carried a wonderfully irreverent cover. General Pinochet had lain in state in a coffin with a glass panel, which allowed his supporters to see his face and the blue and gold collar of his military uniform as they filed past. Photographs of the coffin and its occupant had appeared in all the newspapers. This particular magazine showed the same photograph but instead of both the general's eyes being closed in death, one beady blue eye was wide open. Big Brother was still watching them!

We reach the Pampa, Patagonia

Right Monument to Che Guevara, Havana
Below Ingeniero White Museum

Street tango dancers,
Buenos Aires

Cycling across
the Pampa

The ferocious
Patagonian winds

Above Hansel and Gretel country
Right Waiting to cross Lake Frias

Osorno Volcano on
Lake Lanquihue

Above Changing the guard, Santiago
Below The heroic Lt. Prat, Talcahuano

Below Picnicking in the shade of Pedro de Valdivia

Above Street entertainers,
Plaza de Armas

Above Santa feels the heat!
Below Pinochet, welcome to hell!

Restaurant,
Atacama desert

Baquedano

Christmas crib, Calama

Above The slow FCAB train to Bolivia

Below The silver mountain over Potosí

Above Royal mint, Potosí
Below The silver mines

Above Che Guevara's birth place, Rosario

8. TRAVELLING NORTH

We had been, so to speak, gentlemen of the road ... Not any more.
Now we were just two tramps with packs on our backs, the grime of the
road encrusted in our overalls, shadows of our former aristocratic selves.
(Ernesto Che Guevara)

Not having a funeral to attend, the two ex-bikers spent little time in Santiago before heading north. After their tearful farewells to La Ponderosa, they converted their saddle-bags into backpacks and set off to hitch-hike to Venezuela. They were used to attracting attention in their bikers' gear, and the 'asthmatic wheezing' of their suffering machine had aroused considerable pity. On La Ponderosa, they had belonged to what Ernesto called 'the time-honoured aristocracy of wayfarers' and were offered generous hospitality wherever they went. Now their status had changed. They were just two tramps. They stood for four hours, wearily thumbing, on the road out of Santiago before a lorry finally pulled up and gave them a lift over the mountains to Valparaíso. The driver dumped them on the outskirts of town and sped off into the distance. Left to haul their heavy packs down the streets towards the sea, they were objects of amusement to the few locals who took any notice of them. The majority simply passed them by. They were treated with indifference.

I know exactly what Che Guevara meant. When I'm travelling on my bicycle, everyone is interested. Hotel receptionists, policemen, waiters, tourist information clerks and ladies out shopping are all eager to know who I am, where I come from, where I'm going, what I'm doing and why. I'm offered assistance and lifts, cups of tea and coffee in cafés, drinks in restaurants, and I never lack for a bed. When there's no hotel available, someone will always find somewhere safe for a solitary woman cyclist to stay. Cycling (or at least some sort of self-propulsion on two wheels, as in the case of Ernesto and Alberto) is the key to hospitality's door. More importantly, it's the key to human contact. The bicycle is the great leveller, especially in societies where it's the most common form of transport. People who might shy away from a tourist in a car, welcome a cyclist into their lives. I stay with them. They take me round their schools and hospitals, invite me to their weddings and funerals, and I learn about their daily struggles and their hopes and dreams for the future. For my part, I may not be such an exotic creature as the wealthy Americans who feature in their favourite TV soaps, with their ranches and oil wells, but my modest travel tales still offer them a glimpse of a wider world.

How different it all is without a bicycle! On my fifth visit to Chile, I was planning to continue into Bolivia, where the altitude is taxing, the distances great and the unpaved roads so rough that I would have needed a mountain bike and a mountain biker's skill. So I had flown into Santiago as a normal bikeless tourist.

We all become invisible as we grow older. Instead of finding eager hands to help me pump up the tyres and fix on the panniers, I was just another invisible old ducky trundling her wheeled suitcase through the arrivals hall. I was treated with courtesy, but I was still a non-person. I travelled into town in one of the airport *micros* and presented myself to the hotel receptionist, who handed over my room key and directed me to the lift, his eyes glazed over with indifference. I missed the keen interest and the flurry of activity that always greets my arrival on a bicycle. I felt somehow unconnected. Like the former motorcyclists, I was just a dull former cyclist when I took the bus to Valparaíso, not a member of 'the time-honoured aristocracy of wayfarers'.

Of all the nationalities who settled in Chile and Argentina, the British were the main entrepreneurs. The Spanish conquistadors were usually no more than bounty hunters in search of gold who appropriated, as a sideline, vast swathes of land to be worked by Indian labour – the great estancias which still exist to this day, despite various efforts at land reform. The Germans and Swiss came later, often seeking religious freedom and better opportunities. The majority were farmers, who worked the rich soil themselves and developed the fruit, dairy and beef cattle industries in the centre and south. The Italians were mostly poor migrants, who sailed as labourers, mainly to Argentina, to escape the poverty of Naples, Campania and Calabria, and settled around Buenos Aires. Then there was a sprinkling of other nationalities, all of whom contributed in their various ways. But it was the British in the nineteenth century, with some help from the North Americans, who built the railways, set up the factories, mined the minerals and developed the harbours for their export.

Valparaíso, the port of Santiago, bears their indelible stamp. There is the Plaza Victoria, the Avenida Gran Bretana, streets called Templeman, Edwards, Ross and Cochrane, and the main department store is Johnson's. The fledgling port was sacked by Sir Francis Drake in 1578, but relations had improved by 1815, when the Royal Navy's Pacific Squadron chose Valparaíso as one of its bases. Under the navy's protection, a colony of British merchants settled there, just in time to benefit from the Chilean mining boom of the 1830s, and also the California Gold Rush of the late 1840s, when grain and fruit from Chile were desperately needed to feed the prospectors in the undeveloped American West. The British expanded the port and worked busily to cope with the vast increase in trade but, true to national character, they didn't forget their preoccupation with sport. Passionate cricketers founded a league of local clubs, and British sporting life was complete when the Santiago Wanderers, Chile's oldest football team, moved to Valparaíso to compete with their own Everton. Then the British felt really at home.

Valparaíso is a wonderful shambles. It tumbles down from a ring of 42 steep hills to a narrow strip of land beside the bay, beautiful houses and churches hugger-mugger with tin shacks, all clinging on to the cliffs by the fingernails and all painted in rainbow colours. Viewed from the harbour below, it's a unique sight, like a child's paintbox open to the ocean, a gaudy kaleidoscope, well worth its place on UNESCO's World Heritage List (2003).

The flat bit round the port houses the official buildings, most of them destroyed in the earthquake of 1906 (a whopping 8.6 on the Richter scale) and rebuilt either in fin de siècle or concrete brutalist style. But one of the ugliest hulks, the Chilean Congress building, is far more recent, dating from the height of the Pinochet era.

Valparaíso was, strangely enough, the birthplace of the two most controversial presidents of Chile. They even attended the same school there. First came the socialist Salvador Allende, who was elected in 1970 and led a left-wing coalition, La Unidad Popular. (His communist opponent in the election was no other than Chile's Nobel Prize-winner, Pablo Neruda.) Allende's election, on a radical platform, led to a fall in the stock market and a run on the banks. Agrarian reform proceeded apace and businesses were nationalised, including the entire copper industry, Chile's main money-spinner. Nixon and Kissinger were gravely worried at what they perceived as a threat to the region's stability, especially as Allende was openly friendly with their *bête noire*, Fidel Castro of Cuba. So in 1973, the Chilean armed forces, with backing from the CIA, smashed the populist government. They bombed La Moneda, the presidential palace, and Salvador Allende was either killed by rocket fire or committed suicide. The leader of the

American-backed coup was a relatively unknown army officer, Allende's fellow-citizen from Valparaíso, Augusto Pinochet. As General Pinochet, he took over as president of Chile and the rest is history.

His gift to his hometown was the transfer of the National Congress from Santiago to Valparaíso. It's housed in one of the city's brutalist concrete structures and broods over the Plaza O'Higgins like a sick elephant. The Congress sits there only three days a week, for three weeks in the month during the parliamentary sessions. With the expense of ferrying politicians back and forth from the capital and providing them with two homes, its future looks uncertain, now that Pinochet no longer has any say in the matter.

For times have changed. Chile's president is now a woman, Michelle Bachelet, the first female president of a South American state. She is one of Pinochet's torture victims, a paediatrician by profession, a socialist and a single mother in a basically conservative Roman Catholic country, where the legalisation of divorce was opposed until 2004. 'I am just a Chilean woman, no more and no less than millions of other Chileans,' she said in a recent interview. 'I work, I take care of my home and I drop my daughter off at school. But I'm also a Chilean who feels a calling to fight for justice and for public service.' She is a Chilean, too, who is enough of a pragmatist not to squander the economic progress made under General Pinochet, with the help of Milton Friedmann and his 'Chicago Boys'; and as a former minister of defence, she knows her international politics. Chile could be well on the way to joining the 'top table' under her leadership.

But when the two erstwhile bikers passed through, Chile was a much poorer country than their native Argentina. They installed themselves in a lorry park, where the generous proprietor of a fish and chip shack fed them, free of charge, throughout their stay in Valparaíso.

They were keen to get a passage on a boat to Easter Island, where Chile had its only leper colonies. Alberto followed up the introductions given to them by the doctors they had met in Petrohue, while Ernesto paid a call on an old woman, who used to work as a waitress at the fish and chip shack. He found her lying in a poverty-stricken hovel, suffering from asthma and a weak heart. 'It is in cases like this,' he wrote in his rather tortuous prose, 'when a doctor knows he is powerless, that he longs for change; a change which would prevent the injustice of the system in which until a month ago this poor old woman had had to earn her living as a waitress, wheezing and panting but facing life with dignity.' He was distressed by her illness and, even more, by the acrimony which surrounded her. Her family were too poor to carry a non-contributor. She was a burden and they clearly resented her. She was an example of 'the profound tragedy which circumscribes the life of the proletariat the world over. In these dying eyes there is a humble appeal for forgiveness . . . It's time governments spent less time publicising their own virtues, and more money, much more money, funding socially useful projects.' Ernesto the political reformer was beginning to emerge.

Alberto meanwhile drew a blank with the doctors and the mayor of Valparaíso, who was president of the Friends of the Easter Island Society. He learned that a boat had just left for the island, and there wouldn't be another sailing for a whole year. So the friends abandoned their project of visiting the leper colonies there and stowed away on the *San Antonio*, a ship sailing north to Antofagasta. They were determined at all costs to avoid tramping the 1500 km across the Atacama, the driest desert on earth.

When they were discovered out at sea, Alberto was put to work in the kitchen, while the unfortunate Ernesto drew the short straw. He was made to scrub the decks and clean out the lavatories. But the captain was a genial fellow, who gave them a cabin belonging to an officer on leave and invited them for drinks and a game of canasta in the evenings. So, despite their unsavoury tasks, they still fared pretty well onboard ship and enjoyed the voyage. As they gazed out at night, 'each lost in his own thoughts, on his own flight towards the stratosphere of dreams, we discovered that our true vocation was to roam the highways and waterways of the world for ever'. Ernesto loves his poetic hyperboles. In fact, he had a habit of breaking out into poetry, usually Neruda's, to the astonishment of the more prosaic Alberto. 'I think he knows all the poems of the *Third Residence on Earth* and the *Twenty Love Poems* and *A Song of Despair* by heart,' he wrote admiringly.

I arrived in Valparaíso myself by bus, with a streaming cold, which drained my energy and put me off sightseeing for days. My hotel had cooking facilities and scrubbed tables in the kitchen for the use of guests, so I shopped in the supermarket and ate solitary salad suppers, washed down with whisky and hot peppermint tea. One night I staggered out to a nearby restaurant for cod and chips with a bottle of beer, but fled back rather swiftly when I was chatted up by a Chilean sailor with extravagant tattoos, who was in port on a German ship.

I was not feeling at all sociable, and it was not until my last evening in the city that I felt lively enough to accept an invitation from David, retired from the British Council, to have dinner with him in El Bar Inglés (The English Bar, of course!). David and I had spent the day together in Viña del Mar, the seaside resort where the beautiful people have their second homes. The town has the Palacio Vergara, like a cream Doge's Palace, a casino and the Viña del Mar Gentlemen's Club. While their elegant wives shop, the prosperous businessmen wallow in the club's leather, mahogany and brass under the glittering chandeliers. (I know, because I was cheeky enough to tread the red carpet and climb the sweeping double staircase, before I was asked politely to leave. Meanwhile, David, the well-behaved Englishman, hovered in embarrassment on the pavement outside.) It was a very dignified town, not at all like a European seaside resort. There were plenty of people bathing on the beaches, but I didn't see a single bikini or pair of shorts in the cafés or parading along the streets.

Except at breakfast time, the Chilean guests in my hotel came nowhere near the kitchen, but the four young

Anglophones (British and South African) cooked up a storm every night. Baked fish, roast chickens, mashed potatoes, vegetables, salad, ice cream, beer and wine. They never went out in the evenings, which I thought was rather a pity. And I could never get onto the complimentary hotel internet to send my emails.

'Are you running a business or something from here?' I asked one of the two English gap-year boys. 'You're on the computer from morning till night, non-stop.'

'No. I'm not running a business. I'm just chatting.'

He hogged the computer, chatting in chat rooms, chatting to his family and friends at home and sending them reams of photographs. Whenever I passed the computer room, he was hunched over the machine, and I wondered when he went out to take all the photos he was transmitting. As far as I could see, he never set foot outside the door. It did make me question the value of some students' gap years. For all he saw of Valparaíso and Chile, he might just as well have stayed at home and chatted all day in the flesh to his nearest and dearest – or gone out and earned some money towards his university fees.

'I'm just killing time here,' he said, 'waiting for my flight to Australia. It's cheaper here than Santiago.'

Fortunately for me in my feeble state, there was little serious sightseeing to be done. The flat city centre was a dusty muddle, with horses and carts, men on horseback and load-bearing donkeys trotting along in the midst of the trolleybuses and other assorted motorised traffic. And as in every other city in Chile, the streets were paved with stray dogs, mostly large peaceable males, zonked out fast asleep, or rooting about for scraps and trying to hump anything else on four legs, even other males and the occasional cat – which was a great mistake, resulting in many scratched noses.

The real delights of Valparaíso lay in the precipitous streets, where the multicoloured houses staggered up the cliff faces, and people sat outside on their doorsteps, smoking and chatting with their neighbours, as they do in Havana. Some streets were so steep that they turned into flights of steps. Others were ascended by creaking wooden funicular railways, built in the nineteenth century and still carrying passengers today. I took the Ascensor Reina Victoria and got a splendid view of the city as the car climbed its mountain. But I'm no good at heights and the sight of the cogs and cable unreeling down the drop below me brought on such a severe attack of vertigo that I had to shut my eyes and cling to the bench. After that one experimental ride, I preferred to do my exploration on foot.

Having seen Pablo Neruda's extraordinary Santiago home, La Chascona (The Tangle-haired Woman), named after his third wife Matilde Urrutia, I was interested to see whether his house in Valparaíso, La Sebastiana, would be less eccentric, or more so. Both were built into mountainsides, the one in Santiago climbing up from the foot of Cerro San Cristóbal, and his Valparaíso home perched precariously near the top of one of the steep hills surrounding the bay. They were not houses for the unfit. The rooms ascended into one another by little staircases, rather than adjoining on the same level, as they do in normal houses; and as both places were crammed with a crazy collection of junk, they have somehow merged into one in my memory.

Neruda was a magpie of the first order. Authentic zinc-topped café tables from Paris fought for space with a fair-ground horse, a stuffed lion so long that it entirely covered a single bed, early nineteenth-century mechanical figures in turbans, painted chests, dolls and Japanese screens. There were Classical Greek votive offerings, mosaics, portraits of Admiral Cochrane, a collection of hand-painted plates of hot-air balloons, photographs of Neruda, a painting of the poet in profile cut out of a slice of water melon (his favourite fruit), and – my favourite object – a mechanical picture. It was on a plate showing a village, where the clock in the church tower actually told the time, and workmen were wielding pickaxes, a woman was spinning wool, ducks were diving in the pond and hens were pecking at corn. These were just a few of the items in his overwhelming collections. I enjoyed La Sebastiana more than La Chascona, because the visit was unescorted and I was able to potter around on my own without a guide, peering at the items which really interested me. The most memorable feature was the fantastic panoramic view of Valparaíso Bay from Neruda's fourth-floor study. But for a minimalist like myself, the houses were nightmares. And two of them were quite enough. I never went to see his third residence in Isla Negra.

I've tried hard to appreciate Neruda's poetry, first in translation, then in the original, as my ability to read Spanish grew. He is, after all, Chile's most famous poet, dubbed 'the poet laureate of the masses'. But his works have never spoken to me in any meaningful way. They seem like strings of clever words and images, and I find myself totally unmoved. And having visited two of his three homes, I now see him as an exceedingly vain man and have fallen out of sympathy with him as a person too. Perhaps I would get on better with Gabriela Mistral, Chile's other Nobel Prize-winning poet. I went north in pursuit.

As I travelled up through the Norte Chico (the Little North), I could see why Ernesto and Alberto were so keen to sail to Antofagasta. My bus climbed treeless, shadeless mountains, as empty of life as sand dunes. Occasional patches of tired brown scrub speckled the bone-dry earth and the only vegetation to rise to any height was the cardoon, a tall cactus like a vertically branched tree. There were no houses, no people, not even a goat. It was certainly no country for hitch-hikers – even less for cyclists – and I was glad to be viewing it through a bus window. From time to time, we swept down from this desolation into a valley, a luxuriant oasis of vineyards, ripening corn and orchards dripping with olives, apples and apricots. Then we were back in the mountains again, climbing up to the next arid pass.

I stayed in La Serena in a hotel run, like a number of other businesses in that region, by migrants from the former Yugoslavia. My main purpose there was to visit nearby

Vicuña, where the Museo Gabriela Mistral graces the poet's birthplace. It was a modern building, attached to a replica of the house where she lived as a child, in one room either side of a corridor. There was a good display of photographs, which chronicled her career, both as a teacher and later as an international educationalist and diplomat, and glass cases of her works. In such a small, out-of-the-way town, I was surprised at the large number of people filing through the museum, gazing reverently at the displays. As Chile's first Nobel Prize-winner (1945), her face appears on one of Chile's banknotes and many cities have their Calle Mistral. Unlike Neruda, who was a kind of pantheist and a communist (and therefore anathema to General Pinochet), Gabriela Mistral was celebrated by the regime as a poet who embodied true womanly virtues. So it is her simpler poems about children, motherhood and lost love which are best known today, while her profounder work tends to be overlooked. She is certainly less on display than Neruda in the bookshops.

Vicuña was a relaxed little town, with more Indian faces than I had seen in the big cities. I particularly liked the Church of the Immaculate Conception, whose interior was a show-piece of local woods, laid in imaginative patterns and beauti-fully polished. At the entrance, the usual notice banning ice creams, dogs, pushchairs and immodest clothing had the additional warning: SWITCH OFF YOUR MOBILE. YOU DON'T NEED IT TO TALK TO GOD.

The journey there took me along the fertile Elqui valley, most famous for the production of pisco, the powerful grape spirit which is mixed with egg white, icing sugar and lemon juice to make the national drink, pisco sour (whose invention is disputed with the Peruvians). It was a lovely ride, but my day out was spoilt by a man who harangued me outside La Serena bus station and followed me back to my hotel, raging vociferously.

'We want to know what really happened to Princess Di. She was so beautiful and so good, so kind to the ordinary people. Here in Chile, we think she was killed by the Secret Service, on orders from the Queen.'

'Rubbish!' I said.

'How do you know it's rubbish?'

'Because in England we don't do that sort of thing. We don't live in that sort of society. And the Queen doesn't behave like that. We don't just get rid of people if they're inconvenient, or hold different political views.'

The man was obviously drunk, so it was rather ironic that he went on to say, 'Everyone knows your Queen drinks – gin, like her mother.'

'She may do. And she may drink gin. I don't know. But you're right about her mother. She certainly drank gin – and she lived to the age of one hundred and one! So her gin did her less harm than your pisco sour is obviously doing you. If the Queen drinks, she does it in moderation. What's wrong with that?'

He ranted on. Having defended the Queen, I then ignored him and he finally gave up. But he was voicing the conspiracy theory that I have heard times without number from simpler people abroad. The enquiries into the circumstances of Princess Diana's death seem interminable, and every new twist and obfuscation is dramatised by the tabloid press, both at home and in other countries. The Stevens Inquiry and the aborted inquest have still not established the facts to the world's satisfaction, and British citizens abroad are still plagued by these wearisome accusations.

The next morning, I bought some new socks and a packet of plasters. The underside of one of my toes was badly chafed for some reason and I was worried that the rawness might become infected in such a hot climate. Then I limped into the cathedral, where I was struck with horror at one of the most gruesome paintings I have ever seen. It was hanging in the Chapel of Saint Bartholomew, one of the twelve Apostles, who is said to have been flayed alive. The effulgent saint stands in ecstasy behind a stunted tree, his head in its fork and his skin draped like a fashionable 'throw' over its dead branches. The detail is grisly, down to the floppy skin of his dangling finger ends and toes.

I find it amazing that any religion can relish such horrors, or find faith in them. The painting of Saint Bartholomew rivalled in awfulness a painting of Saint Agatha, which I saw down the Via Appia years ago and remember with nausea to this day. The Saint is screaming in agony, while a soldier hacks off her breasts, which plop onto a plate like twin jellies. And in Santiago, there is the blinded Santa Lucia, who carries her eyes before her on a dish. No wonder the Virgin Mary is so devoutly worshipped by Roman Catholics. She is just about the only holy personage who didn't come to a ghastly end. Her images are always serene and unfrightening.

The indigenous South American peoples had some terrifying gods who demanded human sacrifice. But the dark Hispanic brand of Roman Catholicism, which the conquering Spaniards imposed upon them, was scarcely more consoling. The terrors of the new religion simply merged with the terrors of the old. It was still a religion of blood, gore and suffering.

I think the Orthodox Church has much more to commend it. In pride of place in the Orthodox apse, Christ is shown in His glory as the Pantocrator, the Ruler of the World, not as the man suffering in agony on the Cross. As for the Saints, I always think with pleasure of the Church of S. Apollinare Nuovo in Ravenna. There the white-robed mosaic Saints march confidently towards the altar, each carrying a small symbol of his martyrdom, a little spear, arrow or gridiron. Their suffering is not forgotten, but it is the means to a glorious end, not the main focus of worship, to be dwelt on with macabre fascination. Perhaps the South American peoples would be more cheerful today, if they had been conquered by the mercurial Greeks with their welcoming churches, rather than by the darkly brooding Spaniards.

9. THE NORTE GRANDE

When you actually see the terrain the conquistadors crossed, you automatically raise the feat of Valdivia and his men to one of the most remarkable of Spanish colonisation.

(Ernesto Che Guevara)

Antofagasta made little impression on the two travellers. Alberto, the more practical of the two, gives a few facts. The *San Antonio* docked at two in the morning. They helped to moor the ship, then hid in the captain's cabin while the port officials did their tour of inspection. They were keen to visit the nitrate fields and the copper mines at Chuquicamata, but it took them some time to get the necessary permission documents. So they continued to sleep onboard ship. Ernesto mentions none of this. He simply refers to their 'appropriate send-off from enthusiastic Bacchanalian sailors.'

I travelled overnight to Antofagasta on one of the comfortable, economical intercity buses, which are the main means of transport in Chile. The buses come in several categories, from the standard *clásico* or *turista*, through the *ejecutivo* with slightly more leg room and the *semicama* (semi-bed) with reclining seats to the *cama*, which is like business class on a plane. The seats recline fully to make a flat bed, a pillow and blanket are provided, and meals are served. I treated myself to *cama* for the long ride north from La Serena.

Soon after we left the *terminal de buses*, the conductor came round with our dinners on an aircraft-style tray – smoked ham, salad, a hard-boiled egg, rice, beans and a bread roll, washed down with ginger beer and followed by chocolate gâteau. Breakfast was coffee and a chocolate brownie. The meals were not brilliant, but they were food and they were available. In that desolate landscape, we would have been hard put to it to find restaurants.

During the evening, we continued to travel through the desert of the Norte Chico. It was peppered with low thorn bushes, scrub and cactus – goat country, where roadside shacks advertised goat cheese and *cabritos* (baby goats). Two young women in the bus asked the driver to stop at one of these shacks. They haggled for a while with the family in the doorway, then came back to the bus in triumph, each of them brandishing a tiny kid, which was skinned and ready for the oven.

As we travelled on into the Norte Grande, even the shacks and cactus disappeared until we woke at dawn to the solitude of featureless dun desert. But the night had been extravagant with stars. In the unpolluted air, with no city lights to swamp them, the constellations shone as brightly as street lamps and far off galaxies were sheets of white flame across the sky. You have to go to the world's deserts to see stars. Unsurprisingly, La Serena and the Chilean Norte are home to some of the world's best-equipped observatories. What is disappointing, and much less romantic, is that the astronomers are no longer dedicated visionaries, who sit up all night gazing at the stars through their powerful telescopes. They sleep peacefully in their beds, as earthbound as you and I, while the data is automatically downloaded onto their computers.

Apart from heavy trucks and intercity coaches, there was little traffic on the road, though I did see a young couple on bicycles, with helmets and heavy panniers, pedalling grimly southwards. I didn't envy them. I've cycled across many deserts, but the desolation of the Norte Grande made even the Gobi seem verdant and densely populated by comparison. It was simply amazing to think that the Spanish conquistadors had marched south through those arid mountains wearing quilted doublets and suits of armour, with their brains roasting inside their iron helmets. In some areas of the desert, it never rains, ever. There are a few feeble, spasmodic rivers, around whose estuaries the original inhabitants of the land were able to sustain life. But today water is piped down to Antofagasta from the foothills of the Andes, over 400 km away.

We passed a huge Bio Bio cement plant, its dirty grey concrete merging with the dirty grey desert sand. The only cheerful sights were, paradoxically, the roadside shrines, which marked the spots where fatalities had taken place. These are an art form in South America generally, but the shrines of the Norte Grande outshone all others in fantasy. One was a plastic dome with a collection of toys and a small child's bicycle propped up against it. Another had a blue tin angel on its roof, blowing a trumpet. There was a Crucifixion. There were Madonnas. And one shrine stood in a walled enclosure, its forecourt patterned with pebbles and flying two full-sized Chilean flags. The simpler shrines looked rather like cheerful dog kennels, brightly painted and imaginatively decorated, with the name of the accident victim over the entrance and a vase of plastic flowers in front. Perhaps as a result of all these accidents, the road was being widened and the bus had to make spluttering detours through the sand. I wondered how the road workers survived in the middle of such torrid desolation, and where they slept. There were no signs of camps.

Our bus entered small oasis towns, to drop and pick up passengers. They were desperate places, trying hard to be cheerful in the midst of desolation. The main streets sported brilliant green lawns along their central reservations and sometimes there were clusters of jaunty red geraniums at the roots of the struggling trees. Then we were back in the grey sand, rimed with salt and speckled with low clumps of shrub, like patches of dun-coloured mould.

'Why on earth are you going to Antofagasta?' they had asked me in Santiago. 'Do you have family up there?'

'No. I write travel books.'

'Ah, that explains it! You're going for work. Nobody ever goes there for tourism, or just for a holiday – at least, not if they're in their right minds.'

Travelling through the Norte Grande, I could see what they meant. The only variation to the scenery was the occasional stretch of coastline, where black volcanic rocks rose in giant distorted shapes along the shore. Thirteen hours, even in a comfortable *cama* coach, seemed a very long time. I did a couple of *Times* jumbo crosswords, which I cut out and keep for such journeys, and read a few chapters of a Frederick Forsyth novel I'd picked up in a book exchange, but too many hours of concentration on small print gave me a headache. Also, the silence of the coach was ravaged by constant gunfire and explosions, as one murderous action film after another tore across the TV screen.

About 200 km from Antofagasta, an open-topped lorry had broken down. These are the vehicles in which the really poor travel from city to city, usually standing all the way, because there are too many of them to sit on the floor. They travel in stoic silence, human livestock, crammed together like sheep or cattle on the way to market – or like London commuters on the Tube in the rush hour. These passengers were squatting on their haunches, their hats pulled down over their faces against the glare of the sun. Waves of heat rose from the asphalt and there was not a scrap of shade by the roadside, so our driver stopped to pick them up.

They were all Indian workers on their way to the mines, and they had never travelled *cama* class before. It was a delight to watch them. They were absolutely thrilled, like children waking up to their presents on Christmas morning. They played with the reclining seats, pulling the levers to flatten them out and straighten them up again; they snapped the drinks holders down and up; they poured themselves plastic cups of mineral water from the communal container; they nipped in and out of the lavatory; and they followed the excitements of the television films with popping eyes.

I was just beginning to think that my head would burst with the noise and heat, when we dropped down from the bare desert plateau to the coastal shelf and pulled into Antofagasta, the bustling modern capital of the region. What a relief! It was nice and breezy by the sea and my headache cleared as if by magic. I was not expecting much of the city after the rude comments I'd heard about it in Santiago, but I took an immediate liking to the place. I checked into a hotel near the bus station, went for a leisurely stroll along the main drag, the Calle Arturo Prat, then rested in the leafy Plaza Colón. ('Colón' is a popular name for streets and squares in South America, so I should perhaps explain that Colón is the Spanish version of Columbus and bears no relation to English bodily parts!) I was told that the clock tower in the Plaza Colón was a replica of Big Ben, given by the British community to mark the centenary of Chile's independence, but it was a clunky affair, not nearly as elegant as its slender Gothic original, though its carillon was pleasing. It produced a Christmas carol every fifteen minutes.

What struck me most about Antofagasta was its youthfulness. To date, the staff I'd met in provincial Chilean hotels were of the 'old retainer' variety, the sort of characters Alec Guinness might have played in an Ealing comedy, stooping obsequiously in oversized false teeth and a brown overall. Here in Antofagasta, the waiters and waitresses were brisk young things. There was obviously money to be made in the industrial north.

'Where do you come from?' asked my handsome young waiter that evening, as I tucked into my enormous helping of roast pork and mashed potato. He broke into smiles and English.

'England! Oh, that's brilliant! I'd love to go to England. I love English rock.'

'And what about you? Where do you come from?' I asked. 'Were you born in Antofagasta?'

'No. I come from a poky little village inland. I couldn't believe my luck when I got a job here. It's a fantastic city. Wonderful clubs.'

So much for all those supercilious people in Santiago, who couldn't imagine why anyone would ever want to go to Antofagasta!

Just for fun, because I had a morning to spare, I took the minibus to Mejillones, the local fishing village and seaside resort, soon to be changed forever by the construction of a megaport. I was not intending to ride all the way just to see a popular beach. As I was only a few kilometres south of the Tropic of Capricorn, I thought I might as well visit the monument which was officially opened on the last solstice of the twentieth century, 21 December 2000.

The minibus was a convivial little vehicle. Our first stop was the fruit and vegetable market on the outskirts of Antofagasta. A man was waiting to get on there with half-a-dozen boxes and packing cases. Without being asked and without a moment's hesitation, a young boy on the seat in front of me jumped up and helped the man load his boxes onto the bus and distribute them in convenient places. He had seemed rather a podgy, slug-like boy in his dirty trainers and back-to-front baseball cap, but I had to upgrade my opinion of him when he behaved with such natural courtesy. There was no fashionable teenage 'attitude' about him.

We passed a few market gardens, where lettuces were struggling to grow under awnings in the desert sand. I looked at them longingly, because lettuce was scarce in the Norte Grande. Salad consisted exclusively of avocados and tomatoes. Then we passed some smart seaside housing estates behind high walls. I was sitting just across the aisle from the vegetable man and as there was not much scenery to enchant us, we soon got into conversation. He told me he pushed a fruit and vegetable cart round Mejillones and he'd just been to the market in Antofagasta to buy boxes of avocados, olives and mangos.

'Do you come from Australia?' he asked. 'My two sons are over there now. They live in Adelaide.' He pronounced it as 'Adèle Aïda'.

'No, I'm not Australian. But I've been there. And I've been to Adelaide. It's a beautiful city.'

He rubbed his thumb and middle finger together in the money sign, which is recognised worldwide.

'They make piles of money over there. When they've saved enough, they're going to pay for tickets for my wife and me to go out on a visit. We've never been out of Chile. And we haven't seen our grandchildren yet.'

When I told him I came from England, he said, 'That must be nice too. Is it near to Australia?'

'No. It's on the other side of the world – just about as far as you can go from England. It takes at least thirty-six hours to fly there from London.'

'That's a long way. I thought it must be near to England, because they all speak English there. Where are you going now? Mejillones?'

'No. I'm getting off at the monument on the Tropic of Capricorn.'

He looked amazed. 'That big thing! What do you want to go and see that for? Why don't you come to Mejillones? There's such a clean beach there. It's a beautiful place for a holiday.'

'Some other time,' I said, shaking his hand and hopping off the minibus.

The monument was an interesting set of four vertical greenish stone slabs, two of them concave. It stood within a white stone kerb filled with green stone chippings. I am no astronomer, so I couldn't work out the intended relationship between the slabs, but I understand that they were positioned in such a way that they marked the solstices and equinoxes. It was an impressive monument, standing stark in its isolation against the background of desert mountains, and I thought it would make a good photograph. I prowled around, peering at it from every direction through my camera's viewfinder, until

I found the perfect angle. But after all that trouble, there was no master shot. My camera had jammed.

That was a real disaster, just a week into my trip. I couldn't get the camera repaired in Antofagasta, as the camera shops simply sold new cameras and developed films. So I had to buy a new one. I did the rounds of the shops and department stores, looking for something similar to my Olympus Zoom 115, with which I took the slides for my illustrated talks. But Chile seemed to have gone totally digital and my Spanish was not up to ascertaining if, and how, I could produce 35 mm slides on a digital camera. In any case, a working trip was not the time for experimenting with new photographic techniques. I needed to be sure that my photographs would come out. I eventually tracked down what was probably the last remaining non-digital camera in Antofagasta. It was another Olympus, the Infinity 76, which was an improved camera, lighter, neater and generally more user-friendly. And when I got my January Visa statement, I found it had cost me only £34.87 – less than one-third the price I had paid in London three years ago for my less advanced Zoom 115. I suppose I may eventually have to go over to a digital camera and PowerPoint presentations, but at the moment the lecture associations I visit all have 35 mm projectors, even if they now have the capacity to produce PowerPoint illustrations too. So I can defer the evil day when I have to learn new techniques. I don't enjoy photography. I regard it as a necessary part of my work, and never take snaps for fun.

The day the camera jammed was not one of my best days. On that same morning, I went into a bank to draw some Chilean pesos from the ATM. The writing on the screen was very faint and I had to put my spectacles on to see what I was doing. Then I put them down beside the machine, while I stowed away my money and debit card, and walked out of the bank without them. When I realised what I'd done, I rushed back to the bank and found they had disappeared. The spare pair I always travel with was locked away somewhere at the bottom of my suitcase, which was lodged in the left luggage office at the bus station, and I needed reading glasses urgently for the long bus journey to Calama. So I had to scour Antofagasta for an off-the-peg pair, which I found on a street stall. They were highly satisfactory and cost me just £2.

I'm often asked how I fill in the days on my long solo journeys. Don't I find the hours hang heavy? On that particular day in Antofagasta, locating the minibus depot for Mejillones and tracking down a camera and a pair of reading glasses occupied eight whole hours. And Chile is a comparatively easy country to travel and shop in. Try buying a replacement camera battery in China, or sending a postcard from an Indian post office! Days can pass by in a flash.

The Norte Grande, with its vast copper and nitrate resources, was wrested from Bolivia by Chile in the War of the Pacific (1879–83). Nitrates used to be required for the manufacture of explosives, but these days, synthetics have taken their place, and the desert is littered with abandoned *Oficinas Salitreras*, nitrate mining towns complete with shops, a plaza, workmen's dwellings, quarters for the villas of the bosses and even theatres. One of them, Chacabuco, was used as a concentration camp under the Pinochet regime, and a few of them have inevitably been restored as 'tourist attractions'. But copper is now the main export, shipped in great quantities from the mines behind Antofagasta, along with silver from both Chile and Bolivia, and some nitrates still for fertiliser.

A busy railway, the Ferrocaril Antofagasta a Bolivia (FCAB) carries the copper and other minerals down to the port. Like so many of South America's railways, it was engineered by a British firm in the 1870s. Melbourne Clarke & Co. were granted the concession by the Bolivian government, which at that time held all the territory along the route. In 1887, control passed to the Compania Huanchilaca de Bolivia, which was floated on the London Stock Exchange in 1888 as the FCAB. It returned to British control in 1903, but the Bolivian section of the line was nationalised in 1964, while the Chileans took over their section in 1982, moving the head office from

London to Antofagasta. The railway is now a division of Antofagasta plc, which also has mining interests. It brings silver down from Potosí and Uyuni in Bolivia to Antofagasta, collecting copper from the Chilean mines as it progresses. The FCAB still carries passengers once a week along the mainly Bolivian stretch between Uyuni and Calama, but it is now simply a freight line from there to Antofagasta. I was interested in the railway's chequered history, because I was planning to ride it myself from Calama up into Bolivia, so I went along to inspect the old Antofagasta passenger station.

The station was not open to the public, but the receptionist in the company's offices telephoned around and eventually a security guard in a tin hat arrived to give me a conducted tour. What they thought I might get up to I don't know, but they made me surrender my passport 'for safety'. I found the gracious wooden buildings of the station and offices lovingly preserved. The platform was still there, with the passengers' waiting room and the old porters' trolleys. On the lines, an antique engine was on display, along with some nineteenth-century firefighting equipment and a restaurant car, a cherished relic from the days when The International, as it was then called, was a luxury passenger train. The station even had four of the old red British telephone boxes! Immaculate lawns surrounded the exhibits and gardens luxuriant with palms, oleanders and bougainvillea. While I wandered along the platform, the security gates on the land side of the station opened and a long copper train snaked along past me. Then the security gates on the sea side opened, and the train chugged out and proceeded to chug down the ocean drive, Balmaceda, along with all the motor traffic. Finally, it branched off to the right and entered the security gates into the port.

I was sad that I couldn't ride the train up to Calama, as some of its steepest, most dramatic climbing, 1 in 30 without the aid of rack and pinion, takes place immediately it leaves Antofagasta. The city stands on such a narrow coastal strip that the main streets, which lead gently upwards from the sea, cross only three or four intersections before they swoop up like kites into the lofty coastal range. Shoppers in the Calle Arturo Prat are dwarfed by the towering aridity above them.

In the first 13 km, to Portazuelo, the railway line climbs to a remarkable 555 m. By Baquedano, 80 km inland, it has reached an altitude of 1030 m. Baquedano was once the important railway junction in the centre of nitrate country, where the FCAB crossed the now almost defunct Longino, the north–south railway, which used to run from Santiago to Iquique. It now covers only a limited distance, carrying potassium compounds and coal from Baquedano to the port of Tocopilla.

Once the train has climbed up to this point, it chugs across a bleak plain, which rises steadily from Baquedano to Calama, at an altitude of 2265 m just over 200 km inland. The earth is so mineral rich that patches of nitrate and gypsum show clearly through the desert sandstone. But there is not a single blade of grass. The coastal range behind Antofagasta is high enough to isolate the nitrate lands from any sea-borne humidity, and rain never falls, so that even the hardiest cacti are defeated. (Incidentally, I was amazed at the vast quantity of material about the FCAB amassed by railway buffs on the internet!)

Not being eligible for the excitements of the steep climb from sea level, I had to travel to Calama and the copper mines by bus. We drove along the one strip of asphalt. That and the line of telegraph poles were the only indications that human beings had ever passed that way before. We made a brief stop in the one desert town I really wanted to see, Baquedano. It consisted of a poor main street lined with rickety shops, houses of wood and tin, and a few cafés. It seemed not to have changed much in the fifty years since Che Guevara and Alberto had passed through, except that the shops I saw were general stores and cafés rather than liquor dens. There was a graveyard of rusty engines and rolling stock, optimistically called a railway museum; a brave attempt at a public park with children's swings and slides, offering a small area of green in the middle of the sandy wastes; and, as we left the town, we passed a tumbledown travesty of a tourist attraction, the Nitrate Museum. It was obviously not much of a going concern, as it had a FOR SALE notice nailed to the fence. The whole town was depressing in the extreme.

On that same road from Antofagasta, our two friends, now reduced in status to humble hitch-hikers, hoisted their backpacks and tramped up the mountainside out of town. After waiting most of the day in what little shade was provided by a couple of lamp posts, they finally got a lift in a van to Baquedano – and what would prove to be a defining moment in the life of Ernesto Guevara de la Serna.

10. THE AWAKENING

This strange doctrine (Communism), whose meaning he could never grasp, translated into 'bread for the poor', something he understood and, more importantly, something that filled him with hope.

(Ernesto Che Guevara)

They arrived in Baqeudano in the evening and wandered round the town which was then, as now, little more than a single street of houses with zinc walls. Most of the houses were liquor stores, where the miners and railway workers drank themselves into oblivion. They were hailed by a ragged man, who was sitting with his wife by the roadside. 'Come, comrades, come and eat with us. I'm a vagrant too.' Ernesto lit his little stove and brewed some *maté*, which they all drank, while the couple shared out their fragments of bread and cheese. In my experience, it's usually the world's poorest who are the most generous with what little they have – and the more prosperous, like Ernesto and Alberto, who are often quite happy to take for free what they could well afford to buy. As Ernesto wrote, 'We are not all that broke, but explorers of our stature would rather die than pay for the bourgeois comfort of a hotel.' They showed the same cavalier attitude towards other people's scant food supplies.

The couple by the roadside were Chilean workers, members of the proscribed Chilean Communist Party. The man had spent three months in prison, while some of his friends had disappeared in mysterious circumstances. He suspected that their bodies had been weighted down and were lying somewhere at the bottom of the ocean. Now the couple had left their children in the care of a neighbour and set out to find work in the north. So far, this had proved impossible in the nitrate and copper mines, as it was illegal to employ known communists. But they were heading for a sulphur mine (mercifully now closed), 5700 m up the side of the active Ollagüe volcano, where the terrain was so dangerous, the weather so terrible and the working conditions so appalling that no one needed a permit to work there and no one asked any questions. 'The only thing that counts is the enthusiasm with which the worker ruins his health for a few meagre crumbs,' wrote Ernesto.

Both writers paint a touching picture of the couple as they appeared in the light of a candle, huddled together for warmth in the freezing desert night. The man was describing the harshness of their lives in simple, but impressive language, while his wife, the loyal companion of his misery, was watching him with love and silent admiration. They had no blankets against the bitter cold, so Alberto gave them his, and he and Ernesto crawled together into Ernesto's sleeping bag. They both claim that it was the coldest night they had ever spent in their lives. Ernesto, always a good sleeper, managed to snore his way through it, but Alberto lay wide awake, stiff with cold, watching the slow progress of the moon across the starry heavens.

This meeting with the desperate couple was Ernesto's political awakening. It was his call to arms. Previously, he had been a kind-hearted medical student, sympathetic towards the sick and the poor in the unfocused way of young people generally. He had railed against social injustice and opined that governments should spend more on the poor and less on their own self-glorification. But these were simply lamentations. He saw the problems, but put forward no ideas for their solution. His stance was moral, not political. That night in Baquedano, he began to take a serious interest in communism. 'It's really upsetting,' he wrote, 'to think that they use repressive measures against people like these. Leaving aside the question of whether or not "Communist vermin" are dangerous for a society's health, what had arisen in them was nothing more than the natural desire for a better life, a protest against persistent hunger transformed into a love for this strange doctrine, whose real meaning they could never grasp but, translated into "bread for the poor", was something they understood and, more importantly, something that filled them with hope.'

Apart from his university vacation job as a ship's nurse, Ernesto had led the life of a comfortable middle-class boy in Buenos Aires and Córdoba, two of the most prosperous cities in the wealthiest country in South America. Until he travelled with Alberto, his had been a white man's world. His contacts with indigenous people and *mestizos* would have been on a purely master–servant footing. But on his travels with Alberto, he was by choice a penniless tramp, who met the exploited and dispossessed, for the first time in his life, on their own level and shared his bread with them. As he travelled north through the nitrate and copper belts of the Atacama Desert, and even more so when he and Alberto continued into Peru, he became more and more distressed at the dire living and working conditions of the indigenous peoples, at the same time as he was fascinated by their culture. The descendants of the proud Incas 'look at us meekly, almost fearfully, completely indifferent to the outside world. Some give the impression that they go on living simply because it's a habit they can't give up', while the *mestizos* he describes as 'trapped in the bitterness of their double existence'.

This pity for the exploited went hand in hand with his growing indignation at the capitalist system, in particular at 'the blond, efficient, insolent administrators, the Yankee masters' of the copper mines. But when he was travelling through Northern Chile, he was still simply hovering on the brink of political awareness. He was nibbling at the communist bait, but had not as yet swallowed it.

It's always intellectually satisfying to have a moment of revelation – a blinding light on the road to Damascus. St Paul, in one single flash, was transformed from the most murderous persecutor of the Christians to a man 'filled with the Holy Spirit', who astounded everyone by starting to proclaim Jesus as the Son of God. It was all very neat, too neat. Things are never so simple. There is always a propensity towards change, some inner doubt or dissatisfaction with one's way of life, which is sharpened by chance external occurrences. Transformation is not one single event, but part of a continuous process. The blinding flash is just convenient shorthand. It turns the months or years of woolly pondering into one crisply dramatic incident. In my own modest, non-biblical shorthand, the parable for my change of direction was the moment I looked out of the bus window and saw a lone cyclist pedalling across the immensity of the Great Thar Desert in Rajasthan. I decided then and there that I would give up my job, get a bike and cycle round the world. It makes a gripping tale. It seizes the imagination, but it's no more than an allegory. It's the lazy answer to the question everyone asks: 'Why on earth did you do it?'

Ernesto and Alberto both give detailed accounts of their visit to the vast open-cast Chuquicamata mine and the contrast is fascinating. Ernesto is still the sightseer, the intelligent tourist. His account is mostly a technical description of the copper-mining and refining processes. He alludes, at the very end, to the conflict between the nationalist and left-wing groups on the one hand, who were advocating nationalisation, and the proponents of free enterprise on the other, for whom efficiency was all; they would rather have well-run mines under foreign control than nationalised operations, which would possibly be less efficient. But his concerns are still largely medical. He is distressed, as a sensitive trainee doctor, to see the graveyards crammed with the victims of cave-ins, silicosis and exhaustion, and indignant that the miners have to pay for their hospital accommodation. In fact, he is very critical generally of the lack of facilities in Chilean hospitals compared with those in Argentina: the lack of medicines, instruments and hygiene, even in the operating theatres. The socio-economic injustices of the system worry him less.

Alberto, on the other hand, was a fully fledged communist when he wrote his account years later. He uses the visit as a hook on which to hang one of his lengthy political rants about Yankee capitalism, the exploitation of the Araucanian people (the indigenous inhabitants who are, according to him, the true owners of the mines) and the battles of the union leaders against overwhelmingly unfair odds.

The working conditions in the copper mines were obviously pretty horrendous at the time. But things were very different when I arrived in Chuquicamata to take a guided tour. We assembled in a Codelco (the Chilean Copper Company) office, which also served as a small museum of early everyday life in the mining town. There were dusty bottles of patent medicines, old school exercise books, long-gone brands of tinned food, ancient typewriters, 78s of 1930s dance music and a few photographs. One showed the interior of a general store. Its shelves were stacked with the entire stock of every item for sale, hundreds of identical brown cardboard boxes and cans from the days before the commercial designers got to work. They were basic packets, printed with basic information about the contents and brand, not colourful, eye-catching packages designed to tempt the fickle shopper. In another photo, a group of miners posed in front of an open-topped motor car, proud to feature in the same picture as such a luxurious novelty. We paid about £1 for the tour and were asked, in addition, for a donation towards a Codelco children's charity. We had to wear long sleeves, long trousers and solid shoes.

Our guide arrived – not one of Che Guevara's insolent blond Yankees, but a charming young Chilean metallurgist with the long black hair that seems to be fashionable among the northern miners, Hispanic as well as indigenous.

He explained the background. The Guggenheims, who started up the copper mine, sold out to Anaconda, but the Chilean State under President Frei bought a 51 per cent stake in 1969 and President Allende acquired the rest in 1971. In the disorganised years of Allende's government, copper production in the newly nationalised industry slumped through general inefficiency and the appointment of political henchmen to management positions, against a background of falling world prices. Today Codelco flourishes, thanks to the financial and structural arrangements put into place by General Pinochet after 1973. For all his severity, or perhaps because of it, he was a brilliant manager of the economy.

Then we were given a talk on the copper mining and refining processes, first in Spanish, then in English. The guide showed us a lump of the original rock, the ore which produces one ton of 99.98 per cent pure copper (the purest in the world) from every hundred tons blasted from the earth; and a sheet of the finished product, which is mostly exported to China to be used for their massive national electrification project.

Of course, there's always one on a tour! In our group of 36, he happened to be a North American metallurgist, as tall and stringy as a French bean, with huge teeth and a fixed grin. He asked technical questions on every stage of the refining process – the extraction of the ore, the sulphur baths, the flotation tanks, the smelting and the electrolysis. We all had a violent attack of MEGO (my eyes glaze over), as the poor guide struggled to provide all the information demanded. He had the metallurgical knowledge, but he sometimes failed, naturally enough for a Spanish speaker, to hit on the correct translation. And that produced further questions and objections, until the matter was clarified and the exact English technical term had been agreed on.

'But I don't understand,' said the American, 'why the Chinese are so keen to buy your copper. Haven't they heard of fibre optics? Don't they know they're the thing of the future, not all this copper?'

'I have no idea,' replied the poor, patient young man, 'whether or not the Chinese know about fibre optics. All I know is that they've just signed a ten-year contract to purchase almost the entire output of this mine. That's good enough for me. It will keep us all in work for the next ten years. After that, who knows?'

The little office was as hot as one of the company's furnaces and our legs turned to lead as we stood for half an hour through this American inquisition. Meanwhile, the Spanish speakers, who were already waiting outside in the company coach, were roasting like oven chickens in the shadeless plaza under the full heat of the afternoon sun.

The main Chuquicamata mine, when we finally got there, was an amazing spectacle, well worth the wait. It's the largest hole on earth, said to be one of the two man-made objects (along with the Great Wall of China) visible from outer space. Excavation began 91 years ago and there is still at least another 90 years' worth of copper down there, available for opencast mining, before Codelco has to begin tunnelling. And this is only one copper mine out of many in the area.

We donned hard hats (called 'hammer hats', a term I'd never heard before) and climbed up to the viewing platform. The hole was simply staggeringly immense, over a kilometre deep and 14 km in circumference. I have seen the tremendous Super Pit in Kalgoorlie, Western Australia, but compared with the chasm in Chuquicamata, it was little more than a foxhole. The scores of giant trucks, which circled down into the depths and laboured up again bearing tons of copper ore, looked no bigger than Dinky toys or columns of industrious ants. Dust rose from the workings in a thick brown fog, obliterating the deepest terraces. In the Atacama Desert, water is so scarce that it's recycled eight times in the refining process. For its ninth use, some of the monster trucks carry it down into the depths and spray it over the dust, in an effort to make conditions more tolerable for the workers.

The four newest trucks, bought from Germany, use Global Satellite Positioning instead of drivers and it is hoped eventually to go over to a fully automated system of transport down in the hole. One of the trucks stood beside the viewing platform, dwarfing the visitors who queued up to be photographed beside it. The tyres alone were an astounding four metres tall.

'One of the drivers of these monster trucks is a woman,' said the guide proudly. 'And why not? If we can have a woman president in Chile, why can't we have a woman doing something straightforward like handling a truck?'

Of all the facts and figures which were crammed into our skulls on the tour, one particular piece of information struck me forcibly. A minor by-product of the copper processing is molybdenum. Not being a chemist, I had to look up the uses of this element on the internet, and I discovered that it's used in high-strength alloys. Because it is heat and corrosion resistant, it is vital to the manufacture of aircraft and missile parts, oil pipelines and various types of filament. It serves as a catalyst in the petroleum industry and it forms the anode in some x-ray tubes, particularly in mammography applications. So not only does molybdenum feature in *Times* crosswords (the only places I had met it before), but it is an element with greatly specialised applications. As a result, it fetches such a high price on the international markets ($40 a pound at its most recent high) that its sale funds the entire Chilean copper-mining operation and pays all its employees' wages. So the country's copper is produced virtually free of cost, and the entire proceeds of its sale go into the government's coffers. And the Bolivians – born losers – lost all this potential wealth when they provoked the Chileans into the War of the Pacific and lost the Norte Grande, as well as their access to the sea!

But though the Chuquicamata mines were flourishing, Chuquicamata town was a sad place in December 2006. The streets were deserted, and the houses, shops, community centres and schools were all boarded up. The inhabitants had been transferred en masse to a newly built suburb of Calamata. Their new houses were infinitely superior to their old ones, many of which were the original wood and tin structures, but they weren't yet 'home'. Their lovely art deco community centre had closed down, and the mining families felt lost and uprooted. The newspapers, even the national daily *El Mercurio*, carried articles on the desolation wrought by the transfer. 'The saddest ever Christmas in the mining town of Chuquicamata. They're preparing for the last Midnight Mass in their church.'

Working conditions in the mines have improved significantly since Ernesto and Alberto visited Chuquicamata in 1952. So much so that, paradoxically, the 8000 miners and their families have been forced out of their homes in order to preserve their health. To comply with international standards of worker welfare, they have had to be moved from the vicinity of the mines to the cleaner air of Calamata, 18 km to the south. The move has been an expensive operation for Codelco, but the company hopes it will be good for profits in the long run, as well as beneficial to the workers. At present, the tailings have to be dumped by the giant trucks on top of heaps far away from the mines. This operation is tremendously expensive in fuel. In future, the company plans to tip the tailings over the old township, burying everything but the historic plaza, with its church and civic buildings. These will be preserved as yet another empty 'heritage site', a ghost town which will come to life for a few moments every afternoon, when the Chuquicamata Mine Tour passes through.

I passed the new estate of brick-built houses on my way back to Calama. My visit to Chuquicamata was my last appointment with Che Guevara. He and Alberto were now on their way to Peru and the leper colonies, while I was going to catch the next train to Bolivia and the Mountain of Silver. I had a few days between projects, when I could be completely at leisure, idle with a clear conscience.

When I'd booked my South American flights, way back in July, I had factored in an extra week in Chile before Christmas, as I was hoping to meet Julian there. Since the previous year, when Katherine and I had spent some time with him in Buenos Aires, he had finished building his new boat, *Harrier*, and had sailed her down to Ushuaia in Tierra del Fuego, arriving there at the end of March. His plan was to leave Ushuaia after a couple of weeks and sail through the Beagle Channel, in Darwin's wake, then north through the Chilean fjords to Puerto Montt. Depending on the weather, that leg of the journey could take anything from six weeks to four months. So even allowing for the worst conditions, he expected to have picked his way through the myriad islands and channels of the south to Puerto Montt, then sailed some distance up the coast of Chile to a more northerly port, such as Constitución or Valparaíso, where I could conveniently meet him in December.

But it was not to be. Julian's cooker/heater developed a fault on the way to Ushuaia and had to be returned to the manufacturer in Buenos Aires; there were problems with the echo sounder; and the fuel tank, hoses and filters in the engine needed servicing or replacing. All these technical difficulties kept him prisoner in Ushuaia until October. Then he encountered the worst weather he had ever experienced in all his years of sailing – non-stop sleet, icy rain and constant headwinds. So by the time he had struggled through the desolate fjords to the first habitation, Puerto Eden, about halfway to Puerto Montt, I was already in Antofagasta, way up in the north of that long, thin country. I had run out of time for travelling down to Puerto Eden – even supposing I could find the transport to reach such an inaccessible spot. We had to make do with emails.

There were few tourist sights in Calama. Visitors were usually just passing through on their way to somewhere else. It was once a major Inca crossing, an oasis on the River Loa, where a road from the Altiplano down to the sea met one of their north–south highways. Today its main purpose is to service the copper mines, and its busiest spot is the bus terminal, where the miners arrive and depart and the tourists change onto buses for the new Kathmandu, the currently fashionable desert resort of San Pedro de Atacama.

I always enjoy staying in places where nothing much happens and no one comes to visit. I potter around, chatting to the locals, reading the newspapers over coffee and fruit juice outside the cafés, joining the office workers for lunch-time sandwiches in the square, and I start to feel, rightly or wrongly, that I'm gaining some understanding of what it's really like to live in a country. Cities like Calama are not distorted by tourism.

Strangely enough for such an undistinguished town, it was the only place on my journey where I had difficulty in finding a bed. Everywhere else, I had just turned up, guidebook in hand, and got into my first choice of hotel. But Calama was different. As its life revolved around the mines, there tended to be business conferences in the better hotels, while the cheaper ones were full of transient mineworkers, who rented by the month. I took a taxi from the bus station to the hotel I'd selected, found it was full, dragged my case round to the next one on my list, which was also full, then turned for help to the tourist office. Apparently, there was an international copper-mining conference that week and the only vacancy they could find for me was in the most expensive hotel in town, overlooking the main pedestrian shopping street. But Chilean expensive is not European expensive, and it was a treat to have the excuse for a really comfortable room, as I would be staying there for a few nights. I had a generous armchair for reading in, and a writing desk where I could, in theory, do a bit of work – though I usually gave in to temptation and whiled away my free time with a Tough Puzzle, a crossword or a Sumo Hanji. Puzzles are invaluable to long-distance travellers: they provide hours of entertainment for a fraction of the weight of a novel. Then the hotel offered free internet access and spacious lounges. To complete the pleasure, there was a Bolivian or Peruvian street musician playing heartbreakingly beautiful Andean laments on his pan pipes under my window.

In the evenings, I joined the rest of the citizens in that great South American drawing room, the plaza. Calama had really excelled itself with the Christmas crib in front of the cathedral. It was a large enclosure, with life-sized figures of Mary, Joseph and the Infant Jesus in a real thatched stable. The Three Kings were bowing low, offering their gold, frankincense and myrrh, while a group of shepherds knelt among their sheep. The humans were the usual sort of models. The unique feature of Calama's crib was the animals, which were all real.

There were two goats in a subsidiary pen, while a small flock of sheep, two llamas, an ox and an ass roamed around in the main enclosure. I enjoyed my nightly visit to the crib, amused to watch the different animals and the ways they reacted (or didn't react) to the crowds. The sheep were usually concentrating on their food, all feeding stolidly from the same box and ignoring the people around. The two llamas were usually kneeling side by side, their noses in the air, looking disdainful as camelids do. The ox stood vacantly on its own in a corner. The goats stamped around on the straw in their pen, presumably isolated from the others because their behaviour was untrustworthy. All of these animals carried on with their own lives, caring not a fig for the spectators. But the ass was quite different. He was a dear little donkey, always to be found socialising with the passers-by. He usually stood in one particular corner, where he could push his nose through a small gap in the fence, asking to have it stroked and clearly hoping that people would be kind enough to give him the occasional tasty morsel.

The inside of the cathedral was interesting too. I sometimes stepped in and sat through a part of the evening service. The priest was of white European descent, while the congregation was overwhelmingly indigenous or *mestizo*. The more affluent in South America (and affluence is still closely related to race) are tending now to conform to European patterns of church attendance. Churches are for weddings, funerals and possibly for one service at Christmas. There is the feeling that the Roman Catholic Church is getting out of touch with the real needs of the people. The gap between the grass roots and the Church hierarchy over such vital questions as contraception, abortion and divorce is widening, and evangelists of all creeds are gaining ground. The new Pope Benedict XVI is clearly worried about the South American situation, as he has chosen Brazil for his first overseas visit.

The indigenous peoples have never lost their piety, so they are being specially targeted by Protestant evangelists and Mormons. I had seen four tall, clean-cut young men accosting people in the streets of Calama. Three were blond, one was ginger, and they were all four dressed in grey suits, white shirts and ties, with Bible-sized books under their arms. They stood out a mile from the more casually dressed citizens of Calama, and I knew immediately who they were. They were Mormon missionaries from Utah. I had seen their like in many cities throughout South America and, judging from the number of Churches of the Latter Day Saints, they were having a measure of success. They were exceedingly polite and earnest about their proselytising, but under their neat attire, I was amused to find that they were no different from young men the world over. I happened to be sitting next to them on a bench in the bus station one day and did a bit of earwigging. They were talking about girls!

'She washes her hair from time to time, but as far as I can see, that's about all she does – that and shopping. She seems to be a bit of an airhead.'

'Yeah, but she looks good.'

On Sunday morning, I made an early start, to walk out to the Parque el Loa before the day heated up. I soon left the more prosperous city centre and began to stumble along broken pavements through a poor suburb, where solitary miners lodged in dreary *Residenciales*. They had come to Calama for the work, leaving their families behind. Now it was Sunday morning, the mines were shut, and some of them were standing outside their hostel doors, smoking a cigarette in the morning sun and wondering how they were going to spend the empty day which stretched in front of them. They watched me pass by with idle curiosity. I was alone there, the only person walking down the silent streets, but the atmosphere was totally unthreatening. Anyone I approached for directions struck up a conversation, happy to have been asked. I was an event in a dull day.

I was heading for the Museum of Archaeology and Ethnology, which turned out to be shut on Sunday mornings, contrary to what my guidebook had said. So I had a quick look at the boating lake, a modest pool in the desert, where the trickle of the Loa River had been dammed. The opening engagement of the War of the Pacific had taken place across that river in 1879, though I doubt that was much on the minds of the laughing, splashing children in the park that hot Sunday.

But it was not a wasted morning. Walking back to Calama, I passed an ATM and saw a powerful motorbike parked at the kerb with a sticker of Che Guevara on its windscreen. I hung around outside the bank to accost the rider.

'I see you're a Che Guevara fan,' I said.

'Yes. I've been following the route that he and Alberto took on their motorbike.'

'I've been doing the same thing, on a pedal bike.'

'Over the Andes? Wow!'

He was a tall young Argentine, with gorgeous white teeth and a shaven head. He'd started out from Buenos Aires, where he lives, crossed the pampas and the Andes, then biked up north through Chile. Like me, he'd visited Chuquicamata and was now parting company with his hero. He didn't want to follow him to Peru and the leper colonies, so he was setting off that morning to ride across the desert via San Pedro de Atacama and cross the Andes at the Paso de Sico, back into Argentina. We took a coffee together and swapped tales of our experiences along the road.

I was less lucky with a touring cyclist. His bike was chained trustingly to a lamp post, laden with panniers, a tent and a cooking pot. A bungee held down an oil-splodged copy of the Lonely Planet's guide to Chile in French. I lurked in a nearby café, rehearsing my French questions in the hope of catching him and engaging him in conversation. Touring cyclists in remote places always get very excited at the prospect of meeting a fellow cyclist, and this Frenchman was the only serious tourer I'd come across to date in Chile. But I was disappointed. Three coffees later and he still hadn't appeared, so I lost patience and left.

That afternoon, I found a *micro* to take me back to the museum and wished I hadn't bothered. There was an uninformative display of drab pre-Colombian pots and a few textile fragments, centuries old, but wonderfully preserved in the desert's aridity. A special exhibition told me more about shamans than I had ever wanted to know, and there was a small-sized replica of the adobe Church of San Francisco in Chiu Chiu, one of the oldest churches in Chile, with doors of cactus wood and a thatched roof supported by cactus beams. It was deliciously cool inside and I lingered there, reading the prayer slips below the image of Christ. Among all the usual prayers for recovery from illness, safety on a journey or the gift of a child was one rather more down-to-earth request. In juvenile handwriting, it said: 'Good Christ, we ask you for a bigger hut for our scout troop.'

But the highlight of the visit was finding a market nearby, where I loaded myself up with grapes and mangoes. They were the first fruits, other than tomatoes and overripe bananas, that I'd seen in the Atacama. I made a pig of myself.

These days of enforced leisure in Calama served me well. I was on my way to Bolivia, where I should have to cope with altitudes of 4000 m or more, and I was quite worried. Previously, I had taken high altitudes in my stride, even pushing my bike over the Khunjerab Pass, the highest paved road in the world at 4733 m. On that ascent, I'd suffered none of the symptoms of altitude sickness – headache, nausea, nosebleeds or disorientation – though I had naturally struggled for breath at every step in the thin air, like a fish gasping its life out on a riverbank. But that was ten years ago, before I had blood pressure problems. Now I wondered if my heart would take the strain. I was sanguine enough in the daytime, but terrors balloon in the night and I worked myself up into a fine state of anxiety in the cowardly small hours. What if I had a heart attack in rural Bolivia? Would I be up in the mountains, miles away from a hospital? And if I got to a hospital, what would the doctors be like? And if I suffered from serious altitude sickness, how could I get down to a safer level quickly? There was only one train a week down the mountains and other transport in Bolivia was patchy. But I took some comfort from the reflection that Calama was already pretty high up. It stood at an altitude of 2265 m, and I'd already adjusted to that. I had a headache the first day, but it had soon cleared, and I was already less out of puff than I had been on arrival. It was proving a useful halfway house on the ascent to the Altiplano. Perhaps I would survive Bolivia after all.

Full of confidence in the daylight, I took a *micro* out to Lider, the supermarket in the great out-of-town shopping mall, to stock up for the train journey and beyond. I bought Earl Grey tea, a jar of Nescafé Blend 37, small cartons of fruit juice, health food cereal bars, crackers, cheese triangles (not my favourite type of cheese, but triangles travel well) and, because it was a really big supermarket, I managed to find nectarines and plums, as well as bananas. I filled my rucksack, as I suspected Bolivian shelves would be bare. Then I went out to my favourite Calama restaurant for a fillet steak and a bottle of delicious Chilean wine. It might well be my last decent meal for ten days.

11. THE SLOW TRAIN TO BOLIVIA

These high wild hills and rough uneven ways
Draw out our miles and make them wearisome.

(Shakespeare, *Richard II*)

I knew there was only one passenger train a week from Calama to Uyuni in Bolivia, so I thought I had better book my seat on it as soon as possible, to be on the safe side. I walked to the railway station, immediately after settling into my hotel. The booking office was closed, but I found a young woman rattling away on her computer keyboard in what was obviously the administrative office.

'I'd like to book a seat on the train to Uyuni, please,' I said.

'But the train doesn't go until Wednesday.'

'I know. But can't I book a ticket now?'

'Not until Wednesday – in the afternoon.'

'But I'd like to be certain that I can get a seat. Otherwise, I might be hanging around for days in Calama, and then get no ticket at the end of it. I don't want to run the risk.'

'There are always plenty of tickets for this train. Don't worry. Just come back on Wednesday afternoon.' And she closed the conversation by resuming her typing.

Our exchange reminded me of similar problems over booking train seats in China. In Beijing, the purchase of a ticket took three visits to the railway station, occupying three entire half-days of my life. All that time, effort and frustration just for one simple purchase, which at home we could make over the phone, online or in any railway station in the land in a couple of minutes. Why not just issue a ticket, when a passenger turns up, clutching her money in her hand? Perhaps that's too straightforward a notion for the world's bureaucrats. They like things to be a little more byzantine. Anyway, there was nothing for it but to contain my anxiety until Wednesday afternoon at three o'clock, when the booking office opened.

The train was scheduled to depart at midnight. Having successfully obtained my ticket that afternoon, I arrived at the station at 11.30 and couldn't believe my eyes. The platform was still locked, so the waiting room, station steps and even the pavements of the approach roads were jammed with Bolivian women in brown bowler hats, each of them transporting at least fifty sacks, cartons and other miscellaneous packages of goods. There were sacks of rice, cases of Sprite and Coca Cola, toilet rolls by the gross, packets of powdered milk, Nescafé, McKay's biscuits, powdered mashed potato in great cartons (for a country which grows hundreds, perhaps thousands, of varieties of potato!), socks and pullovers, blankets and towels, even a litter of Labrador puppies, one month old, according to the girl who had bought them. While we waited to get onto the platform, I chatted to one of the bowler-hatted ladies.

'Do you live in Uyuni?' I asked, in the usual conversational opening.

'Yes. I come down from there to Calama once a fortnight on the train,' she told me. 'We have nothing in Bolivia, absolutely nothing. So I go to Lider (the Chilean version of Tesco's) and buy as much as I can pack into my nephew's van. He works in Calama – fantastic money in Chile! And he's a good boy. He helps me. He drives me to the station, I load everything onto the train, then I sell it on my market stall in Uyuni. We're all doing the same thing.'

So many women and such piles of goods had spilled out of the station that I couldn't get anywhere near the entrance. Then at 11.40, the door to the platform was unlocked and pandemonium ensued. The ladies started to fight their way through, pushing and shoving their giant packages towards the train.

When I finally reached the platform myself, I saw an engine and one, just one, carriage. It was divided into two compartments and there was one central flight of three enormously steep steps, up which all the Bolivian ladies had to manhandle their goods. Once inside, they filled the luggage racks, the spaces under the seats and the entire centre aisle, so there was nowhere to put your feet and any progress down the carriage involved clambering over mountains of Sprite and mashed potatoes.

The very short man who sold us our numbered tickets must have harboured a grudge against tall people. He had given me a window-seat in a section for four passengers. When my three companions joined me, they turned out to be three European backpackers – delightful boys, but twice the height of the stocky, short-legged Bolivian ladies. So the four tallest people on the train had been allocated seats in the same cramped section. How we managed to manoeuvre our long legs and big feet into a space the size of a medium suitcase I shall never know. It was the last train before Christmas, so every seat was taken and none of us could move elsewhere. We knew we were in for a very uncomfortable night.

Considering the vast quantities of merchandise which had to be loaded onto the train, it did surprisingly well to pull out of Calama station at 12.05. We trundled slowly out of town into the star-spangled blackness of the desert night.

My three companions were a French boy, a Belgian and a German, but at first they foxed me, because they were all conversing together in Spanish.

'Well, we have three languages between us,' they explained. 'French, German and Flemish. We met on an intensive Spanish course in Santiago and after three months of speaking nothing but Spanish, it's become our *lingua franca*.'

They had made friends on the course and now they were backpacking and camping together around South America. The fact that their packs, with a year's worth of clothing, three tents and three sets of cooking utensils, were the size of small houses didn't help in that overloaded compartment. Gilles, the Belgian boy, was even carrying a set of juggling clubs. I had to take my suitcase down from the rack and put it under our feet, so that one at least of the mammoth rucksacks could be stowed up there, out of the way.

They invited me to join them in a game of cards called 'Shit Head'. Neither Gunther, the German, nor I knew how to play it, so Gilles proceeded to explain the rules to us in Spanish. I'm not very keen on cards at the best of times and I'm afraid I switched off in the middle of his lengthy explanation and pretended to go to sleep.

The train's progress was agonisingly slow, as it crawled like a lame beetle up the walls of the Cordillera of the Andes. It was such a pity that we were travelling through the night. I'd read on the internet that the line skirted San Pedro and San Pablo (Saints Peter and Paul), two active volcanoes, and cut across the vast lava bed spewed out during their frequent eruptions. Near San Pedro, great reservoirs had been blasted out of the rock, and these were the source of the water which ran from the taps in Antofagasta, almost 400 km away. When we reached Ascotán, the FCAB was at its highest point in Chile (3956 m). Then the train was said to chug past a lake surrounded by the most dramatic mountains, snow-capped at their summits and glittering with weird metallic colours further down their flanks.

We missed all these marvels as we tried to doze our way through the long uncomfortable night. Our guidebooks had told us that the train was unheated and the temperature could drop as low as minus 15°C. We had been advised to keep our sleeping bags to hand. It never got icy cold on that midsummer night, well inside the Tropic of Capricorn, but it was still a great comfort to be able to snuggle up in goose down. The four of us even managed, with some ingenuity, to rest our sleeping-bagged feet on the opposite seats, two pairs of feet alternating cosily with two bottoms in each direction. It was no occasion for modesty.

We reached Ollagüe on the border with Bolivia at the scheduled time of 8.30. It had taken us just over 8 hours to travel some 195 km. Ollagüe was a small Aymara village of tumbledown houses in the middle of desert and salt flats. Fortunately, about twenty passengers disembarked in the bleak railway yard and were picked up by friends and relations, together with all their booty from the Calama Lider. Their departure left a little room for the rest of us to spread out, so I sprinted across the compartment and seized an empty seat in a six with five short Bolivian ladies.

'It's not that I don't love you,' I explained to the boys. 'But I can't stand the heat through that eastern window. The sun's too strong for me.'

It all worked out well. I sat in greater comfort, with somewhere to put my big feet, while the three boys were joined by a young Spanish backpacker, eager to make up a four at 'Shit Head'.

The Chilean conductor in his white hard hat ushered us all to Chilean Immigration and Customs. He had a printed list of our names and, with Chilean efficiency, lined us up in alphabetical order. We were soon stamped out of the country and shepherded back onto the train. Then, his duty done, the conductor joined the Chilean driver in his cab, the engine was uncoupled and we watched in consternation as the two of them drove off together, back to Chile, abandoning us in a siding to wait for our Bolivian engine.

The minutes turned into hours. We all sat in the carriage or wandered around the derelict buildings, whose mud bricks were fast crumbling back into the desert sand from which they had been formed. Ollagüe was once an important junction, but the great days of South American railways were long gone and it was now just a desolate dot on the map. There was no café, not even a stall where we could buy a morning coffee or replenish our supplies of bottled water. The sun grew stronger and we all sweltered in the heat.

'Whatever happened to customer information?' asked Gilles.

There was a moment's excitement when there was a crash, the carriage rocked and we heard the clank of couplings. We rushed outside to look, only to find that a second carriage was being attached to ours, while the engine which had delivered it was being uncoupled again. It chugged away and our spirits fell. Now we were two carriages in an oven of a siding, not one. But I suppose this flurry of activity did demonstrate that the station was still staffed.

The one good feature of the delay concerned hygiene. Our carriage had one lavatory for about 150 passengers. There was no water to flush its tin tube and that, along with the floor, had become unspeakably disgusting by the time we reached Ollagüe. The delay in the station meant that I was able to avoid that stinking horror completely by prowling round the ruins and finding a discreet spot, far away from the train, behind a tumbledown wall.

At something like 11.30, a buzz went round the camp that the Bolivian engine was due at 12.30. Twelve-thirty came and went, and there was still no sign of an engine. At this point, Gilles decided to put on an entertainment for the troops. He got his juggling clubs down from the luggage rack, and fished in his backpack for a set of juggling balls. He climbed down onto the station sands and went into action, soon drawing an appreciative crowd. He was so adept, and it looked so easy, that the other backpackers thought they could juggle too. Balls and clubs flew wildly across the station yard, and that added greatly to the entertainment.

'Do you do this for money?' I asked.

'Occasionally – when I'm strapped for cash, or I've got it in the bank and can't find an ATM. But today's a free show. I have a strict rule though. I never compete with any of the locals. I only juggle for money when there are no other street entertainers around.'

'Why's that? Don't you like competition?' In retrospect, that was rather an unkind question.

'No. It's not that,' said Gilles, taking no offence. 'I may be an impecunious student by European standards, but compared with the poor devils who scratch a living on the streets, I'm a wealthy man. I'm careful not to take the bread out of their mouths.'

He was a strange sight with his dusty, straggling blond dreadlocks, threaded with red and yellow plastic beads, but his heart was in the right place. He was always the first to jump up and lend a hand with the ladies' packages.

At two o'clock, a Bolivian official came into the carriage and apologised for the delay. He stated the obvious. The engine had unfortunately not arrived yet.

At 3.30, they seemed to give up on the engine they were expecting from Uyuni and decided to attach the two passenger carriages to the back of a long snake of a freight train, which happened to be passing through from Antofagasta. And at 3.55 we finally set off – but only across No Man's Land to Bolivian Immigration and Customs.

With no efficient Chilean conductor to line us up, the Bolivian Immigration Office became a frenzied 150-woman rugby scrum. All the bowler-hatted ladies tried to elbow their way to the front, only to be given forms to fill in. There was nowhere to write, except on one window sill, and few people had biros. As a writer, I always carry a stock, so I handed them round to speed up the procedure. With only one immigration clerk on duty, it was painfully slow. The Bolivians entered their country for free, which I suppose was fair enough, while we foreigners were charged about £1.50 for an entry stamp.

As we were carrying such huge quantities of goods, I was dreading the Bolivian customs. But the officials never so much as cast an eye over the sacks and packages. They knew from experience what was in them – desperately needed foodstuffs, cleaning materials and household linens. The ladies were performing an invaluable service for their fellow Bolivians, while keeping the Chilean supermarket tills ringing away merrily. So everyone was happy.

It would, of course, have been a different story, had I been travelling in the opposite direction. The Chilean customs always do a thorough inspection of goods entering from anywhere else, but especially from Bolivia, the main source of smuggled coca. They also destroy any foodstuffs, from meat and vegetables down to opened packets of biscuits. Agriculture and fruit-growing are major Chilean industries and they are fanatical about protecting their money-spinners from beetles and blight. Like the Argentines, they are particularly jealous guardians of their ancient, pre-phylloxera French vine stocks.

Despite the laid-back attitude of the inspectors, it still took us over an hour to clear Bolivian customs and, miraculously, I got all my biros back. The girl with the litter of Labrador pups had been giving them a little run out in the yard, and we had to help her catch them and bundle them back onto the train. Once they were all on, the whistle blew, the train lurched forwards and everyone cheered. But before we could get too excited, it stopped again at a platform, a few minutes down the line, where a group of new Bolivian passengers were waiting to pile into the second carriage. We finally chugged out of Ollagüe. It was 5.05 in the afternoon. We had been waiting in that benighted desert outpost for just over eight and a half hours.

The train had climbed the Andes to an altitude of some 4000 m and, from now on, the run to Uyuni would be along the flat, with a fine view of the Ollagüe volcano, its fumarole sending a column of white smoke into the cloudless blue sky. But the real spectacles were the salt flats: on our right the Salar de Chiguana and on our left the Salar de Uyuni, the highest and largest salt lake in the world, twice the size of the Great Salt Lake in the United States. The effect of the sun on the salt was dazzling. The train trundled along a corridor between the wide expanses of blinding whiteness. It was a strip of absolute desert, where the only vegetation was the occasional splodge of moss, which lay over the sand edging of the salt flats like livid green cowpats. For most of the 200 km crossing, there was nothing and nobody to be seen.

In a dot on the map called Rio Grande, there were great piles of salt waiting to be ground and iodised, and nearby there were a few men in hard hats, but they stopped working to watch the train go by, so it was impossible to tell if they were salt miners or maintenance staff on the line. We stopped at villages, some almost deserted, but bravely sporting a football pitch or basketball court, which were no more than shadeless expanses of sand with wonky goalposts and punctured nets. I thought how depressing it would be to live in such a place.

I would not have spotted them myself, but with eyes used to the glare, my Bolivian neighbours nudged me in excitement to point out a distant herd of vicuñas, the smallest of the South American camelids. Their wool is the finest and lightest in the world. It was so prized in Inca times, that only royalty were allowed to wear vicuña garments. But the softness of their wool has been a near disaster for the animals. They never breed in captivity, so they have been hunted to the verge of extinction. Recent legislation has rescued the remaining few (estimated at only about 6000 in 1965) and they are beginning to claw their way back up the survival ladder. But they are still very rare, shy creatures and I felt privileged to have caught a glimpse of them, wavering in the distant heat haze.

When I saw the vicuñas and their larger brethren, the llamas, grazing on what looked like wastes of stone and salt, with no vegetation to speak of, I was reminded of journeys I have made on the backs of the greatest of their species, the camel. I have ridden a camel for five days across the Great Thar Desert in Rajasthan and I have galloped in the tracks of Lawrence of Arabia down Jordan's Wadi Rum on an excruciating wooden saddle, like a baby's high chair. So I was prepared for the motion of the train.

No metal can withstand the extremes of temperature across the salt flats. They range from 30°C in the afternoons to minus 25°C at night. The result is uncomfortably buckled rails. We rode our seats like camel saddles, bucking and jolting, and trying to avoid the parcels which came flying down from the racks.

More passengers alighted at villages and by the evening I had a section for four all to myself. I could finally stretch out and, being alone, I could have read in peace for a while, had there been any lights in the compartment to read by. As we neared Uyuni, my bowler-hatted friend, who had described stocking up in the Lider supermarket, decided to assemble all her purchases in my section, as it was near to the exit. I watched in dismay as she surrounded me, carton by carton, with a Great Wall of China. I was imprisoned behind a barricade of toilet rolls, powdered mashed potatoes, Coca Cola and underpants.

'Don't worry!' she said. 'My family will help me move all this stuff in no time.'

Meanwhile, night had fallen and I was in the situation that always makes me slightly nervous. I was in an unknown country, heading for an unknown town, on my own, in the dark. To make matters worse, the boliviano is not a hard currency, so I had been unable to buy any in advance either in London or Chile, and there had been no bank on the border. I had not a single boliviano in my wallet.

At times like this, I hate not being on my bicycle. My bicycle gives me control. I arrive in a town at more or less the time I plan to arrive, and never in the dark. But trains and buses leave me powerless. Their schedules are out of my control. I'm a leaf blowing in their wind. The other disadvantage is the luggage. My bicycle is the perfect porter's trolley, on which I can wheel my belongings effortlessly into the town centre, checking out the hotels as I go, until I see one I fancy. But in Bolivia, without my faithful Condor, I was lumbered with a backpack, a sleeping bag, a handbag and a suitcase.

When we pulled into Uyuni, a mob of her relations did in fact board the train, as my friend had promised, shoving cartons down the steps and out of the window to others waiting on the platform. The Great Wall of China was dismantled, brick by brick, in the most efficient manner. Then it was my turn to manhandle my possessions down the steep steps. I managed that without too much difficulty. But then my troubles began. The exit was across the line from our platform and, this being Bolivia, there was no underpass, overpass, or even a few helpful steps, and the drop was fearsome. I sat on the edge of the platform and shuffled down onto the track, pulling my luggage behind me. The platforms were almost level with my shoulder and I could never have managed to climb up the opposite side had it not been for the kind attentions of my backpacking friends. They hauled up my luggage and even pushed and pulled my own great frame up from the track to the exit platform.

I knew from my guidebook that there were a couple of hotels almost opposite the station, so I hoisted up my backback and trundled my wheeled suitcase across the cobbled yard, pursued by desperate touts, who wanted to sell me tours of the salt flats – at 10.30 at night, when I had just been looking at salt flats for the last fourteen hours! Outside the station, the street was unpaved, so I had to carry my suitcase, which was quite an effort at that altitude. I staggered into a perfectly reasonable little hotel, where there was a vacant double room with private bath for 40 bolivianos. The manager insisted on cash in advance and, to my relief, was willing to accept US dollars. The equivalent to 40 bolivianos was $5. I could see that Bolivia was going to be cheap.

Having had nothing to eat all day but a few biscuits, an apple and a couple of plums, I had to venture out into the night to search for food. My hotel didn't do meals, but Uyuni's pleasant little plaza was just around the corner and one pizzeria was still open. I was served with what I think was the soggiest pizza I'd ever eaten in my life, washed down with a bottle of Bolivian beer. But it was food, and I was in good company, because all the other non-Bolivian survivors of the train journey were eating in the same restaurant. The four backpackers and I were joined by a charming family from Chile, who had borrowed one of my biros in Immigration. We were all in high spirits, happy to have escaped at last from the dreadful train. Even the three young children from Chile managed to smile and get through their slices of pizza without grizzling, though they were reeling with tiredness and finding it very difficult to keep their eyes open. I didn't know how comfortable my $5 bed would be, but it turned out to be excellent. So, after a night sitting wide awake, blinking like a poached owl, I decided to give myself two nights' rest in Uyuni to gather my strength for the Bolivian unknown.

12. FIRST TASTE OF BOLIVIA

When awful darkness and silence reign
Over the great Gromboolian plain,
  Through the long, long wintry nights; –
When Storm-clouds brood on the towering heights
Of the Hills of the Chankly Bore: –

(Edward Lear, 'The Dong with a Luminous Nose')

It was not exactly my first taste of the country. In 1979, I'd been given a sabbatical term before I assumed my responsibilities as a headmistress, and I had chosen to spend the recreational half of this generous gift of time crossing South America on an overland package. We entered Bolivia from Paraguay and moved as swiftly as the terrible roads would allow to Cochabamba and La Paz, before visiting the ruins of Tiahuanaco and sailing across Lake Titicaca. But moving along in an organised group is not really travelling. We were nannied in our own coach from one tourist site to the next, where we met no Bolivians at all, except for the sellers of postcards and the bowler-hatted ladies offering us *chullos*, those multi-coloured knitted caps with ear flaps, and jerseys with hectic patterns of llamas marching across their beige chests – the sort of gear which looks charming in the high Andes, on holiday, but is totally unwearable at home. We were in and out of Bolivia in about five days.

All this happened long ago, so long ago in fact that it seems like another life. I was finding it hard to remember which places were in Bolivia and which were in Peru, as the Altiplano is uniform in its drabness, the kind of featureless flinty landscape which Paul Theroux has likened to 'kitty litter'. So I was looking forward to refreshing my memory of the country and getting to talk to a few Bolivians.

As soon as I left my hotel the next morning, I saw that I had parachuted down in one day from the First World to the Third. Plastic bags were bowling along the street in the chill wind and garbage filled the gutters, some just thrown out to rot and some tied up in bags, which had been torn open in the night by foraging dogs or rats. Manholes had lost their covers, or had them stolen for the metal, and no attempt had been made to put up a barrier or even a warning notice. The unwary could easily find themselves down in the sewers or up to the waist in a refuse-clogged hole. What flagstones were left on the derelict pavements were all smashed up and tilted at crazy angles. They looked as if they'd been specially designed with ankle-breaking in mind. The roads were potholed, but they seemed on the whole to be less hazardous than the pavements, so I leaped over the gutter garbage and took to the highway. Fortunately, traffic was thin.

Before I could buy any breakfast, I had to get myself some bolivianos. I crossed the Plaza Arce and found the main street, the Avenida Potosí. The bank didn't change money and, in any case, it was not open yet, but I found an exchange shop, where I changed my remaining Chilean pesos, plus a 20 US dollar bill. No rates were posted and there was no competition, so I just had to hope that the rates were not a rip-off. There was a large army barracks in Uyuni and as I left the shop, about two hundred squaddies jogged past me down the Avenida, clomping along in their heavy boots and chanting slogans, led by a plump young sergeant, a girl who was only half their size.

Uyuni consisted of three streets running east to west, parallel with the railway track, intersected by three north–south streets and the 'square', which was in fact a long, thin pedestrianised rectangle. So exploring the town after breakfast took no time at all.

In most countries, national costume is seen only at jolly folk festivals put on specially for the tourists, or in the pages of the *National Geographic* magazines. In Bolivia, almost all the women wear national costume in real life. The women of Uyuni were dressed in short, flouncy, many-layered skirts over thick knitted wool stockings and flat pumps. They wore dark-brown bowler hats or straw sun hats and carried everything – babies, vegetables and shopping generally – in shawls on their backs. These were woven in dazzling geometric patterns of purple, pink, magenta, green and blue. Each region of Bolivia is said to have its own unique designs and colour combinations, though you would have to be an expert to distinguish between them. The men of Uyuni were drabber. City dwellers, they sported baseball caps, jeans and shabby Western jackets, rather than the traditional tunics and ponchos of the field workers of the Altiplano.

Apart from the fact that hats are essential protection from the intensity of the sun's rays at that altitude, they have always been of the greatest importance to the indigenous peoples of South America because they cover the head, the most sacred part of the body. In earlier days, they indicated social class, type of work and prosperity. For instance, in Inca times, a fisherman would wear a hat of a particular pattern and design, to show that he was a fisherman. But if that hat was made of wool, it showed that he was a rich fisherman, as he could afford to trade with wool producers. The women's multi-layered skirts were copied from the dresses of sixteenth-century Spanish ladies, but their bowler hats are of more recent origin. They first appeared in the 1930s, possibly in imitation of the hats worn by the European engineers and mine superintendents, though one account has it that a wily importer ordered too large a consignment of bowler hats and got rid of his surplus stock by persuading the locals that they were the height of fashion for European ladies. There are said to be over a hundred traditional styles of bowler hat and top hat in Bolivia, and I did notice how the hats changed in shape, decoration and colour from area to area as I travelled around the country – though today, among the younger women, the baseball cap is sadly beginning to supplant this rich and significant variety of headgear, thanks to the cultural dominance of the United States.

The older people in Uyuni were generally toothless and many had the bow legs of childhood rickets. Malnutrition was rife, and I spotted neither a doctor's nor a dentist's surgery in the town. That was hardly surprising, as 22 per cent of the population has no access to medical care, according to a survey in 2002, and there are only 1.7 hospital beds to 1000 people. I just hoped I wouldn't get ill there or break a tooth!

To my relief, after all my nightly panics in Calama over my blood pressure, my heart seemed to be coping perfectly well with the altitude (3665 m). I'd passed a fairly restless night (one of the symptoms of altitude sickness) and woken at five o'clock with a parched mouth and a headache. But it was probably just dehydration after the lack of fluids on the train, because I drank a large mug of water with two aspirins, and slept very well after that until about 7.30. My head was perfectly clear and I was only slightly out of breath as I ambled around the town. I was obviously going to live, even if my hair was literally standing on end with electricity in the thin, dry air. No wonder there were so many hairdressers! It's amazing what the human body can adapt to. My dinner-time beer frothed uncontrollably and, when I took my aspirins in the night, I noticed that the bubbles in the bubble-pack were tiny balloons, blown up to the point of bursting. I popped a couple and the tablets shot straight across the room like little white bullets. If the altitude could do that to a simple bubble-pack, what on earth was it doing to my own complex system? And yet I felt fine.

Most of the shops were open-fronted shacks, halfway between market stalls and tin huts. As I passed along a row of these, I heard someone calling me. It was my friend from the train. She was busy opening a carton of pastel-coloured toilet rolls and setting them out temptingly on the trestle tables which served as her shop window. Having sampled the scratchy local variety, I could well understand the demand for her rolls from Lider. They were gossamer by comparison.

'I hope you found a hotel last night. Where are you staying?' (A useful way of finding out how much money I had!)

'I'm staying at the Hotel Avenida.'

'Oh, very nice,' she said. 'But they don't do breakfast there. You'll need some biscuits.'

I bought a packet of lemon creams, which looked the least sickly of her selection. She was a good businesswoman, brisk and cheerful, like all the neighbouring stallholders, all of them women. As far as I could see, there was little work in Uyuni for the men. It used to be a major railway junction for international trains entering Bolivia from Chile and Argentina, but the railways are now in a state of terminal decay. So unless they worked in the salt mines, joined the army, or were educated enough to act as tour guides, the men simply hung around in the plaza. It was the women who ran the stalls, while the children shone shoes, or sold lottery tickets, sweets and cigarettes. Some toted ice creams around in wooden boxes on shoulder straps. Although education is theoretically compulsory for six to eleven year olds, it is reckoned that only about 40 per cent of that age group attend school regularly. The rest work. In the last survey, in 2002, illiteracy still stood at 6.9 per cent for Bolivian males and 18.4 per cent for females.

When I'm travelling, I usually have a snack lunch of bread, cheese and fruit, so I looked for something to eat with my remaining Chilean crackers. But in Uyuni there were no refrigerators, even in the few proper shops, so no cheese, fresh milk or cold drinks were available. Some of the women arrived in the plaza on tricycles, loaded up with home-made snacks and Thermos flasks of coffee. I went over to inspect. The cups were cracked, and they were dipping the cutlery and plates after use in a bucket of scummy water – in a country where tap water is unsafe, even when it's freshly drawn. I decided I would probably die of the plague, or at least suffer a severe attack of Montezuma's revenge, if I ate one of their messes of sweetcorn, so I lunched on dry crackers. As for fruit on the Altiplano, forget it! The vegetable stalls were piled high with potatoes, carrots and a few tomatoes. When I managed to track down two more or less undamaged mangoes in the early evening, it was quite a triumph. Loving my food and drink as I do, I could see deprivation looming in Bolivia.

The town's economy depended on the women traders. They used money to buy and sell, but their system of mutual dependency was so simple that they could equally well have bartered. The woman who sold rice and pasta bought tomatoes from the woman selling vegetables, who bought socks from the clothes seller, who bought biscuits or toilet rolls from my friend, who bought a new knife from the woman selling hardware, who bought rice from the woman selling rice and pasta. It was the same pathetically small sum of money which was doing the rounds from the rice seller, back to the rice seller. The only possible sources of outside cash were the foreigners, who stayed in the local hotels and might be persuaded to take a tour of the salt flats. But that week there were only a handful of us, and we were just passing through, staying in Uyuni for one or two nights to recover from the train journey. My backpacking friends did take an afternoon trip, speeding across the crackling salt in an open-topped jeep, but the Chileans and I stayed put.

Apart from the Guianas, Bolivia has the smallest economy in South America, and is reckoned by Transparency International to be one of the world's most corrupt – which is saying something. It has been blighted since independence by political instability, earning a place in the *Guinness Book of Records* for the greatest number of military coups d'état in history – 188 between 1825 and 1982! As a result, it ranks between Afghanistan and Mozambique in the world's poverty league. It is estimated that 70 per cent of the people live below the poverty line, despite the country's vast mineral resources and its wealth of natural gas, and despite the fact that it receives more aid from international sources than any other country in South America. The Gross National Income is less than $900 US annually per capita. In 1985, inflation hit 24,000 per cent and, until recently, Bolivia's external debt was so high ($5,762 million in 2000 and still rising) that over 30 per cent of the entire GDP went to service it. But, in 2005, the country was included in the debt cancellation plans of the G8. It remains to be seen whether or not the government will have the expertise to profit from the reduction in interest payments. At least there have been relatively stable civilian governments since 1982, with peaceful democratic transitions between presidents, so maybe things are beginning to look up.

Politics used to be the sport of the white European elite, a minority pursuit from which the indigenous peoples were excluded. Presidents came in with bloodshed, disappointed their supporters and left in haste with their profits. For the Indians, the struggle to keep body and soul together went on regardless. But in 1952, they were finally given the vote. At 55 per cent of the population, they outnumber the Europeans and *mestizos* combined and in 2005 Evo Morales, leader of the Movimiento al Socialismo (MAS), became the first elected Indian president.

Evo, as he is affectionately known, is a colourful character, a former llama herder, who used to played the trumpet in a local band. He came into prominence as leader of the *cocalero* movement, the loose confederation of coca-growing campesinos, and, in April 2000, he was one of the organisers of the mass demonstrations, roadblocks and running battles in protest against the takeover of the Cochabamba water works by a large international company, Aguas de Tanari. Water prices were to be increased and laws passed to make it illegal to catch and use rainwater, which would have put water out of the reach of the majority of campesinos. The protest movement was a success and Bolivian water stayed under Bolivian control.

A popular figure in his trademark hand-knitted Altiplano jumpers, Evo masterminded an extremely clever ceremony before his inauguration as president. He appeared on the stage dressed in the *Unku*, the ancient robe of the high priest of the Collas, one of the Aymara-speaking peoples. He had modified it by adding Amazonian anacondas to the traditional decoration of mountain condors, to emphasise that he represented the peoples of the Bolivian lowlands as well as those of the Altiplano. For the same reason, he had his staff carved out of lowland wood, decorated with the traditional mountain silver and gold. All this was powerful populist symbolism. But his most striking gesture was the immediate slashing of his own presidential salary from his predecessor's 34,900 bolivianos a month to 15,000 (about £900) and persuading his ministers to take similar pay cuts. 'We need six thousand more teachers,' he said, 'and there's only the money to pay for two thousand two hundred.' He promised that the savings from government salaries would be used to create a fund specifically to employ extra school staff. His actions have endeared him to the struggling masses, but his renationalisation of the Bolivian natural gas industry has done him no favours internationally. Foreign investment in the country has dropped as a result. But things may stabilise. When the Europeans have made such a poor fist of governing Bolivia in the past, Evo can hardly do worse.

Uyuni is notorious for its bitter winds and harsh living conditions, isolated as it is in the remote south-western corner of Bolivia. To the north, between Uyuni and La Paz, stretches the bleak Altiplano, 800 km of barren plain, caught between the two major cordilleras of the Andes, with not a single tree to break the monotony. It hardly ever rains, and what little rain falls has no way of escaping through the ring of mountains, so it evaporates and forms salt pans. It is a region that not even the martial Incas managed to subdue, as is clear from the survival there of the Aymara language, rather than the Inca Quechua. To the south, towards the border with

Argentina, the plateau rolls on, equally high and desolate, but now pierced by dramatic red rock formations.

Fortunately, the howling winds were still. Had I been on my bicycle, they would not have been so kind. Winds love to torment cyclists. They would have delighted in blowing a gale straight into my face. But the sun at 3665 m was so intense that I felt it stinging my back through my shirt, jersey and fleece. The archaeological museum was closed, so I went on a tour of the town's other attractions, its four monuments. They were all strung out along the Avenida Ferroviaria, parallel to the railway line. There was a shiny steam engine, made in Yorkshire; the statue of an armed miner, commemorating the revolution of 1952, which resulted in the enfranchisement of the indigenous peoples; the statue of a giant woman in a long skirt, stretching her arms out in front of her, made entirely of scrap metal – a clever way of disposing of all those derelict bits of railway; and a monument outside the barracks to 'Uyuni, *Hija Pridilecta de Bolivia*' (Uyuni, Bolivia's Favourite Daughter), a title bestowed on the town in gratitude for the help given to the wounded soldiers returning from the disastrous Chaco War with Paraguay (1932–5), when Bolivia lost 55,000 men and almost the whole of the potentially oil-rich Chaco region. Monuments throughout Bolivia commemorate this war, as if it were a triumph, when in fact it was just another occasion – like the War of the Pacific against Chile, the two wars against Peru and the border skirmishes with Argentina and Brazil – when the country lost a rich chunk of land to one of its neighbours. Since independence in 1835, Bolivia, always the loser, has lost over half its original territory, including the mineral wealth of the Atacama Desert, access to the sea and large tracts of the Amazonian rubber forests.

In the afternoon, I went on a visit to El Cementerio de Trenes. At least Uyuni had the honesty to call it a 'train cemetery', rather than a 'train museum', as elsewhere. To get there, I had to walk eastwards as far as the army barracks, then continue along the train line. My two guidebooks described it as a 1 km walk, or a walk taking fifteen minutes. I can only marvel at how speedy the authors must have been on their feet. I'm no snail, but the further I walked, the further the railway line seemed to recede into the distance, while the engines and rolling stock in the cemetery were barely visible in the far clouds of dust.

The railway track was raised on a low embankment with a ditch on either side, where all the town's garbage was piled high in stinking heaps – at least, all of it that had not been left to rot in Uyuni's gutters. The smell was overpowering. At that altitude, there were few flies, which was a blessing, but there were packs of scavenging dogs. I left the last houses behind and walked on into open desert. No one was around except the dogs, some of whom growled and bared their teeth at me, and a few solitary lurking men. I'm not of a nervous disposition. I usually walk along resolutely, quite confident of my safety. If you look like a victim, you will soon become one. But out there, on my own and very conspicuous in the empty land-scape, I did start to feel a little uneasy, especially as I was carrying my passport, credit cards and reserve funds in the body-belt under my jersey. I picked up a couple of stones from the track, in case the dogs went for me. But what about the prowling men? I was new to Bolivia and didn't know what sort of behaviour to expect. I just had a hunch that these men were too furtive for comfort. I decided to give up. Why run into danger to look at a bunch of rusty engines, when I didn't know one type of engine from another, and didn't much care? I took two long-distance shots of the train cemetery through my zoom lens (though I guessed I was still too far away for the photos to come out), then beat an unhurried retreat, so as not to excite the dogs.

I was disappointed not to get my own photo of an engine I'd seen on a postcard that morning. It was a shot of a disintegrating heap of rust, crumbling away into the desert sand, and someone had painted in bold letters on its boiler, 'Life's like that!' That philosophical engine was my main reason for wanting to visit the yard. To make up for the lack of my own photo, I scoured Uyuni all evening, searching for that market stall with the postcards, without success. I'm not a keen shopper, but I really must school myself to buy what I like when I see it. I so often miss the chance and end up full of regrets.

I was having quite a sociable time in Uyuni. Everywhere I went in such a small town – restaurants, cafés, shops, the internet centre – I bumped into the four backpackers, the Chilean family or my bowler-hatted friend, and we stopped for a chat or took a coffee together. But two nights were enough. I had to move on. The train service to Potosí was now freight only, so I had to travel there by bus.

Bus travel in Bolivia was the other terror that had been keeping me awake at nights. I remembered with fear and trembling the journeys I'd made in 1978, when our tour bus had climbed incredibly high mountain passes on narrow roads, negotiating landslides and teetering along the edges of preci-pices. For a vertigo sufferer, it had been a waking nightmare. Now I had no choice but to repeat the horror.

The offices of all the intercity buses lined both sides of the street just north of the Plaza Arce. There were dozens of them and just like competing bus services the world over, they all left for the same destinations at the same times. I've never been able to understand why they don't stagger their departures, to give the passengers a wider choice. For Potosí, every single bus left either at 10 a.m. or 7 p.m. The four backpackers were strolling up and down the street, casting a critical eye over the buses. They had decided to leave at 7 p.m. that evening, as a night journey would save them the expense of a hostel. I was aiming for ten o'clock the next morning. I wanted to see the scenery – but also the very thought of a night journey along those scary mountain roads filled me with dread. I should be safer in the daylight.

Although it had stayed dry in Uyuni, I knew that it was the rainy season in that corner of Bolivia. I also knew how little tarmac there was on the roads (some 93 per cent of them are still unpaved), and how soon the dirt tracks could dissolve into skidpans in a downpour. So inspecting the tyres on the buses was my top priority. Some were as bald as eggs. The rest had shallow undulations, which might once in the distant past have been treads. It was all very unnerving. The buses themselves looked elderly, and I had no way of checking the condition of their engines or the skill and patience of their drivers, but I could at least peer through the windows. Some had reasonable seats and some had their springs poking through. I settled on the company that seemed to have the most modern buses and hoped for the best.

The next morning, we joined the procession of buses leaving Uyuni at 10 a.m. Inside the town, the road was paved with small hexagonal stones, once beautifully cut and laid, but now sticking up in all directions like the spines of turbulent hedgehogs. It was actually quite a relief to leave the bumps behind and roll onto the narrow dirt road. We drove through a flat desert landscape covered in plastic bags and rusting tins, passed a stony valley where nothing grew but tall ithyphallic cacti, and soon reached Pulcayo.

As there are few tourist attractions in this barren corner of Bolivia, the Proyecto Turistico Pulcayo is making the most of its tenuous connection with the notorious bandits, Butch Cassidy and the Sundance Kid. Pulcayo's silver mines once employed twenty-thousand men, but mining ceased fifty years ago and the place is now a virtual ghost town. It stands on a dusty hill, its shacks listing crazily near the crown and a few brave terraces of greenery striping its lower reaches. At its base, a stream no more than a foot wide, still discoloured by the seepage from the old mines, trickles along between towering multicoloured cliffs. It is a desolate spot, but it has one sight which they hope will bring the tourists flocking. In yet another train museum stands the train which Butch Cassidy and the Sundance Kid are said by some to have robbed. Its wooden railcar is riddled with their bullets.

The story goes that the manager of the Aramayo Mining Company was taking the payroll of one of the company's mines to Quechisla, some time in 1908. He was travelling by train and was unescorted, when he was held up and robbed by two outlaws, reputed to be Butch Cassidy and the Sundance Kid. They fled north with their loot in the direction of Uyuni. It had always been their dream to own a smallholding and live peaceful farming lives, but Pinkerton's Detective Agency was on their tail for a string of robberies committed in the USA. They made a number of attempts to settle down in Argentina, but every time they put down roots, they were discovered and had to move hurriedly on to somewhere else. It has been conjectured that this train robbery was intended to be their last. The aim was to finance their rural idyll in some secret location in Bolivia. Hunted by the authorities and bands of furious armed miners, whose pay they had stolen, they went into hiding in the remote mining village of San Vicente. There they were recognised and the house they were staying in was surrounded. Rather than surrender, Butch shot his partner in crime, then turned the gun on himself. They were buried in unmarked graves in the San Vicente cemetery.

Argentine Patagonia and Bolivia are littered with locations where Butch and the Sundance Kid are said to have farmed, worked in the mines or robbed banks. As for the place where they met their doom, San Vicente is only one of many candidates for the distinction. An exhumation of bodies in the cemetery in 1991 proved inconclusive. Like Elvis, the pair seem to have been sighted in dozens of locations throughout both north and South America, years after their supposed demise. It has even been claimed that they fled to Paris under assumed names and were gunned down there. With so much competition, it was hardly surprising that Pulcayo's tenuous connection with the two outlaws failed to excite the passengers in my bus. None of us got out to see the train which they might or might not have robbed.

After Pulcayo, the land became more sandy. We wobbled on boulders across dry riverbeds that were hemmed in by sand dunes. In the distance we could see naked mountains. Some had a grey-green tinge, and their tormented strata reared up at 45-degree angles. Others were eroded sandstone formations, which rose in fantastic columns from the plain, like the 'fairy chimneys' of Cappadocia. Anthony Trollope says in his book on Australia and New Zealand: 'I doubt whether I ever read any description of scenery which gave me an idea of the place described.' That's how I feel about the Altiplano. Any attempt to describe it is bound to fail. Unless you have seen its terrible aridity for yourself, you can get no conception of its desolation from a book. I was reminded constantly of Edward Lear and his great Gromboolian plain where 'awful darkness and silence reign . . . on the towering heights/Of the Hills of the Chankly Bore'. The only way I could cope with its awfulness was by making a joke of it.

There were a few pathetic trickles of rivers, which supported some agriculture down in their valleys, mostly maize and wheat, but it was impossible to tell how many people lived in the villages. These consisted of small clusters of mud-brick hovels, some thatched and some roofed with tin or corrugated iron. But whatever the roofs were made of, they all needed stones to hold them down and prevent them from sailing away on the fierce winds which howled down the valleys. As the houses had no windows, only gaps boarded up with wood or blocked with clumps of brush, it was difficult to see whether or not they were inhabited. Window glass and curtains were obviously unaffordable luxuries in that poverty-stricken environment, and no one had the means or the will to give doors a coat of paint or grow a few flowers. The countryside seemed empty.

It was not a ride to lift the spirits. As we neared Potosí, there was marshland where llamas and sheep were grazing, and we passed one herd of pigs and two donkeys. Then we started to climb. The winding mountain roads were diabolical. They were so narrow that one side of the bus almost scraped the rock face, while the other gave horrifying views down to the chasms beneath. We juddered along over stony corrugated surfaces, our driver sitting firmly on the tail of another Potosí-bound bus and hooting in irritation. It was a more ramshackle conveyance than ours and much slower, but there was no room to overtake and our driver was getting frustrated. So, added to my vertigo, was the fear that he would suddenly lose patience and attempt some reckless manoeuvre. Fortunately, there was little traffic and we managed quite well until we came to a really tight bend on a steep descent. There we met a wide oncoming truck. Our driver had to go into reverse. Our bus groaned its way back up the slope, pulling in as close to the rock face as a ditch would allow. The bus in front of us did the same. Then the truck inched its way round the corner and climbed up almost to our level. There was a precarious little shelf overhanging the abyss, just wide enough to take the truck and allow us to crawl past. I was glad it was the truck that had to perch there, not our bus because, although it was wide enough for the truck, the shelf was not nearly the right length. The truck driver braked hard against the slope, crossed himself, then sat there with two of his rear four wheels sticking out into thin air.

At 12.30, we stopped at a tin-roofed café. It advertised coffee, *maté* (herbal tea), *caña* (a sort of cane alcohol) and *chicha* (fermented maize beer) to wash down its empanadas, but it was so desperately dark and dingy inside, with no electricity and no covering on its dirt floor, that I gave the refreshments a miss. I joined the rest of the passengers for a comfort stop behind the crumbling walls, men to one side, women to the other, then retreated to the relative salubriousness of the coach for a lunch of biscuits and Tampico Citrus Punch, a very pleasant Bolivian soft drink I had discovered in Uyuni.

The afternoon turned nasty. There were black storm clouds ahead and distant lightning tore across the bruised sky, but we beat the rain to Potosí and the safety of the city's tarmac roads. Our bus treads were the best I had seen in Uyuni, and I suppose they would have coped with manoeuvres on tight bends in the rain. I was just relieved that they weren't put to the test while I was a passenger. Bolivia was not motoring country. Even if the roads were paved, the mountain passes would still be hazardous. The Incas had the right idea, laying a network of pavements for travellers on foot. Even today, Bolivians give the distance in walking time rather than kilometres. If you ask the way, the answer is 'Turn right and it's twenty minutes' walk along the railway track.' Like the Ethiopians in similar terrain, they think nothing of walking tremendous distances.

Potosí, at 4090 metres, is the highest city in the world, so the bus had a considerable climb to reach its terminus on the outskirts. I'd intended to make enquiries about my onward journey as soon as I arrived, but I couldn't summon the energy. I was gasping for breath at that altitude and, travelling alone, I had no one with me who could keep an eye on my luggage. I quailed at the thought of hauling it breathlessly along the rows of ticket offices in the filthy chaos of the bus station. I would have to come back another day and book my ticket without it. I looked for a taxi to take me to the hotel I had picked out of my guidebook, but there were none to be seen, so I boarded a minibus bound for the city centre. The climb continued. Up and up went the minibus, toiling through narrow cobbled streets, past sumptuous churches and seething Christmas markets. Then, with a final puff of exhaust fumes, it came to a halt in the Plaza de 10 Noviembre, opposite La Casa Real de la Moneda, the Spanish Royal Mint. I had arrived at the start of my second historical route in South America.

13. THE MOUNTAIN OF SILVER

Soy el rico Potosí, del mondo soy el tesoro; soy el rey de los montes, envidia soy de los reyes.

(I am rich Potosí, the treasure of the world; I am the king of the mountains, the envy of kings.)

(Coat of Arms of the City of Potosí)

It seems fitting to begin the story of a legendary mountain with a couple of legends.

Many years ago, Huaya Ccapac, the eleventh ruler of the Inca Empire, was making a grand tour of his gold and silver mines when he saw a magnificent mountain. It towered in grandeur over one of the starkest plains in his Andean kingdom, a huge perfect cone in a delicate shade of pink.

'Such a marvel of nature must have silver at its heart,' he announced, and he ordered his vassals to go to the hill and find it. They hurried there with their flint tools and began to dig exploratory passages in the mountain, searching for its silver veins. Suddenly, a voice like thunder echoed through the landscape. 'Do not take the silver from this mountain,' it roared. 'It is destined for other masters, who will come from afar to claim it.' The terrified miners rushed to report this supernatural occurence to the Inca. Being a religious ruler – in fact the earthly incarnation of the Inca God of the Sun, Inti – Huaya Ccapac declared the mountain sacred and gave the order to cease mining operations.

That was supposed to have happened some time in the middle of the fifteenth century – around 1460, if the reigns of the Inca rulers have been dated correctly. The Inca ruler's orders were obeyed and the mountain lay undisturbed for almost a hundred years. Then in 1544 or 1545, depending on which account you read, a llama herder named Diego Huallpa was grazing his herd one evening on the lower slopes of the mountain, when two of his llamas made a bid for freedom. They ran far away, at great speed, and Diego spent hours looking for them. By the time he had found them and led them back to join the rest of the herd, night had fallen. At that altitude, the hours of darkness are bitterly cold, even in summer, so he lit a fire. As he gazed into the flames, he was astonished to see molten silver trickling out of the ashes.

Diego decided to keep his find a secret. He joined forces with his friend, Chalco, and together they began to mine for the silver. Here the versions of the legend diverge, as usually happens with legends. Some say that Chalco had a row with Diego over the division of the spoils; others that he had rather too much to drink one night and started to boast within earshot of the Spaniards, who by that time had conquered the Altiplano. Whichever it was, accounts agree that Chalco, either deliberately or through drunken indiscretion, leaked the discovery of the silver. He and Diego never made their fortunes, for the Spaniards banished them from the mountain and commandeered it for themselves.

At that time, the name of the mountain was Sumaj Orcko and the city of Potosí did not exist. But when the miners were reporting their supernatural experience to the Inca, they were heard to use the word 'potocsi', which still puzzles etymologists. Was it Quechua, the language of the Incas, or was it a word in Aymara, the other major language of the Altiplano?

And did it mean 'thunder, burst, explosion, ruin, spoil, spring, source of silver . . .'? No one knows. But what is certain is that the city which grew up at the foot of the mountain was called by the Spaniards Potosí, while they named the mountain itself Cerro Rico (Rich Mountain).

Indian legends about 'Children of the Sun', who were destined to come from far away to conquer their lands – and in the case of the Cerro Rico, to exploit their wealth – are one of the reasons why such powerful and well-organised king-doms as those of the Aztecs and the Incas, fell so easily into Spanish hands. The indigenous peoples and their rulers, deeply religious then as now, seem to have resigned themselves to what they perceived as the will of the gods and given in without much of a struggle.

The Incas were less passive than the Aztecs. They put up a bit of a fight, but it is still one of the amazements of history that Francisco Pizarro, with a mere 180 men and 27 horses, could conquer an empire which stretched from Quito in modern Equador down to northern Argentina and Chile. Of course, there were other factors at work, apart from South American legends and superstition.

It was a time of great energy and confidence in the developed world. There was something special shimmering in the air. From the strength of China under the Mings, through the glories of the Ottoman Empire under Suleiman the Magnifi-cent, through the Renaissance in Italy, the seeds of the Reformation and the growing power of the European mon-archs, success was sweeping the globe. The Tudors had stabilised England after years of conflict, Louis XI was on the throne of France and the whole of Europe was buzzing with ideas, with the excitement of new sciences and new worlds. And no country was more fired up than Spain. The Catholic monarchs, Ferdinand and Isabella, had succeeded in driving the last of the Moors out of the Iberian Peninsula, and their ships (albeit under the command of an Italian, Christopher Columbus) had achieved the seemingly impossible. They had crossed the Atlantic and discovered the West Indies. Cortez had already conquered Mexico and the Spaniards were cock-a-hoop. Nothing and no one could halt their progress.

When they met the Incas, they were buoyed up with inner confidence, but that was not their only advantage. They had firearms, technically sophisticated crossbows and suits of iron armour, against which the simple Inca bows and arrows were completely useless. Then the appearance of the Spaniards inspired the Incas with dread. They had never seen white faces before, and horses were unknown in South America. When Pizarro and his men first came riding into Cajamarca, the Incas thought the horses and men were one and the same animal, some hideous four-legged beast with a man's head and trunk, a kind of centaur with the ashen face of a corpse. Then, to their horror, one of the cavalrymen dismounted, and the fantastic creature seemed to split in two and still go on living. The Inca warriors dropped their bows, arrows, clubs and spears, and fled in terror. These must indeed be the 'Children of the Sun', the gods from distant lands who were destined to take over their empire.

Pizarro was a lucky man. He and his troops filled the Incas with religious awe and psychological dread, and infected them with smallpox, measles, influenza and other European diseases, at a time when they were lacking firm leadership. Huaya Ccapac had died and bequeathed his newly conquered kingdom of Quito to Atahuallpa, his son by a Quito princess, while his main kingdom, based on the Inca capital, Cuzco, was left to Huascar, his legitimate heir. In the civil war that inevitably followed, Atahuallpa was the victor, but the fighting between the two half-brothers had left the empire in disarray. So in 1533 Pizarro and his men were able to march from Tumbes, where they landed on the coast of Peru, up into the Andes to Cajamarca, watched curiously by the Inca spies, but not attacked.

Unlike 'stout Cortez', the Conqueror of Mexico, who was an educated man, Francisco Pizarro was illiterate. An illegitimate son of a minor nobleman from Trujillo in Extremadura, he had grown up in poverty and gone out to the New World as a young man to seek his fortune – like many others from that stony, sun-baked region of Spain. So Cortez was able to write his own account of his dealings with Montezuma and the Aztecs. He has left us his commentaries, which provide us with a window into his mind, through which we can glimpse his strategy and his motivation. But Pizarro left nothing on paper. We have only factual accounts of his actions, written by others. We have no inkling from Pizarro himself of his thoughts and motives. In his case, we can only speculate. And he does seem to have played his cards shrewdly. He seems to have recognised that he could survive with such a small force only if he appeared friendly towards the locals. So he treated those he met with civility, and sent messages to the Inca, assuring him of his peaceful intent. Any fighting or cruelty by his soldiers on the march was severely punished.

The Spaniards were cordially received everywhere. When they arrived in Cajamarca, the Inca Atahuallpa was taking the waters at a nearby spa. Pizarro sent ambassadors to offer him the assistance of the Spaniards against his enemies, and the Inca returned the compliment by inviting Pizarro and his men to make themselves comfortable in his palace in Cajamarca; he himself would return the next day to welcome them personally. But Pizarro arranged his own welcome party. When the Inca and his nobles walked unarmed into the palace, they were ambushed. Atahuallpa's army was slaughtered to a man and he himself was offered his freedom for an enormous ransom. A room in the palace was to be filled from floor to ceiling, once with gold and twice with silver. Atahuallpa gave the order, and his people came from all corners of his kingdom, bearing gold and silver jewellery, goblets, plates and religious artefacts, all exquisitely crafted. Some of the most spectacular treasures were sent to Spain with Hernando Pizarro, Francisco's brother, as the King's share. The rest of the objects were simply melted down by troops indifferent to their beauty and the precious metals divided up between them.

Although he had faithfully kept his part of the bargain, and even converted to Christianity, Atahuallpa was still burned at the stake and one of his brothers, Toparca, was set up as the Spaniards' puppet Inca. Pizarro proclaimed that he came in the name of the Holy Vicar of God and the Sovereign of Spain and required obedience. The Incas understood not a word he was saying, but their silence was taken as acquiescence and they were attested by a notary to be subjects of Spain. So ended the mighty Inca Empire, in fraud and a broken promise.

In 1537, shortly after the conquest, Pope Paul III issued a papal bull, Veritas Ipsa (The Very Truth) which 'solemnly recognises those Indians as true men . . . and the said Indians and all other peoples who at a later stage might come to the knowledge of the Christians, even if they should be outside the Christian faith, should not be deprived of their freedom, nor the enjoyment of their possessions, and should not be reduced to slavery'. And it is true that there were some devout and benevolent Spanish churchmen, who went out to South America to convert the people and care for them. But the vast majority of Spaniards went out to Peru and Bolivia (then called Alto Peru) as adventurers, to amass considerable fortunes. They returned home with their loot, built palaces and lived the lives of Spanish grandees. As Gaspar de Espinosa, the Spanish Governor of Panama, wrote to the Emperor Charles V, 'The greed of Spaniards of all classes is so great as to be insatiable: the more the chiefs give, the more the Spaniards try to persuade their own captains and governors to kill or torture them to give more.' More picturesquely, 'Their bodies swelled with greed and their hunger was ravenous,' wrote Ernando Diaz.

In the end, greed and the struggle for power led to the assassination of Francisco Pizarro in a political uprising led by Diego de Almagro, son of Pizarro's former rival, the conquistador who first discovered Chile. 'El Mozo' (The Lad), as he was called, killed Pizarro in his palace in the city he had founded, Lima, the capital of Peru. But before his death, Pizarro had the satisfaction of being ennobled as the Marqués de la Conquista by the King of Spain, who also declared his children by a daughter of Atahuallpa to be his legitimate heirs. The illiterate, illegitimate child who grew up in poverty in Extremadura would be a proud man today, if he could return to his birthplace and see his dramatic equestrian statue dominating the medieval plaza of Trujillo, in front of the flamboyant Palacio de los Marqueses de la Conquista.

Once the Spaniards learned of the rich veins of silver in Cerro Rico, their greed knew no bounds. They founded the city of Potosí in 1546 as a mining town, giving it the grand name of the Villa Imperial de Carlos V de Potosí. Within 18 months, the Silver Rush had attracted a population of 14,000, which soon exploded to 120,000, making it the largest city in the Americas. The mountain provided easy pickings. There were copious surface deposits with a high silver content, which were worked very easily by the indigenous miners, even though they used basic tools and primitive smelting techniques. Potosí became the biggest source of silver in the world. Hence the Spanish boast that they could build a bridge of silver all the way from Potosí to Spain and still have plenty of silver left to carry across it.

But the rich surface deposits were used up within twenty years and the miners had to begin the slow process of digging shafts. The silver content of the underground ore was lower, and the city went into decline. But a new Viceroy of Peru, Francisco de Toledo, came to the rescue.

Francisco de Toledo, Count of Oropesa, was a nobleman from Seville, a cousin and close friend of the Emperor Charles V. An austere figure, as his portraits show, dressed entirely in black with a white ruff, he arrived in Lima as viceroy in 1569 and immediately set about reforming the government and setting up an efficient system of administration. He was a man of unbounded energy, the only viceroy ever to travel extensively throughout his realm. Inspecting, fact finding, taking a census of the different ethnic groups, and at the same time consolidating the authority of the Spanish Crown, he covered over 8000 km. He has been described as one of the greatest and most prolific administrators in history. A recent collection of his regulations runs to almost a thousand pages of fine print. Yet he is, sadly, a man who has lapsed into virtual oblivion. I'm ashamed to say that I had never heard of him, until I came across him in my current researches. *Sic transit gloria mundi.*

As a member of the religious-military Order of Alcantara, he was particularly keen on the conversion of the Indians and seems to have taken their welfare very seriously for a man of his times. He even promulgated laws that applied equally to Indians and Spaniards – a practice that did not endear him to the *encomenderos*, the great landowners, who lost some of their privileges as a result. They were partly responsible for his recall to Spain in disgrace by King Philip II in 1581.

But still in Peru, between regularising the State accounts, founding a navy to keep out Sir Francis Drake and other buccaneers, improving the roads, building bridges, reforming the University of San Marcos in Lima and setting up the Inquisition, Toledo arrived in Potosí in 1572 to focus his towering intellect on the problems of the silver mines. His most important contribution to the industry was his knowledge of the newly discovered technique of refining silver by amalgamating it with mercury – a metal that he protected by making it a royal monopoly. This technique greatly improved productivity. Then, appalled at the lack of proper controls and the general chaos in the city, he went to work with his usual vigour, regulating the administration and modernising the entire mining and smelting operation.

He first persuaded the mine owners to invest in a system of dams and artificial lakes in the surrounding mountains, with aqueducts to bring down the water that would power the wheels that crushed the ore. He introduced legislation to regulate property rights, and so ended the fights and bitter squabbles between the mine owners. He established the Royal Mint, to stamp coins and standardise the silver into accurately weighted ingots, 20 per cent of which went to the Spanish Crown. Then he turned his attention to the system of forced labour, the Inca *mita*.

Under the *mita*, the land between Cuzco and North Argentina was divided into sixteen districts, which were forced every year to send a proportion of their male population, aged between eighteen and fifty, to work for their rulers. Some authorities claim that Toledo introduced the system to the mines; others that the system was already in place and he tried to mitigate its hardship. He knew that he could not abolish the system altogether, as that would produce a severe labour shortage, but he did reduce the proportion required to one-seventh of the population, tried to ensure that the workers would not be drafted too far from their native villages and ordered that they should be recompensed for their labour. Even so, the *mitayos* were still paid such miserable wages that they could not subsist on them, and had to be supported by their families at home and their working conditions were as appalling as ever.

Thanks to Toledo's reforms, the boom times returned to Potosí, generating even more fabulous wealth than before. Calculated in marks (a mark is usually taken to be 8 ounces), the silver mined from the Cerro Rico rose from around 130,000 marks a year in the early 1550s to 1 million marks by 1592. If this was not the Spanish dream of El Dorado, it was the nearest they had ever come to it. Lured by this incredible wealth, speculators flocked from Spain and every other part of South America. Potosí's population grew to more than 160,000 residents, including 6000 black slaves. In size, its only rivals in Christendom were London, Paris and Seville. According to John Hemming in his *Conquest of the Incas*, there were 14 dance halls, 36 gambling houses, 700 or 800 professional gamblers, a theatre, 120 prostitutes and dozens of baroque churches. In 1658, to celebrate the Feast of Corpus Cristi, the streets were literally paved with silver ingots. The world was to see nothing like Potosí's riches and extravagance until the wild days of Klondike and the California Gold Rush. In Spanish, *vale un Potosí* (it's worth a Potosí) became a common phrase to describe fabulous wealth.

The Incas called gold 'the tears of the sun' and silver 'the tears of the moon'. If the moon could mourn, she would have shed rivers of tears over the indigenous people of Bolivia and the black slaves. While the Spaniards were revelling in their wealth, the workers were dying in their thousands. The conditions in the mines were absolutely horrendous. The miners were made to stay underground for weeks on end, forced to meet ever larger quotas on pain of death; while the *mitayos* who worked overground in the foundries died of mercury poisoning. The silver ore, crushed to powder by the hydraulic machinery, was mixed with mercury and trodden to an amalgam by workers with their bare feet. Then the mixture was heated to drive off the mercury, producing toxic vapour. It is claimed that 80 per cent of the male population of the 16 districts lost their lives on the Cerro Rico. 'Every peso coin minted in Potosí has cost the lives of ten Indians, who have died in the depths of the mines,' wrote one of the Spanish priests, Fray Antonio de la Calancha, in 1638.

Figures are always difficult to come by, but it has been estimated that in the three centuries of Spanish colonial rule, some 8 to 9 million Indians and Africans were sacrificed to the gods of greed. The Bolivian countryside was emptied of men, a demographic collapse from which the Altiplano has never recovered. In Potosí's heyday, a Franciscan friar, Fray Fernando de Armellones wrote: 'Under the Incas' rule, the Indians were daily on the increase ... We cannot conceal the great paradox that a barbarian, Huaya Ccapac, kept such excellent order that the entire country was calm and all were nourished, whereas today we see only infinite deserted villages on all the roads of the kingdom.'

They say that wealth doesn't bring happiness. Their own personal affluence, and the power and respect it brought them, may have been a dream come true to hordes of individual Spaniards, but the sudden oversupply of silver coin did little to benefit mankind. Peru and Bolivia were awash with money, at a time when the villages were so depopulated that they could no longer produce food and other necessities. Prices soared to dizzying heights and hyperinflation set in, further impoverishing the indigenous peoples.

Unlike the migrants to North America, who went there to escape religious persecution or simply in search of better lives for themselves and their families, most of the Spaniards who ventured to South America in the sixteenth and seventeenth centuries went out there with the sole purpose of making their fortunes. The Europeans in North America settled down, ploughed the soil, established manufacturing industries and built roads and railways. They were industrious people, who settled on land that was relatively poor in natural resources and by their own labours made a prosperous country of it. The conquistadors, on the other hand, simply exploited the riches and plentiful slave labour of South America and returned home to Spain as wealthy men. They did little to improve conditions in the country – in fact, their activities led to its almost terminal decline.

Inevitably, the curse of inflation spread to Spain, and from there to the rest of Europe, as the continent was suddenly flooded with silver coins. Their ready availability gave a boost to trade, both within European markets and between Europe and Asia, as demand for silk, spices and other exotic imports grew. But many at the bottom end of the scale were impoverished by rising prices. Then the nouveau riche arrived home, weighed down like donkeys with sacks of silver, and like donkeys they started to fling it around. Many of them were peasants from the poverty-stricken Extremadura and, like today's lottery winners, they built themselves mansions, even palaces, rode around in grand carriages, dressed themselves in extravagant finery and generally vied with one another in the purchase and display of luxury goods. In their day, they were the world's great shoppers.

As for their monarch, King Philip II, he grew richer than the legendary Croesus of Lydia on his 20 per cent rake-off of all the silver and gold produced in the New World. But he was not a prudent spender. He perceived his mission in life as the defence of the True Faith against the rising tide of Protestantism and threw vast sums of money into financing wars in Europe, including the failed attack on England by his Spanish Armada in 1588. His father, the Holy Roman Emperor, Charles V, was constantly setting armies on the march and launching battle fleets, financed by loans from the banking house of the German Fugger family. But Charles was always able to repay his debts. His relationship with the Fuggers, who charged him anything from 12 to 50 per cent interest, depending on the level of risk, proved highly satisfactory to both parties. Charles strengthened his grip on his extensive empire and the Fuggers grew rich. By contrast, Philip II, who had unimaginable wealth pouring into his treasury from Peru, still managed to go bankrupt twice, in 1575 and 1596. He defaulted on loans from the Fuggers, and that signalled the beginning of the end for the once profitable relationship between private capital and the European monarchs.

Undaunted by such minor setbacks as bankruptcy, King Philip continued to feed the flames of inflation with his grand schemes, in particular by the wealth he lavished between 1563 and 1584 on the construction of his hubristic palace-cum-monastery of San Lorenzo del Escorial. This gigantic edifice of yellow-grey granite must be just about the coldest, most forbidding building in Europe. A morbid man, King Philip had it designed in the shape of the gridiron on which Saint Laurence suffered martyrdom. He planned it, not only as his palace on a lonely site north of Madrid, but as his own grandiose tomb and the mausoleum of Spanish kings. With its Rotting Room, where the bodies of dead royals were left to decompose before being transferred to the richly decorated marble Pantheon, the Escorial is a house of horrors from which tourists escape with sighs of relief, to revive themselves in the nearest bar. While Queen Elizabeth was down at Tilbury Docks, dressed in a suit of gleaming armour 'like an Angell bright', inspiring her fleet to repel the Spanish Armada, Philip II was at prayer in El Escorial's Basilica, where there were 44 altars, so that several Masses could be celebrated simultaneously. Visitors to El Escorial are shown his bedroom, where he died of some hideously painful and fetid skin disease. Double doors open out from this simple whitewashed chamber into an oratory behind the high altar, so that the King could follow the Mass on his bed of pain. Despite the many splendid works of art in the palace, its gloom is indescribable. King Philip II of Spain was for four years, until her death in 1558, married to Queen Mary I, Mary Tudor, the daughter of Henry VIII and Catherine of Aragon, and was therefore King of England. I can only think that the accession of Queen Elizabeth and her refusal to marry was our lucky escape. King Philip would not have made a 'merrie monarch'!

But silver profits of such prodigious magnitude could not last indefinitely. By 1650 or thereabouts, the richest ore had been mined from the Cerro Rico and silver output began to fall. The city shrank, as the mine owners drifted away to seek more profitable ventures elsewhere, and their departure reduced the need for a large labour force of *mitayos*. To add to the general decline, two natural disasters struck. The restraining wall of one of Toledo's artificial lakes burst in 1626, and a great tide of water thundered down from the mountains, sweeping away whole areas of the city and drowning at least 4000 inhabitants. Then in 1719 an outbreak of typhoid killed an estimated 22,000 people. By 1750, the population was down from its peak of 160,000 to 70,000, and by the 1780s it stood at a miserable 35,000. The loss of revenue from Potosí's silver hit the whole of Peru and Bolivia very hard. All the other cities went into decline, except La Paz. The King of Spain, Carlos III, tried to help out by reducing his cut from 20 to 10 per cent. He established an academy for the study of metallurgy and built a new Royal Mint, but the glory days were over.

The city was saved by tin, a humble metal which was beneath the notice of the Spanish conquistadors. As silver production declined, the profits from tin rose, until the world price collapsed through over-supply. But though the city was limping along from one crisis to the next, with only fifty working mines left in the Cerro Rico, it was still a prize worth fighting for in the Wars of Independence. Potosí was besieged several times and bounced like a yo-yo from the Argentine Freedom Fighters to the Royalists and back again. On each occasion, there was mayhem and looting in the city. The glorious baroque churches were stripped of their treasures by the soldiery and the citizens became more and more despondent and intractable. The last straw was the decision of the Argentine commander, General Manuel Belgrano, to keep the Mint out of Royalist hands by blowing it up. The besieged Argentines lit the fuse and fled from the city, giving the residents a chance to put out the flame. They saved their most prestigious building in the nick of time, but in their anger at General Belgrano, they abandoned their previous idea of joining neighbouring Argentina. With its population reduced to a mere 9000, and its wealth a thing of the past, Potosí and its Mountain of Silver became part of the newly independent state of Bolivia in 1825.

14. CHRISTMAS IN POTOSI

Does the road wind up-hill all the way?
  Yes, to the very end.
Will the day's journey take the whole long day?
  From morn to night, my friend.

(Christina Rossetti)

The bus had climbed up to the bus station, the minibus had climbed up to the centre, and there was still more climbing to be done. I hauled my luggage down to the pavement and looked around me. The plaza in most cities occupies a flat central space – and so it did in Potosí. But Potosí clings to such a steep rise that the Plaza 10 de Noviembre had been excavated from the mountain side to form a plateau. The roads and pavements rose like ramps on either side of it, climbing up to the Plaza 6 de Agosto, the neighbouring square which loomed still higher. The better hotels were even further up this ascending scale. Panting like a donkey with lung disease, I staggered into the first one I came to, the Hostal Colonial, which happened to be the most expensive in Potosí, but I was too exhausted by the climb to care about the price. The altitude was taking my breath away.

As the name suggests, the hotel was a beautifully restored colonial mansion, set around two cobbled courtyards with fountains. It had a spacious vestibule, a salon (which was closed for refurbishment) and was visually charming. But my bedroom was poky for the price. There was no chair or writing desk, and not enough space between the two beds to swing a mouse, let alone the proverbial cat. If I wanted to write, I would have to migrate to a café. I took the room temporarily, resolving to look for more spacious accommodation the next morning, when I'd recovered from the journey. But the next day dawned and I didn't have the energy. I just couldn't face the thought of dragging my luggage up and down that hill. I was settled by then, with my toiletries spread out in the bathroom. My torch, books and the small travelling alarm, which was bought in Peru years ago and still goes everywhere with me, were arranged on the bedside cabinet in their usual formation, and my coat was on its hook. The room was mine now, for better or worse, and it was far less exhausting to stay put. I went down to the hotel restaurant for breakfast.

'I don't believe it. Not you again!' I opened the restaurant door, and there were the Chilean family tucking into their scrambled eggs. They all greeted me warmly. We were the only residents in the hotel, so we could converse across the tables. In fact, it seemed as if we were the only tourists in town, as the four backpackers were nowhere to be seen. They had perhaps taken one look at Potosí and moved on. Despite the grandeur of its architecture, it was a depressing city.

With its 32 sumptuous baroque churches and 2000 or more registered Spanish colonial buildings, Potosí was declared a world heritage site by UNESCO in 1987. The cobbled streets are lined with the former mansions of wealthy mine owners and the façades of magnificent churches. But they are also lined with beggars, women in bowler hats and multicoloured shawls with their broods of ragged, runny-nosed children. They sit on the dank pavements of the city centre from early morning until late at night. In the evenings, the small children are sent into the restaurants, to beg at the tables. They are soon chased out by the waiters, who sometimes, when the boss isn't looking, press a sneaky crust of bread or a stale cake into their grimy little hands.

Most of these women have been widowed by the mines, or are caring for invalid husbands. Mining methods have changed little over the centuries. The miners still hack away with primitive tools, in tunnels so tight that they have to crawl through mud and water to reach the seams, then crawl out again with the excavated ore on their backs to reach the waggons. These are manhandled from the mines to the crushing machines. Where the tunnels are too low or narrow for adults, children wriggle inside to extract the ore. The temperatures range from below freezing to 45°C on the fourth or fifth levels down, and the air is thick with dust, chemicals and deadly gases, including arsenic, silica dust, asbestos, acetylene vapours and carbon monoxide.

The great tin crash of 1985 caused the mines of the Cerro Rico to close down, but the government introduced new incentives two years later and unemployed miners trickled back, setting up co-operatives. These days, there is little silver to be found and they scratch around for tin, wolfram, zinc, lead and antimony, metals below the notice of the Spanish conquistadors. The miners who are members of the co-operatives do have some basic sickness and pension arrangements, but these men constitute barely 20 per cent of the work force. The other 80 per cent are children and peasant migrants from the north, casual labourers, who earn next to nothing and have no safety nets of any kind. Women are employed too, to pick through the tailings in case any scraps of valuable ore have been rejected. Before they begin their ten-hour shifts, the miners chew coca leaves for an hour or two, and it is coca that keeps them going underground, banishing fatigue and hunger. Life expectancy in the mines is ten to fifteen years. Those who are not killed by rock falls or the collapse of ill-constructed tunnels die of silicosis. It is estimated that two-thirds of the population of Potosí suffer from respiratory illnesses of one sort or another.

The sun was shining, but it was cold, with a bitter wind. I lent my guidebooks to the family from Chile, who were planning to do a tour of the major churches. I had read about them, but was not tempted. A little overblown, gold-encrusted baroque goes a long way with me, even when it's graced with solid silver altars and sacred vessels of great magnificence. Apart from the architectural excesses of the churches, I simply couldn't face another dose of Spanish Catholic morbidity. The Convent of Santa Teresa was said to have a superb collection of flagellation instruments, presumably used in the old days to keep any wayward nuns in order. The Convent of San Francisco housed the miraculous crucifix of El Señor de la Vera Cruz (The Lord of the True Cross), Potosí's patron, which was found in front of the church in 1550. Our Lord's beard was said to be made of real human hair, which grew and had to be trimmed from time to time, while His Cross was supposed to dip a few centimetres nearer to the church flagstones every year; when it finally extended to the ground, the superstitious claimed that the world would end. Then the Church of San Agustín was so spooky, with all its crypts and catacombs, that ghost tours were led around at nights.

I gave all these gruesome sights a miss by staying out of the churches, though I did enjoy the exterior carvings in the mestizo-baroque style. These were extravagantly executed by indigenous craftsmen and featured their traditional wealth of tropical leaves, vines, exotic birds and naked-breasted women, with the sneaky addition of such pre-Christian images as the sun, moon and stars. Viceroy Francisco de Toledo, eagle-eyed as always, spotted the symbols and was shocked. He issued yet another of his edicts, banning their carving. But the priests must have turned a blind eye. If this Inca symbolism kept the people docile and helped to reconcile them to their forcible conversion, why not let it pass? Religious syncretism can be a useful tool.

The one thing that really puzzled me about the churches was their orientation. I thought I must have lost my sense of direction, until I got out my compass to check. I was expecting the high altars to be at the east end, with the main door of the church facing west, the usual direction for Roman Catholic churches. But in the majority of cases, the churches of Potosí were built on a north–south axis. This, I later learned, was because the Cerro Rico lay to the south of the city. The high altars were therefore positioned at the north end of the churches, so that their main doors could lie open, and the priests could offer up their prayers towards the Mountain of Silver, the source of Potosí's riches! With slave labour to line their pockets with silver and slave labour to build their churches and mansions, the Spanish conquistadors had plenty of reasons for thanking their God, who ruled in their 32 churches, while the Devil was said to be laughing in their 6000 mines.

As I was giving all the churches a miss, I was left with nothing much to do in Potosí. Window-shopping was out, for there were few shops. One street, called by the locals El Boulevard, was lined with modern shopfronts along its pedestrianised length, but the shops were mostly takeaways, patisseries and money exchanges. There was little of interest to buy. As for the historic centre, its colonial mansions were built like fortresses, with blank exterior walls enclosing inner courtyards. They couldn't easily be adapted to provide shopfronts. There were just a few holes in thick stone walls, which led down steps to a tour operator's office, or a crowded dungeon where I could have bought silver coffee spoons and a knitted Andean bonnet with ear flaps. Some descended to well-patronised underground internet cafés.

These days, I rely on emails to keep in touch, and in South America there are so many internet cafés that I'm never more than a few doors away. (They often have charmingly incongruous names, like the Bethlehem Internet Café.) But on this journey, I was having problems. The emails I sent from both Chile and Bolivia were sometimes arriving, sometimes not, and I didn't always receive the customary message that contact had failed. So I was writing at length to my family and friends, and had no idea that the letters weren't getting through until I got a panic stricken: 'Where are you? We haven't heard anything for three weeks. Are you all right?'

Twice in Bolivia, I had a bizarre experience when I was trying to email one particular friend. On each occasion, I typed out my letter and clicked 'Send'. But instead of sending it, the computer produced a box on the screen, which told me that I was not allowed to communicate with pornographic sites. It then swallowed my letter, with no possibility of retrieval – at least not by me. The joke was that the intended recipient was a lord of appeal. I rather liked the idea of a law lord operating a pornographic site!

Like everyone else in Bolivia, the people of Potosí shopped on the streets. In the run-up to Christmas, the pavement stalls were doing a frenzied trade in cheap toys, wrapping paper, Christmas cards with snow and robins, and lovely long strands of fresh greenery, traditionally used to decorate the houses on Christmas Eve. But I was looking for food, so I made my way to the city's covered market, where I bought a large panettone, the light Italian version of Christmas cake favoured by the South Americans – and by me. I didn't know it at the time, but this purchase was to be my salvation.

On Christmas Eve itself, I went on a guided tour of the Royal Mint – and who should appear at the ticket-counter but the family from Chile! By this time, I knew much more about them. They were not Chileans at all. Sven was a tall blond German, working in Chile, and his gorgeous, elegant, raven-haired, cream-complexioned wife, whose name sounded like 'Lady', was Bolivian. Their three young children, aged nine, seven and five, attended the Swiss School in Santiago and were bilingual in Spanish and German, with a bit of English and French thrown in. They said 'Good morning' and 'How do you do' very politely.

'This is a farewell visit to my in-laws in Bolivia,' said Sven regretfully. 'I'm being posted back to Germany, to Hanover. We don't know how we're going to cope. Saxony is so flat, and we all love the mountains – the walking and skiing. Even in the middle of Santiago, you can walk down the city streets and see the peaks of the Andes.'

It took us all morning to do the tour of La Casa Real de la Moneda, as it covers an entire city block with its two hundred rooms set around five internal courtyards. It was built to house all that silver, so its walls are a metre thick, and the few tiny windows overlooking the street are heavily barred. Entrance to the complex is through just one thick wooden door, covered in iron studs, under an ornate stone portico.

The compulsory guided tour was led by Julio, a charming young *mestizo*. The rest of our party, with the exception of the Spanish-speaking family from Chile, were all Bolivians, and the tour was to be conducted in Spanish. Julio was worried about me, but I assured him that I would be able to manage, provided he didn't speak too fast. So he spoke slowly for my benefit and, once he had asked my name, addressed all his explanations to me personally. Every sentence began with 'Ana' or 'Señora Ana,' while the rest of the group were virtually ignored. It was very well meant, but rather embarrassing.

La Moneda is now a museum and art gallery, instead of a mint. There are many paintings by the most famous of the indigenous artists, Melchor Pérez de Holguín, born in Cochabamba, whose religious works found their way into most of Potosí's churches and convents. But the most famous painting in the collection is by an anonymous artist. It is *La Virgen del Cerro*, painted probably in the eighteenth century. The Virgin is portrayed as the Cerro Rico itself, her head and shoulders appearing from the peak of its perfect cone, as if the mountain were her full skirt. In heaven, the Christian Trinity, accompanied by a retinue of angels and archangels, are placing a crown upon her head, while on the earth below, the powers spiritual – the Pope, an archbishop and a priest – kneel in adoration on the left, and the powers temporal – the emperor, a city councillor and a knight of Santiago – kneel on her right. But there are pre-Christian undertones. The Virgin herself can be seen, and worshipped, as Pachamama, the Andean Earth Mother. To the left of the mountain shines the Inca deity, the god of the sun, and to the right the Inca goddess of the moon.

On the slope of the Cerro Rico, the 'skirt' of the Virgin (or Pachamama), there are flocks of llama grazing, Diego Huallpa sits beside the fire which revealed to him the existence of the mountain's silver, princely Spaniards ride on horseback and, perhaps most importantly, the Inca Huayna Ccapac appears, he who forbade the mining of the Cerro's silver. It's a most complex picture, and one of the most perfect expressions of that syncretism, which has enabled the Andean peoples to reconcile Christianity with their old religion and avoid the wrath of their ancient gods of nature.

I was fascinated by *La Virgen del Cerro*, and charmed by a series of paintings in the council chamber depicting battles between Europeans and Ottoman Turks. The local artist had never seen a horse. No doubt one of his Spanish patrons drew a general sketch for him to go on, an outline of a horse's shape and its size in relation to a man. But he gave him no clue as to the horse's face. So the artist used his imagination and gave the horses human features. They are charging into battle with furrowed brows and looks of extreme anxiety in their very unhorsey eyes.

We toured the original silver smelting and laminating equipment, the giant wheels made of wood, iron and llama leather, which were turned by mules plodding round in a blinkered circle on the stone floor of the storey below. For a while, the Spaniards imported African slaves to do the work but, according to Julio, their blood cells were unable to cope with the lack of oxygen at that altitude and they soon died. Even the mules, usually so long-lived, suffered so much from the altitude and the arduous work that they survived for only two to three years. The mules were imported from Tucumán, and I was pleased to receive this confirmation of the historic trade route I intended to follow through Argentina. The Tucumán mules were eventually replaced by steam power, then by electricity at the beginning of the twentieth century. Now the Mint no longer functions as a mint. Bolivian coins are minted in Germany and the notes are printed in France.

Julio was a lively, amusing companion and he was kept on his toes by my namesake, Ana, the seven-year-old daughter of the family from Chile, who was full of questions and comments. At the end of the tour, I asked Julio about visiting the Cerro Rico. The tour operators run visits to the mines, which take you inside the tunnels to talk to the miners and see the horrendous conditions under which they work. One operator advised that they were not tours for 'wimps or woosies', or people with heart or breathing problems, or claustrophobia. Being a bit of a coward, I decided I fitted into all of those categories. I just wanted to visit the Mountain of Silver and see it close up with my own eyes. I had no wish to enter the labyrinthine tunnels. While I was talking to Julio, the Chileans came up and joined in the conversation. Like me, they wanted to visit the mountain, but going on one of the mine tours was out of the question when they had three little people in tow.

'I live quite near to the Cerro Rico,' said Julio. 'As it's Christmas Eve, I'm finishing work here today at one o'clock. If you meet me outside the gate, I'll be happy to take you there.'

This was a wonderful offer. We knew there would be minibuses to the mines, but which ones, and where to catch them? At that altitude, none of us fancied tramping around the streets making enquiries. We were all surprised at our tiredness. We accepted our guide's offer eagerly.

I didn't bother with much lunch, so I was the first to arrive and I had a long chat with Julio. His English was basic, but he was keen to practise.

'I studied for five years to qualify as an official guide,' he told me, 'but it's not very well paid. So I have a night job too, in a hotel. I didn't learn any English at school. I have a course on tapes with a grammar book, and when it's quiet in the hotel in the middle of the night, I can concentrate. And I sometimes meet English speakers there. I try to talk to them, to get some real live practice. Usually, they're Americans, which is fine. But I'm so pleased to have the chance today to listen to someone from England.'

The Chileans arrived and we walked a couple of blocks to the bus stop. The minibus was crowded, but they found a seat for me next to a large lady, who was cradling a delicate little bird's nest with two toy birds in it. It was delightfully whimsical and I admired it. The woman beamed. 'It's for my granddaughter, for Christmas. She's just four and I think she'll love it.' ('And she'll break it in no time,' I thought, but the woman was so pleased with her purchase that I kept that thought to myself.) We went on talking about Christmas throughout the bus journey and I suddenly realised that I was speaking Spanish naturally, without much of an effort. After years of struggle, had I finally cracked it?

I've always had a problem with Spanish, as I speak Italian, and the languages are very similar. In the past, whenever I opened my mouth to say something in Spanish, the words would come out in Italian, unless I was concentrating really hard. It never mattered. If I used the Italian word '*preferisco*' instead of the Spanish '*prefiero*' for 'I prefer', everyone knew quite well what I meant, but I was always disappointed with myself. That day on the minibus, Spanish began to flow and I found myself concentrating on the content of the conversation rather than the process. I was so delighted, I could have hugged my voluble neighbour.

We reached the Cerro Rico, where not a soul was in sight. Were all the miners underground, or had they gone home on Christmas Eve? We walked under the iron entrance arch and wound our way up the dirt track which snaked up to the workings. And we wandered straight back into the Dark Ages. The mountain, whose summit gleamed rosy pink from the city below, was a filthy grey-black mess on its lower slopes. It was riddled with holes, the narrow entrances to the myriad tunnels, and the heaps of tailings were leaking scummy, polluted water down to the stream below. The buildings were primitive corrugated-iron structures, so rickety that they looked as if they were teetering on the edge of collapse. If the outside of the mines was such a scene of Stygian horror, I could scarcely imagine the hell of the interior. But the Cerro Rico was still the mountain of dreams. Miners still worked underground in deadly conditions, driven on by the hope that one day they might strike silver, and at night the slopes were alive with scavengers sifting through the tailings.

A flight of concrete steps led down from a cluster of ore-crushing sheds. As we stood at the bottom, two miners appeared at the top, both of them drunk. One was absolutely legless and was being helped along by his slightly less inebriated workmate. Halfway down the steps, the worse of the two toppled over and they both came crashing down the unforgiving concrete flight and landed, grazed and bloodied, in a cursing heap at the bottom. Coca leaves and cane spirit. But how else do you deal with such desperate conditions, from which there is no escape?

The miners throughout Bolivia are famous for their colourful fiestas, which are now great tourist attractions. High on drugs and alcohol, they perform their masked dances in fantastic costumes, sometimes honouring the Christian saints, sometimes sacrificing llamas to Pachamama and El Tio (Uncle), their euphemism for the devil of the mines. In mining traditions, as elsewhere in South America, Christianity is entwined with a desire to placate the ancient gods of the land. When life is so precarious, it's wise to honour both. The miners of Potosí make offerings of coca, cigarettes and alcohol to El Tio at the weekends, in the hope that this lord of the underworld will help them find his treasure, or at least spare their lives so that they can go on seeking it. Of course, the weekends bring pay day and the miners celebrate, taking a share of the coca and cane spirit themselves. The pair who flung themselves down the concrete steps had obviously just been communing with El Tio.

The Chileans and Julio continued to climb the mountain, to see some of the higher workings, but I had seen enough. I decided to walk back into town. As I neared the bottom of the Cerro Rico, I was joined by a small boy, who tried to sell me a nugget of 'silver'. It was probably lead or pyrites and I had no intention of buying.

'Where did you get it from?' I asked.

'From the mine.'

'How? Do you work inside, down below?'

'Yes. I'm a miner. I can crawl into some of the smallest tunnels,' he said proudly.

'How old are you?'

'Ten.'

It was heartbreaking. Pedro was one of the 1000 or so child miners in Potosí. He had never been to school. He told me he had already worked in the mines for three years. He was just a little cypher, an unregarded component of the 30.8 per cent of the population of the Potosí department who were illiterate. He was a statistic, doomed to die an early death, before he had even started living.

Modern prospecting techniques have revealed that the Cerro Rico still contains at least as much silver as the Spaniards extracted from it, with the richest ore concentrated in its peak. The cheapest way to mine the silver would simply be to lop off the peak and transform the mountain into one huge open-cast mine. But that would destroy a national emblem. A poll was carried out among the people of Potosí, and 97 per cent of them said they would rather starve than see the silhouette of their great Mountain of Silver destroyed. UNESCO backs them. UNESCO would prefer a horizontal shaft, so that the ore could be extracted without damaging that perfect cone.

The miners are understandably bitter. Jaime Villalobos, a geologist and former minister for mines, understands their feelings. The Cerro Rico has been mined by the Spaniards, the Bolivian Mining Corporation and the private sector. All have taken valuable non-renewable resources from the area and left nothing in return but contamination and poverty. 'However it is managed in the future,' he says 'the project should have a built-in guarantee to create some wealth for Potosí itself and its people.'

As the Cerro Rico towers above the city to a height of 4845 metres, the return was mostly downhill, so I walked back to my hotel for the exercise. First I crossed the city's outer ring, the poverty belt. There the migrant workers, who have fled the hunger of the countryside to sell themselves in the mines as casual labour, have built their unregulated shacks. Then I came to the middle ring of more substantial buildings, the homes of the workers in the co-operatives, where the streets were paved and there were proper markets. As I continued downhill, I finally reached the city centre and the grand houses of the conquistadors, now inhabited by Potosí's small middle class. A last burst of energy took me uphill, past the two plazas and into my sanctuary in the Hostal Colonial, where a night's accommodation probably cost me as much as one of those miners would earn in a year. Not for the first time on my travels, I thought how extremely lucky I was to have been born in England, in the twentieth century.

I had one more task to perform that Christmas Eve. We had been advised to bring sleeping bags for the long night on the train to Bolivia, when the temperature could fall below zero, and I'd ferreted out an old one, a relic of the days when I used to go on archaeological digs. I was newly graduated at the time and it was the only sort of holiday I could afford. In its day, my sleeping bag was the best available. Made by Blacks, it was very efficient, but heavy and bulky compared with the stream-lined models of today. I had kept it in the back of a cupboard for years, not knowing what to do with it, but now I had the perfect use. I brought it to South America with the intention of swathing myself in it on the train, hanging onto it until I was sure that my hotel in Potosí was adequately heated, then passing it on to someone who needed it. I had picked out just such a person.

She sold newspapers in the Plaza 6 de Agosto. No matter how early I went out in the mornings, she was already there, sitting on the cold flagstones, and, when I walked back to my hotel after dinner, she was still sitting there, trying to sell off her last copies of *El Diario*. She wore the flouncy, many-layered skirt of the Altiplano (useful protection against the chill of the pavement) and a narrow-brimmed beige bowler hat of the Potosí type, more of a sugarloaf in shape than a true round bowler. She was lame and bow-legged from a serious case of rickets.

'I've brought you this for Christmas,' I said. 'It's filled with goose down and it will keep you really warm in the winter.'

She looked at me in total disbelief. Then her toothless mouth broke into a huge grin. She said nothing. She was a Quechua-speaker, with only enough Spanish to sell newspapers. But she took the sleeping bag and put it behind her, so that she could lean against its soft warmth instead of the cold, hard wall. It was probably the first time for years that the poor woman had had anything to smile about. We exchanged Christmas greetings and I left her sitting there on the pavement, still looking bewildered at such a remarkable stroke of good fortune.

Bolivia is not a gourmet's delight, but I had found one decent restaurant in Potosí. Unfortunately, Christmas Eve is the time when South Americans eat their family Christmas dinners, so the restaurant was closed, as were all the others in that street. I searched around, and the only place I could find that was serving anything resembling a meal was a takeaway chicken outlet with a few formica-topped tables. I ate my quarter chicken with chips, tomato ketchup and a bottle of beer under the curious gaze of a few solitary men. But worse was to come.

On Christmas morning, the hotel staff were serving breakfast as usual. The Chilean table looked like a war zone, with reindeer wrapping paper and ribbon strewn over the toast and cornflakes, as three excited jammy-fingered children opened their presents. Then the family drove away to spend the rest of their holidays with Lady's parents in Sucre and I was left alone, the sole guest in the hotel. I suppose Bolivians were at home for Christmas and El Colonial was too expensive for the travelling young.

Outside, the streets were surprisingly busy, thronged with people showing off their new Christmas finery. Many little boys were dressed in white suits, while little girls danced along in a froth of white organdie, surrounded by their families in their best clothes. Christmas was a popular time for Confirmation and the celebration of First Communion – and in poor communities, where life is so bleak, celebrations sacred and secular are always lavish occasions, seized upon as shafts of light in a grey existence. No expense is spared.

The little boys who were not being confirmed were buzzing along on new skateboards, obviously the favourite Christmas present that year. But they hadn't really got the hang of them. Most of them were sitting down and paddling them along the pavements with their hands. For the girls, the great treasure was a Barbie doll. There was something faintly incongruous about little black-haired, black-eyed Indian girls sitting with their bowler-hatted mothers in a plaza on the edge of the Bolivian Altiplano, lovingly dressing these blonde, long-legged representatives of North American commercialism. With her ballgowns, bikinis, mortar board and astronaut's space suit, Barbie was so far removed from the lives that awaited little girls in Potosí as to seem almost bizarre. She was probably too remote even to inspire their dreams. Yet how pervasive are the tackiest aspects of a culture!

A corner shop was open and I found, to my delight, that there had just been a delivery of tomatoes, a rare treat on the Altiplano. I bought half a kilo. They were the first fresh fruit I'd seen since the two mangoes I bought in Uyuni. I love my fruit and vegetables and always eat masses of them at home. In Bolivia, they were very hard to come by, and my system was growing increasingly rebellious at the plates of eggs, pizzas, fried chicken and chips, with not a green vegetable in sight. I was feeling vaguely out of sorts, a combination of the discomfort and lack of energy caused by my diet, and breathlessness from the lack of oxygen in the air. I couldn't wait to move on to Tupiza, my next stop, at 2990 m a full thousand metres lower than Potosí.

But first, I had to get through Christmas Day – and it was not exciting. I'd intended to fill the afternoon with work, but after wandering round Potosí looking for fruit and sending a couple of emails, I was too exhausted to concentrate on writing. I tried to take a siesta, but sleeplessness is a problem at that altitude, so I got up again and settled my hotel bill, ready for an early departure next morning. I was conscious of killing time, which I never like to do. When I'm travelling on my bicycle, rest days are bliss; and there are many small, absorbing tasks to be accomplished: tyres to be checked, brakes to be tightened, panniers to be unpacked and repacked more efficiently, maps to be studied. I'm never lonely on my bicycle, because my life is so busy and I spend so long on the road. But bus journeys are quick. They leave oceans of time to be filled at every stop, and I really miss company when I'm stuck in a town with nothing special to do. I'd come to Potosí with specific objectives, and I'd achieved those. There was nothing else I needed to do and, as it was Christmas Day, nothing was open anyway. There was nowhere to while away a few hours. The museums were shut, and the churches so full of treasures that they had to be kept locked up when there were no services in progress. Had the buses been running, I would have moved on.

Anyway, I was stuck in Potosí for the rest of the day, and all I had to look forward to was my dinner. The hotel restaurant had closed down after breakfast – which was hardly surprising when I was the only guest in residence. So at seven o'clock, I sallied forth into the chilly streets, full of anticipation. They were almost deserted. The little kiosks in the plaza, where you could normally buy soft drinks and sweets at all hours, were boarded up for the night. My nice restaurant was closed. Even the takeaway chicken outlet was shut. There was not a restaurant, café, shop or kiosk open in the whole of Potosí's city centre. I trudged back disconsolately to my hotel, where my Christmas dinner, which should have been the crown of my day, consisted of the remainders of snacks I was carrying in my rucksack: five dry cream crackers, three tomatoes, a slab of panettone and a bottle of Bolivian beer out of my minibar. I enjoyed this feast in solitary splendour. It was a Christmas Day to remember.

15. THE TUPIZA VALLEY

Kennst du das Land, wo die Zitronen blühn?
Im dunkeln Laub die Gold-Orangen glühn,
Ein sanfter Wind vom blauen Himmel weht,
Die Myrte still und hoch der Lorbeer steht –
Kennst du es wohl?

*(Do you know the land where the lemon trees bloom? In their dark
foliage the golden oranges glow. A gentle wind drifts down from the
blue heavens. The myrtle is still and the laurel stands tall. Do you know
it well?)*

(Goethe)

My O Globus bus had decent treads, which was as well, because we had another long, tortuous road ahead of us. We drove out through the slums at the base of the Cerro Rico and I had my last view of the Mountain of Silver, grey, murky and deserted in the dawn light. The road was paved for about an hour out of Potosí and, after that, great stretches of highway had been constructed with concrete slabs, but for some reason we were not allowed to travel along them. We had to stay on the parallel grit. Where work was ongoing, the labourers were dressed in very fetching buttercup-yellow overalls, with matching buttercup-yellow sunhats.

There had been a shower of rain, so the cacti had burst into bloom. White, pink and red flowers, which seemed ridiculously small and delicate, perched alone on the top of great thick trunks; and yellow flowers brightened the flat ground-level succulents. When we descended into a valley, there were llamas and goats grazing, even a few cows in mossy hollows, and the general impression of the surrounding mountainsides was one of greenness. But then we climbed back into stony aridity. Our road was the usual Bolivian nightmare – a narrow dirt track with vertiginous drops just a few centimetres away from our wheels. And it seemed to get more terrifying as we went on. We passed a bus, just like ours, which had gone over the edge and was lying upside-down in the gulley below. Everyone crossed themselves, including the driver, which was somewhat unnerving on such a dangerous bend.

The countryside was deserted. Village houses were boarded up and the land uncared for, because subsistence farmers had migrated in droves from the harsh lands of the Altiplano down to the rain forests of the Chapare Region in the Upper Amazon Basin, or the subtropical valleys of the Yungas, where the Andes tumble eastwards in cascades of clear water and densely wooded slopes. Statistically, two-thirds of the population of Bolivia were still living on the Altiplano, but I don't know where they were hiding. There was no washing hung out to dry, no one working in the fields and the herds of llamas seemed to be managing on their own, untended. The country people had left, joining the impoverished miners from ghost towns where the tin seams were exhausted, in search of an easier, more prosperous existence. And the overwhelming attraction was the cultivation of coca.

The man sitting beside me in the bus was chewing coca leaves, as he was legally entitled to do in Bolivia. Coca is the drug of choice among the indigenous peoples, who recognise its benefits when properly used. The abuse of its derivatives is a North American and European problem, for which the peoples of South America are taking the blame and the punishment.

The little green coca leaf has been so revered throughout the centuries that it has been given the name of Coca Mama and is considered to be a beneficent goddess, the daughter of Pachamama, the Great Earth Mother. In Inca times, its use as a recreational drug was restricted to the king and his court, though priests could chew it in religious rituals. The famous teams of Inca runners were allowed to use it too, to give them the endurance to cover great distances up and down the Andes at speed. Chewing coca leaves serves as an appetite suppressant. It numbs the senses, while at the same time stimulating the nervous system. When the Spaniards took over the country, they realised that coca could be enormously useful in the Potosí mines. Chewing it would stave off hunger and fatigue, so that the miners could work all day without a lunch break and without getting weary. Their productivity would rise at the same time as they became more docile and contented. So the Spaniards commercialised its production, establishing large plantations of coca bushes in the Yungas to supply the mines. In a nice example of Christian hypocrisy, the priests named it 'the devil's leaf', and banned its use, except in the mines!

Today, coca leaves are sold by the kilo in Bolivian markets, as openly as carrots or tomatoes. It's sold together with *legia*, an alkaloid usually made of a mixture of lime, potato and quinoa ash, which draws the drug from the leaves when they are chewed. I've chewed coca once myself, in Peru. It was not unpleasant in taste and at first I wondered what all the fuss was about. Nothing seemed to happen. But after about half an hour's steady mastication, the gums of the side of my mouth where I was rolling the wad around began to go numb. Gradually, the numbness spread to the side of my tongue. Then across the whole tongue. Then it began to seep down my throat. At that point, I decided enough was enough. I'd made my experiment and it was very interesting, but I'm not a risk-taker where my health is concerned. I spat it out before the numbness could spread any further. My mouth felt dead, as if I'd just been to the dentist – and, of course, the chief medical use of cocaine is as a local anaesthetic. The leaves are also useful, brewed up in the herbal tea, *maté de coca*, as relief for altitude sickness. In themselves, they seem to be broadly beneficial. They contain minerals, salts, vitamins and even a little protein, all useful adjuncts to the sparse, unhealthy diet of the Altiplano, where people survive on potatoes and a few other root vegetables, with a bit of goat or llama meat on high days and holidays.

Chewing coca leaves is as much a part of daily life among the indigenous peoples of South America as smoking a cigarette or drinking a cup of coffee. The Potosí miners share it in a Friday ritual with El Tio, the devil of the mines, to keep him friendly and increase their chances of a lucky strike. They offer leaves to Pachamama, when she's hungry, and to the spirits of the mountains, when they look threatening. They place bunches of coca leaves in the foundations of their houses; under a rock at the start of a journey, to smooth their way; and farmers offer them up to the gods of the countryside when planting, to ensure a good harvest. Traditional healers use them as remedies and also to cast magic spells. Among the Yunga and Aymara peoples, they even measure distances in *cocadas* – the number of wads of coca leaves you will chew your way through on your journey from A to B. The conquistadors and later European settlers despised the chewing of coca as a dirty local habit, tied up with pagan superstitions, but I'm told it has lately come into fashion among the Bolivian urban young.

Coca first arrived in the West in 1862, when an Austrian expedition returned from Peru with a bundle of leaves. German chemists analysed them and isolated an alkaloid, which they called *cocain*. At first, it was tried as an antidote to heroin and alcohol addiction, and as a cure for hay fever and other allergies. Then its value as a stimulant was realised and it was recommended as a tonic. Sigmund Freud tried some himself and called it a 'magical substance'. No one outside the business knows the recipe for Coca Cola, but it is widely believed that some by-product of the cocaine refining process still goes into the world's most popular drink, to pep up its consumers.

All was well until the West became addicted to cocaine as a recreational drug. A huge demand erupted, which the South Americans were quite happy to meet. In Bolivia, the coca leaves grown in the Yungas are the ones that the locals chew. But to meet Western demand, production has spread to the Chapare Region, particularly around Cochabamba, where the leaves are less pleasant to chew, but make perfectly acceptable cocaine. The smallholders, who fled the Altiplano and its hardships, can carry out their part of the process with ease. They grow the bushes, harvest the leaves and soak them in a pit, in a mixture of water and sulphuric acid. A bit of stirring and a bit more mixing with other chemicals, and a liquid is produced which curdles into small granules of cocaine. These are carried over the border into Colombia to be refined into white powder and flown in the drug barons' private planes to North America. It is reckoned that in 1995, at the height of coca production, one in eight Bolivians depended on coca for their livelihood.

Coca is a wonderful crop. It can be harvested four times a year and will flourish on the same patch of land for fifteen years or more, without exhausting the soil. No other crop is so easy to grow – or so lucrative. It's hardly surprising that poor farmers show little enthusiasm for crop-substitution schemes. Even landless labourers can earn around $10 a night for treading the coca leaves in the pits, the sort of wages that workers in other industries can only dream of.

Alarmed at the quantity of illicit cocaine flooding North American cities, and the crime which inevitably accompanies such traffic, the United States in 1997 threatened to ban all aid to Bolivia, unless the coca crops were destroyed. The government of Hugo Banzer could not withstand this level of pressure and promised 'Zero Coca' by 2002 – even though most members of his government were known drug traffickers! Under what was called the 'Dignity Plan', government drug-control troops (UMOPAR) were sent in to root out the coca bushes. The farmers, acting in well-organised syndicates, resisted with roadblocks, rioting and fights to the death, but by

2001, the government claimed to have destroyed 90 per cent of the country's coca. It was a victory for the United States and Banzer's government, but the loss of the $600 million of coca export (as much as the value of all other exports combined) sent the country spiralling into recession.

There was great popular unrest. Resentment at the destruction of the coca trade, combined with widespread economic hardship, brought forth a new political force, known as 'the coca politicians'. Their leader, Evo Morales, himself a *cocalero*, was elected president in 2005 on the policy of 'Zero Cocaine' and 'Zero Drug Trafficking', not 'Zero Coca' – a policy he has tried to get the United States to back. Meanwhile, in the search for other licit uses of the plant, he has negotiated a loan of $250,000 from Venezuela to build two coca-processing factories in Chapare and Las Yungas. They should be up and running by the autumn of 2007, producing *maté de coca* (coca tea) and *trimaté* (a herbal drink made of aniseed, camomile and coca leaves), for which Venezuela will probably be the chief export market. Meanwhile, since the Zero Coca 'victory' of the United States in 2001, the growing of coca bushes for illicit purposes has moved out of the traditional regions and production has begun to climb again.

Despite the sacrifices made by Bolivia, demand for cocaine in the West continues to grow. And as long as there is demand, suppliers will be found. Bolivia was forced out of the market, so Colombia stepped up production to fill the gap. It remains to be seen whether or not Bolivia will salvage its ruined economy by creeping back into the illicit trade. But one thing is clear. Unless North America and Europe make a serious attempt to stamp out drug addiction and its causes at home, uprooting coca bushes in South America and heroin poppies in Afghanistan will only inflict suffering on subsistence farmers without solving the underlying problem. The West is the culprit in this damaging trade.

By the time we reached our lunch stop in Santiago de Cotogaita, we had begun the descent into lush, green valleys.

The main street was lined with stalls selling mangoes and tiny apricots, no bigger than cherries, but wonderfully sweet. Fruit at last!

We wound our way down to the Rio Tupiza, where the city of that name shelters in a bowl formed by the vivid red, brown, grey, purple and green mountains of the Cordillera de Chichas. It was a delight. We drove into town along the riverbank in the shade of orange, banana and mango trees, past fields of maize and market gardens full of lettuces. My hotel had a lawn and a roof-top terrace with tables and chairs under awnings, and there was an outdoor swimming pool. From my window, the view was stunning. The tropical gardens held my eyes for a moment, before they ranged across the verdant river valley to the backdrop of fiery red mountains striped with green, where the streams cascaded down to join the Tupiza River. I'd been struggling for weeks with the climate – first the heat and glare of the Atacama Desert, then the bleak, perishingly cold Bolivian Altiplano. In Tupiza, my body surrendered to the enveloping warmth. I was transformed. A relaxed, indolent creature, I threw off the jersey, anorak and fleece-lined trousers, which had been indispensible so far in Bolivia, and luxuriated like a cat in the sunshine. At 2990 m, over a 1000 m down from Potosí, my breath came easily and I knew I should sleep well.

My bedroom was furnished with cardoon cactus wood. It was golden in colour, and looked just like leopard skin, except that it had holes where the spots should be. There was an efficient desk lamp, also made of cactus wood, and I thought how pleasant it would be to spend a few days sitting at that speckled desk and drafting a chapter or two. In fact, the whole ambience was so agreeable, that I could imagine myself spending an entire English winter there when I had another book to write. The climate was wonderful and the Mitru was a really good hotel, which charged ludicrously little by European standards. Its buffet breakfasts were a feast: freshly squeezed orange, grapefruit and guava juice, and huge bowls of pineapple, mango, melon and papaya. Fruit at last, and as much of it as I could eat! The one fly in the ointment would be my evening meals unless Tupiza, with its wealth of vegetables, turned out to be an improvement on the rest of Bolivia.

There was a terrific thunderstorm that evening, while I was unpacking my case. Lightning illuminated the crimson mountains and the downpour was so torrential that it was almost exhilarating. I watched the storm from the safety of my room. The rain beat like a million hammers on my picture window and water seeped under the door across my tiled floor. I was relieved that the storm's fury had come down on me in Tupiza and not on the bus journey. The road through the mountains had been bad enough dry, without lakes of mud to contend with. When I went out to dinner, the rain had stopped, but the roads were still fast flowing rivers, over which the citizens of Tupiza were leaping like gazelles.

My guidebooks had both recommended a particular Italian restaurant, so I gave it a try. A nice bit of chicken was served with both chips and rice, but there was not a scrap of vegetable or salad in sight. Washed down with a small carafe of the local wine, which was tolerable but expensive, the meal was adequate, but it answered my query. If that was the best fare Tupiza could offer, I would not be rushing to spend a winter there.

Tupiza had recently joined the 'gringo trail', so there were other tourists in the restaurant. Two English girls were sitting at the next table, and one of them was talking almost non-stop with the kind of fluency I always envy. I watch such girls in the Tube sometimes and wonder what on earth they can be talking about with such enthusiasm for such a long time. By comparison, my friends and I seem to be tongue-tied dullards. The tables were quite close together, so here was my opportunity to do a bit of earwigging and find the answer to the puzzle. While I waited for my chicken to be served, I amused myself by timing the eloquent speaker. According to my watch, she spoke excitedly for twenty minutes, scarcely drawing breath, about rubbish collection in Derby and the difficulties her father was having with his wheely bin!

As I walked out of the restaurant, a four-wheel drive clanked by decorated with tin cans and white balloons. The newly weds sat inside, looking a bit sheepish. It was a mild evening, so I wandered along to the Plaza de Independencia and saw what seemed to be a conveyor belt of weddings in progress in the church. The next brides and grooms were queuing outside on the steps, while the current couple were being married inside. The pews and pillars were decorated with swags of white net curtain and, by the light of the white candles at the pew ends, I noted with interest that the ladies had taken off their bowler hats inside the church.

Like most of the old mining centres in Bolivia, Tupiza had seen wealthier days. This was reflected in the grandeur of the city's neoclassical church with its two great bell towers, and the imposing fin de siècle civic architecture. The city was once home to one of the country's wealthiest mining dynasties, founded by Jose Avelino Aramayo, whose statue gleams in the middle of the plaza's palm trees. It was an Aramayo payroll that tempted Butch Cassidy and the Sundance Kid into their last fatal hold-up.

According to the version favoured in Tupiza, the outlaws' first plan was to rob the bank in the city, but they were deterred from that by the presence of Bolivian troops. So they lay in wait in a mountain pass north of Tupiza for a payroll that was being carried to one of the Aramayo Company's mines in Quechisla. Everyone wants to make the most of the legend in a region where, apart from the rugged landscape, there is little to captivate the tourist. In Pulcayo, they claimed that the manager of the mining company was carrying the payroll by train, and the one attraction of that mining ghost town was the railway carriage supposedly riddled with the outlaws' bullets. In Tupiza, they wanted to keep the legend nearer to home, by claiming that the payroll was being carried by a string of mules through the Pass of Huaca Huanusca when it was ambushed. It was there, they claim, that Butch Cassidy and the Sundance Kid stole the payroll, plus one of the company's mules to carry it. But both accounts agree that the bandits fled to San Vicente, a remote mining village some 100 km north-west of Tupiza, where they were surrounded, committed suicide and were buried in the cemetery.

The 1969 Hollywood film *Butch Cassidy and the Sundance Kid*, with Paul Newman and Robert Redford in the title roles, was being shown free of charge in Tupiza's tourist hotels and tour operators were offering Butch Cassidy and the Sundance Kid Trails. I was not tempted. I'd already seen enough of that 'Wild West' landscape out of bus windows, with more to come on the way to the Argentine border. I had no wish to spend good money on a tour of yet more stones, canyons and cacti. As a townie, born and bred, I much preferred to wander round the pleasant city. Its days of splendour might be over, but it was still a flourishing agricultural centre, bolstered by serious wages from a YPFB oil refinery, antimony mining and tourism. It was a place where employment prospects were good and, unlike the chilly Altiplano, it was hanging on to its young people.

The tour that would have interested me, had I had the time for it, was the newly established Che Guevara Trail in the Santa Cruz Region. Che was a romantic. The invasion of Cuba with Fidel Castro in November 1956 and his subsequent glittering successes as a guerrilla leader were the high points of his life. But after the overthrow of the Batista regime in Cuba, the hard, humdrum work began. Castro set about reorganising the administration of the island on communist lines and his former guerrilla commander was at first quite happy to assist him. But life as a government minister in a suit was not nearly as dashing as the life of a revolutionary in the jungle, and Che Guevara soon became bored. His experience of guerrilla warfare had turned the one-time doctor and Marxist intellectual into an action junkie.

He first abandoned Cuba to go and fight for the communist revolution in the Congo. But that was just an exciting sideshow, a bit of guerrilla practice to keep his hand in before he turned his attention to South America. His dream was to bring the whole of his continent together as one great Marxist state. Thinking that his native Argentina was too prosperous and middle class for the grand vision to take root there, he led a small group of revolutionaries into Bolivia. As the poorest country in South America, it seemed to offer the most fertile ground. Unfortunately, he picked rather a bad time. The Bolivian military dictator, President Barrientos, was a fluent Quechua speaker, and he had won the support of the peasant federations by promising not to go back on previous agrarian reforms. They had signed the Pacto Militar-Campesino. The result was that Che Guevara failed to pick up any support from the local peasantry and he and his small group of warriors were isolated in the remote region south of the town of Vallegrande.

Suffering from severe attacks of asthma, for which he had run out of drugs, El Che was captured in the hamlet of La Higuera and executed without trial on 9 October 1967, by the Bolivian army. As proof of his death, his body was displayed to the world's press. The photograph of his face, looking serene and almost Christ-like, has become another of the iconic images of our time. To prevent his grave from becoming a place of pilgrimage, he was buried at dead of night in an unmarked spot on the edge of Vallegrande's airfield, where he stayed until 1997, when his remains were exhumed and reburied in Santa Clara, Cuba, the arena of his greatest victories.

The Che Guevara Trail is tough. Like the visits to the mines in Potosí, it's not for 'wimps or woosies'. It's a circuit of 815 km, along dirt roads passable only on foot or muleback, with accommodation in basic lodges and campsites. The trail winds through the sub-tropical jungle on the borders of the Santa Cruz and Chuquisaca regions, visiting Che's base camp and passing through the battle grounds where his guerrillas fought the Bolivian army. It ends in Vallegrande at the site where Che Guevara was buried. The Guaraní people, who live along the route, are amongst the poorest in the country. They are subsistence farmers, without running water or electricity, who scratch a living from the cultivation of maize. The Che Guevara Trail is a community support project, financed in part by international aid agencies, in the hope that it will bring tourists and jobs to this remote, backward region.

When Paul Theroux wrote *The Old Patagonian Express* (first published in 1979), he was able to travel by rail all the way from his home in Boston to Esquel in the foothills of the Andes, just above the 43rd Parallel. From Massachusetts to deepest Patagonia. The trains may have varied in comfort and the services in efficiency, but at least the railways were still in operation.

One of the trains he enjoyed was the luxurious Panamerican Express from La Paz, the capital of Bolivia, through to Tucumán in the north of Argentina. How I would have loved to ride that train, with its first-class Pullman sleeping compartments and its liveried waiters in the restaurant car! But El Panamericano is now a thing of the past. Trains no longer run out of La Paz, nor is there a service connecting Bolivia with North Argentina.

Yet Bolivia is still better served by rail than many countries in South America. A private Chilean company, the Empresa Ferroviaria Andina, took over the moribund Bolivian State Railways (ENFE) in 1995 and now operates two pretty efficient services. One of them, the FCO (the oriental region), runs from the eastern city of Santa Cruz to Brazil. The other, the FCA (Andes region), crosses the south-west Altiplano from Oruro, some 230 km south of La Paz, to Villazón on the Argentine border. The FCA was obviously the line which interested me. Its two trains, El Nuevo Expreso del Sur (the Southern Express) and the weirdly named Wara Wara del Sur are both modern and both run twice a week, via Uyuni and Tupiza. Of the two, I was told that El Nuevo Expreso del Sur was faster, more reliable and more luxurious, with heated carriages and even a dining car with waiters in bow ties.

Quailing at the thought of another ride over mountains in a Bolivian bus with worn treads on its tyres, I decided to travel in style and comparative safety. I walked along to the railway station to check the timetables. To my disappointment, I found that I'd just missed an Expreso del Sur departure for Villazón, which had passed through Tupiza at 2.30 that very morning; and the next train, a Wara Wara, was not due until Sunday. I did a quick calculation. If I hung around in Tupiza until Sunday, I should not have enough days left to visit all the places I wanted to visit in Argentina before my flight home from Buenos Aires to London on 10 January.

I rushed to the bus station and bought a ticket to ride to Villazón that same afternoon, thinking back regretfully to my first cycle ride around the world. On that journey, I was absolutely free, with no timetables and no commitments. If I had to wait a fortnight for an onward flight, the start of a festival, or the arrival of a friend who was coming out to join me, it didn't matter a scrap. I had all the time in the world. Now I had a contract to finish a book and a string of lectures to give in the New Year, so I had to travel with an eye on the calendar and get home in good time. It seemed to be one of life's ironies that my original escape to travel had turned into a travel career, which was now interfering with my freedom to travel!

Before I left Tupiza, I particularly wanted to make some local enquiries about the Silver Road from Potosí to Buenos Aires, which I knew passed through the city, and I was lucky enough to meet Señora Fabiola Mitru T. de Sánchez. Her grandfather was a Bolivian success story. He had migrated from Chalcis on the Greek island of Euboea and arrived in Bolivia, via the Pacific and Chile, in 1908. There he had prospered in the mining industry, before turning his attention to establishing hotels in the delightful Tupiza valley. The family still owned the hotel where I was staying and ran one of the major tourist agencies in town, promoting what Señora Fabiola called 'the industry without chimneys'. She had just written a well-researched book on the history of the city and the places of tourist interest in the surrounding countryside. I was happy to be presented with a copy of *Tupiza y Turismo*, 'from one writer to another', as she put it. I scuttled off to catch my bus with this useful gift in my backpack, to distract myself from the dangers of the journey. In fact, the climb out of the Tupiza valley was so scary that I couldn't even read. But once we reached high ground again, my vertigo began to relax and I was able to dip into the book between shutting my eyes over precipices. Every now and then we crossed the railway track, which looked so safe and sturdy that I would have glided along it to the Argentine border without a tremor, had time been on my side.

After my short break at a comfortable altitude, I was up to 3443 m again in Villazón and I noticed the difference immediately I collected my case and hauled it up the step to the pavement. Breathless and bad tempered, I beat off the importunate bus touts, who descended like a flock of vultures, squawking in a mixture of foreign tongues. They flashed glossy brochures in front of our eyes, dazzling us with photographs of sleek Argentine coaches. Their standard of elegance and comfort struck the Bolivian passengers with awe, used as they were to ramshackle contraptions like the one with the broken windscreen that had just carried us over the mountains from Tupiza. I shooed all the touts away, as I was not intending to catch a swift intercity coach direct to Buenos Aires or Tucumán. I planned to cross the bridge into Argentina by taxi and spend the night in La Quiaca, the small town on the other side of the border, before travelling at a leisurely pace through the beautiful Quebrada de Humahuaca. But the pictures in the brochures had given me heart. Buses with treads on their tyres and roads with tarmac for them to run along! My Bolivian travel jitters were over.

But first I had to cross the border. There was not a taxi in sight, so I trundled my wheeled suitcase across the small town, then downhill to Bolivian Immigration on the north bank of the Rio Villazón. I was in and out of the office, my passport duly stamped, in two minutes flat. Then I crossed the road to the Argentine building, where the experience could not have been more different. The Bolivians didn't care who left their country, or what they took out with them. But the Argentines, like the Chileans, are very particular about whom and what they let in. They are anxious to protect their pre-phylloxera vines, their crops and their cattle from imported agricultural pests and diseases. They have laws to prevent illegal immigration from less-developed South American countries. And on the borders with Bolivia in particular, the customs officers are hawk-eyed. They don't want illicit coca entering their countries.

There was such a mob outside the Argentine Immigration and Customs that six policemen were needed to direct new arrivals into the correct channel and keep them in order. It was a painfully slow process, as most of the people in the queues were Bolivian workers, returning to Argentina after their Christmas holidays. They were loaded up with Christmas presents and stacks of household goods and toys. which they had bought in Bolivia, where prices were lower. In addition to having these mountains of gear searched for smuggled coca, they all had to have their work permits checked. We shuffled along in our queues, baking in the strong afternoon sun. I was lucky to be standing next to a charming white-haired Bolivian father and his English-speaking daughter, on their way to stay with relations in Jujuy, so I was able to do a bit of chatting to pass the time. Then there was a group of German backpacking boys, who kept coming up to me in turn and asking most kindly if I was all right and if there was anything they could do to help me. I didn't quite know whether to be touched by all this concern for my well-being or annoyed. Did I really look so decrepit?

After a wait of three hours, I had just reached the entrance to Immigration and was standing under the shelter of the glass roofing over the road, when the sky turned black and a sudden hailstorm erupted. The police took pity on the two hundred or more people behind me in the queue and herded them into the road under the glass roof. Of course, that caused chaos, as they all lost their rightful place in the queue and started elbowing their way towards the door. I managed to stand my ground and about fifteen minutes later finally inched my way inside the building. I was astonished. There was just one poor harassed clerk on duty behind the counter, frantically trying to process that milling multitude single-handed! On my previous visits to Argentina, I had thought them an efficient people. So how could they have allowed such ridiculous understaffing?

I got through Customs on the nod, then went back to the shelter of the glass roof until the storm had passed over. By that time, night had fallen. There was a lake beside Customs, which had once been a gritty yard, and it was there that the taxis from town picked up their passengers. There was no queue and no system. As soon as a taxi appeared, everyone rushed through the water to grab it. Those who were travelling in groups, or at least in pairs, were able to leave one person guarding the luggage, while another did the sprinting. On my own, having to run with my suitcase through the puddles, I was at such a disadvantage that I despaired and decided to walk across the bridge. The pavement was uneven, the little wheels on my suitcase couldn't roll, and the bridge looked awfully long. So I went back to the lake, where I struck lucky. A young woman on her own, with only a briefcase for luggage, had managed to grab a taxi. I banged on the window, imploring her to let me share it. The selfish creature shook her head, but the taxi driver took pity on me standing there in the drizzle and opened the front door.

I'd expected a bank or exchange bureau at Argentine Customs, but had been disappointed. So I found myself in the worrying situation of sitting alone in a taxi at night in an unknown Argentine town without a single Argentine peso to my name. Surprisingly, the cabby refused to take American dollars, but said he would accept 10 bolivianos if I had those. I had just one 20 boliviano note left in my wallet. I told him to keep the lot. It was worth only about $2.50 anyway – a modest sum to pay for what in fact turned out to be quite a long ride. But he did a rapid calculation and insisted on giving me the equivalent of 10 bolivianos change in Argentine pesos.

Then he carried my suitcase into the hotel and stood beside me at the desk until he was sure I had a room for the night. Like the German backpackers, he was looking after me.

Cold, hungry and exhausted, I changed out of my wet clothes and went down to the restaurant. By then, it was 8.30. It had taken me 6 hours to cover just 100 km and get myself through Immigration. I celebrated my arrival in Argentina with one of their magnificent steaks and a half-bottle of delicious Malbec wine. The steak came with two fried eggs on top, a plateful of chips and a basket of rolls. I was obviously still too near the Bolivian border to be served any vegetables or salad! Half the steak, one egg and a few forkfuls of chips later, I fell into bed, only to lie awake half the night with indigestion. I'd forgotten the altitude, which plays havoc with stomachs, even those as resilient as mine. But warmth, comfort, fruit and salad awaited me, as I travelled down to sea level in Buenos Aires, and that thought was immensely cheering.

16. THE SILVER ROAD

I could not print
Ground where the grass had yielded to the steps
Of generations of illustrious men,
Unmoved.

(William Wordsworth)

The Spaniards in Potosí were awash with silver. They had so much of the metal that they even, in fits of extravagance, paved the streets with silver ingots and shod their horses in gleaming silver shoes. But they wanted to get the bulk of it home to Spain, to dazzle the neighbours with their new found wealth; and their kings needed their 20 per cent cut to finance their wars of religion in Europe. The problem was the inconvenience of the location. The silver mines were high up on the Bolivian Altiplano, or Alto Peru, as it was called in those days, and the nearest Spanish port of any size was Callao, the port of their South American capital, Lima. This was a journey of almost 2000 km, and it involved a climb over the Western Cordillera of the Andes. The silver was carried at first by llama train to Lima and Callao, and later by surer-footed mules imported into Bolivia from what is now north-west Argentina.

Once again, the Spaniards struck lucky. By the time they arrived in the New World, the Incas had conquered all their neighbours and established a vast mountain empire, which stretched from modern Equador, through Peru and Bolivia to central Chile and north-west Argentina. Having acquired all this territory, they had to administer it and keep their assorted peoples in order – and they realised that good communications were the key. So they set about building a network of all-weather roads with the same discipline and meticulous care that they had applied to the business of war. This network of fine roads, so brilliantly constructed that the world had not seen their like since the days of the Roman Empire, fell very conveniently into the hands of the Spaniards when they defeated the Incas.

The achievement of the Incas was arguably greater than that of the Romans. Compared with the cordilleras of the Andes and the flood plains beside the Pacific Ocean, the Romans had quite easy terrain to cross. The road through the Great St Bernard Pass, the highest paved road built by the Romans, climbs up to a mere 2469 m, whereas there is no pass leading out of the Altiplano that is lower than 4000 m. Hernando Pizarro, the brother of Francisco, the Conqueror of Peru, was moved to exclaim: 'Such magnificent roads could be seen nowhere in Christendom in country as rough as this. Almost all of them are paved.'

The centre of the spider's web was the Inca capital, Cuzco, 'the navel of the world'. From there, roads spread out like tentacles to all corners of the territory. As it was an Andean empire, which snaked along the mountainous backbone of the continent, it was long and thin. At the time of the network's greatest extent, there were two main highways from north to south, with plentiful connecting roads between them. The mountain road through the Andes, stretches of which still survive to this day, ran from Quito in Equador, through Cuzco, La Paz and Tupiza, then down the Quebrada de Humahuaca into north-west Argentina. The second highway ran beside the Pacific from Tumbes, the Inca city in the north of Peru where Pizarro and his conquistadors first landed, followed the Peruvian coast, crossed Chile's Atacama Desert and continued south as far as the Rio Maule, which flows into the sea at Constitutión, about 250 km south of Santiago. As ancient roads always follow the line of least resistence, their course is built upon over and over again throughout the centuries. The original Inca coastal road is the obvious way to go, so it has now evolved into the Pan-American Highway. (Most of the above place names are, of course, the names given by the Spanish to the cities they founded along the routes.)

The peoples conquered by the Incas already had well-established paths between their settlements. As they followed the natural contours of the land, the Incas inherited a ready-made system of communications. Their achievement was to take these rough paths and turn them into works of art. There were no horses in South America at the time, so the Inca roads were built for travel on foot. This meant that they could be quite narrow, usually only about one metre wide, but they had to be smoothly paved with flagstones, to be kind on travelling feet. They also had to manage the dizzying climbs over the Andes in a way that took account of human frailties, including breathlessness at high altitudes. The surveyors who worked out the gradients were men of genius. Their roads climbed the mountains in comfortable zigzags, with flights of steps, tunnels and stone embankments to ease the way over the steepest climbs and ensure that, even in the winter, the highest reaches would not be impassable. They filled in dangerous chasms with rubble and masonry, and wove fibre suspension bridges across mountain torrents. Rafts with sails stood ready to take travellers across calmer rivers and lakes.

The coastal highway presented a different set of problems, which were tackled with equal ingenuity. Where the land was liable to flooding, the road was built up on a causeway, defended on both sides by a parapet of clay; trees and shrubs were planted alongside, to provide the traveller with shade; and across sandy wastes, where road-building was utterly impracticable, the Incas drove in lines of piles to indicate the route.

All the Inca roads had stone pillars at intervals of about 5 km. Then there were small buildings about 8 km apart, where the official runners, or *chasquis*, stayed. These men provided the imperial postal service, running with government messages from one halt to the next. Running in relay, they could cover about 250 km in a day. As well as messages, these *chasquis* carried fish from the coast up to the royal table in the mountains, or game and ice from the mountains to the coast, when the Inca and his court were travelling through the lowlands. To keep them running at the speed required for such missions, the *chasquis* were allowed to chew coca leaves, which suppressed their hunger and enabled them to take high mountain passes without tiring.

In addition to the *chasquis'* quarters along the road, there were *tambos* (inns) about 20 km apart, erected to house government ministers and army personnel. Beside them stood rows of rectangular storehouses, which the local populations were obliged to keep serviced and provisioned. They also acted as emergency stores for the people themselves in case of crop failure.

The Incas had inherited basic pathways from their predecessors, which they enhanced to construct a brilliant system of communications. They spanned their empire with fine all-weather roads, introduced a postal service and comforted the medieval traveller with the level of amenities provided only centuries later in Europe by coaching inns and motorway service stations. All these wonders dropped like ripe plums into the hands of the lucky Spaniards. Their horses found the flights of mountain steps difficult to climb and even more difficult to descend, but that was a small disadvantage compared with the general convenience of the roads.

The Incas knew their empire as Tawantinsuyo, the Empire of the Four Quarters, as it radiated outwards in four directions from Cuzco, the centre of their world. Of these four quarters, the two which were of immediate interest to the Spaniards were Chinchaysuyu, which stretched north-west from Cuzco and contained Pizarro's capital of Lima with its port of Callao, and the Collasuyu, stretching south-west from Cuzco and holding Potosí.

When Christopher Columbus arrived in the New World in 1492, his first landfall was on the island of Cuba, and from there Spanish domination of the region gradually spread across the Caribbean. Even though Keats was mistaken and it was Vasco Nuñez de Balboa, not 'stout Cortez', whose eagle eyes 'stared at the Pacific – silent, upon a peak in Darien', the result was the same. In 1513, Balboa chanced to climb a hill at the narrowest point of the isthmus of Panama and, to his great surprise, discovered a new ocean. Raising a cross there, he and his followers sang a Te Deum, then claimed the ocean and all its surrounding territories for Spain. There too, he heard from the local people of an empire to the south, which was fabulously rich. These rumours sealed the Incas' fate, for the Spaniards began to explore the Pacific coast in search of this empire and its legendary wealth. Within twenty years Pizarro had found and conquered it. Meanwhile, in 1521, Hernando Cortez had laid waste Tenochlitan, the capital city of Mexico, and overthrown Montezuma and his Aztec kingdom. This meant that the Spaniards had an unhampered overland journey on ready-made Inca roads from Potosí on the Altiplano, via Cuzco and Lima to the Pacific. As the ocean was controlled by their ships, they then had a clear sea passage for their Inca loot northwards to Panama or Mexico, where they had only to haul it across the isthmus to reach the Caribbean and the ships bound for Spain. It was a safe journey, but long and arduous.

During this momentous half-century for Spain, the world's most experienced navigators, the Portuguese, were also turning greedy eyes on the New World. The rivalry between the two countries became so serious that the Pope was called in to adjudicate. Under his Treaty of Tordesillas, in 1494, an imaginary line was drawn down the globe 370 leagues west of the Cape Verde Islands (roughly 48 to 49 degrees west of Greenwich). West of that line, all territories and all trade routes were to come under the undisputed control of Spain;

east of it, the world and its trade would belong to Portugal. The kings of the two countries signed up willingly to this demarcation. Portugal already dominated the lucrative trade with Africa, India and the Spice Islands. Now the Treaty of Tordesillas gave them the monopoly over it, with leave to subdue any countries they chose in the name of the True Faith. Meanwhile, the Spanish kings gained the monopoly over conquest and trade in the New World. Or so they thought! What no one knew in 1494 was that the New World stuck out into the South Atlantic far east of the line drawn by the Pope.

It was the Portuguese navigator, Pedro Alvares Cabral, probably blown off course on his way to the east, who first came upon this huge shoulder of land in 1500. He thought he had struck an Atlantic island and claimed it for the Portuguese Crown. The King of Portugal, Manuel I, was intrigued and early next year sent Gonçalo Coelho with the Florentine navigator, Amerigo Vespucci, to explore that rough general area. On 1 November, All Saints' Day, 1501, they sailed into a magnificent turquoise bay, dotted with 38 sandy islands, which they named, appropriately enough, Bahía de Todos Os Santos. Overlooking the bay was an easily defended flat-topped cliff, and on this the Portuguese later built Salvador, their first capital of Brazil. So the Portuguese, quite legitimately, but contrary to the intention of the Treaty of Tordesillas, gained control over a huge chunk of the New World and the trade routes between Europe and its long Atlantic coastline. Their South American empire extended from the mouth of the Amazon in the north almost to the River Plate in the south (named the 'Silver River' by Sebastian Cabot because he mistakenly thought there was silver to be found on its banks). And by one of the quirks of fate, it was a minor character in this great epic of Iberian discovery and conquest, the Italian Amerigo Vespucci, who gave his name to the entire continent of North and South America. Eat your heart out, Christopher Columbus!

*　*　*

With the Portuguese in control of the known Atlantic coast and its hinterland, the Spanish had no choice but to continue to transport Potosí's silver along the Inca roads from the Altiplano via Lima to the Pacific. But attempts were being made to reach Peru from the River Plate and its tributaries. Asunción, on the Paraguay River, was successfully founded by the Spanish in 1537; Santa Fe, a port on the Paraná River at a convenient spot between Asunción and the coast in 1573; and Buenos Aires, at the second attempt, in 1580. In addition, the Spanish conquistadors were moving down along the ready-made highways through the Inca Collasuyu Region into what is now Argentina, founding Santiago del Estero (1553), Tucumán (1571), Córdoba (1573), Salta (1582), La Rioja (1591) and Jujuy (1593) on the way. They were keen to protect their precious Potosí from the south and also to secure the routes over the Andes between Upper Peru and Chile.

Within a century of Columbus' first landfall, the energy of the Spanish conquistadors, and their lust for gold and silver, had driven them through the entire South American continent from the Caribbean and Mexico in the north to the River Plate in Argentina and Chile's River Bio Bio in the south. Only the inhospitable lands of the pampas and Patagonia, and the ice fields at the extreme tip of the continent remained to be colonised.

The territories between the Altiplano and the Atlantic having been subdued and settled, the way now lay open for the Spanish to transport Potosí's silver to Buenos Aires. It was a route with many attractions. Once they had toiled over the mountains between Tupiza and the River Villazón, which today forms the border between Bolivia and Argentina, the journey to the Atlantic was almost entirely downhill. It took about fifty days by mule train, so it was further to walk than the mountain passes through Cuzco and Lima, but the terrain was gentler, the climate more temperate and there was food and water in abundance for both men and mules. The silver could either be carried overland all the way to Buenos Aires or loaded onto boats in Santa Fe to complete its journey by floating down the Paraná River. From Buenos Aires, it could then be shipped direct to Spain. Compared with the complications of carrying tons of heavy metal over the Andes to Callao, shipping it to Panama, unloading it and carrying it across the isthmus, then loading it up again onto ships bound for Spain, the Buenos Aires route was simplicity itself. It was the natural way to go.

But the hand of the Spanish Crown lay heavy on its colonies. The King and his administrators were determined to maintain the supremacy of Lima, so all imports and exports to and from the Spanish Viceroyalty of Peru had to be channelled through the capital. The export of silver from Buenos Aires was specifically banned by the Crown, as was trade in general between Buenos Aires and Alto Peru. An exception was made in the case of the African slaves required to work in the mines. Their life expectancy on the Altiplano was so short that a constant supply of fresh manpower was needed, so in 1595 Spain gave permission for Buenos Aires to import African slaves from Brazil. In 1602, flour, dried beef and tallow were added to the slaves, making a limited list of items that could legally be traded between the two Atlantic neighbours. But the doors to this sensible expansion were soon slammed shut. Lima's merchants, jealous of their monopoly, opposed what they saw as rising competition and, in 1622, the Spanish Crown banned all trade between Buenos Aires and Brazil. Buenos Aires was limited to a yearly traffic with Spain of two 100-ton merchant vessels to provide essential goods for its own citizens.

Such a ridiculous situation could not last. It was not possible for the Spanish Crown to maintain Buenos Aires as an important strategic post on the estuary of the River Plate, while at the same time crushing its commercial development. The ban was an open invitation to Buenos Aires to turn to the contraband for which it was ideally situated. The Brazilian port of Colonia do Sacramento lay just across the estuary and was the perfect smuggling depot for illegal traffic with Brazil and Portugal.

Buenos Aires had many advantages over the port of Callao. There were fewer pirates lurking in its vicinity; less seaweed at that latitude to clog the hulls of the trading ships; the overland journey to Alto Peru, though longer, was easier and cheaper than the mountain route through Cuzco; and the greater distance of Buenos Aires from Lima meant that contraband was more difficult for the Spanish authorities to control. Trade expanded steadily.

As Potosí needed mules for the mines, and agricultural produce to feed the miners, trade between the cities of North Argentina and the Altiplano was allowed. This permission to trade did not extend southwards to Buenos Aires, but the stream of mules, livestock, cotton and cereals which flowed from the fertile lowlands up onto the Altiplano brought a wealth of silver and gold down from Potosí. This currency was traded in Buenos Aires for clothing, domestic items and weapons from Europe, all of which were shipped from Portugal via Sacramento or Rio de Janiero to meet the demands of wealthy Potosí Spaniards. In Lisbon, the arrival of so much silver from Peru enabled the Portuguese to finance their penetration of India and China. Silver was traded for silks and oriental spices, which inevitably became part of the contraband traffic with Buenos Aires. Potosí was a boom town, where purses were deep and the hunger for both European and oriental luxuries insatiable.

There was no stopping Buenos Aires. It was in a prime position and it soon became a magnet for traders from other parts of the Spanish Viceroyalty of Peru and also from abroad. Between 1713 and 1739, there was a significant influx of British merchants, who brought with them their experience of international commercial practice. While Lima's population stagnated at around 55,000 to 60,000, in the century between 1740 and 1840 the population of Buenos Aires leaped from 11,000 to 65,000. Little by little, trade with North Argentina, the Chacos and even Chile drained away from the capital and fell into the more efficient hands of the merchants of Buenos Aires. In 1776, Spain bowed to the inevitable and elevated the port to the Viceroyalty of the Rio de la Plata. The city that was once despised and almost crushed out of existence by the Spanish Crown became the bustling, sophisticated capital of Argentina, while Lima is now just a crumbling relic of its former glory, the capital of one of South America's most backward states.

With Buenos Aires growing rapidly in importance, the Spanish had to improve communications between the two Viceroyalties. So they used the Inca roads as the basis for their own system, widening them to take carriages and carts and establishing post houses at regular intervals along the way. Later on, in the nineteenth century, the same routes through Bolivia and Argentina were used in the construction of the rail network, for which most of the capital was raised in London by British promoters and investment bankers.

The road from Potosí to Buenos Aires was one of the most significant in the history of South America. Because of its gentle topography, it was the obvious route to take. It was trodden first by the ancient peoples who preceded the Incas, then by the feet of the Inca warriors and runners themselves. Then it served the hooves and wheels of the Spaniards, who carried their silver along it, and provided the line of least resistance for the laying of railway tracks. That same route, now a ribbon of smooth tarmac with internationally recognised road signs, is still used today by every traveller from Bolivia down to Buenos Aires. The Silver Road – layer upon layer of history, like an ancient palimpsest. I couldn't imagine a more fascinating road to follow.

17. THE INCA ROAD

Sightseeing is the art of disappointment. But, fortunately, Heaven rewards us with so many agreeable prospects and adventures along the way; and, sometimes, when we go out to see a petrified forest, prepares a more delightful curiosity in the form of Mr. Evans ...

(Robert Louis Stevenson)

When I travelled through Patagonia, I found villages full of Mr Evanses, descendants of the Welsh settlers who arrived there in 1865 with the non-conformist minister, Michael D. Jones. My taxi was driven by a Mr Davies and my bags were carried up to my room by a boy called Williams. Their great-great-grandparents had fled to Argentina to be able to practise their non-conformist religion freely and escape the tyranny of the English language. Now they all speak Spanish, but they keep their little corners of Wales alive by selling Welsh farmhouse teas and cakes to the tourists. What saddened me in those villages were the lists of Welsh names engraved on the war memorials – all the young Evanses and Davises, conscripts who had died in the Falklands War, fighting for Galtieri's Argentina, some of them no doubt against the invading Welsh Guards. Welsh against Welsh. The waste of war.

There were no Mr Evanses in La Quiaca, though North Argentina had its share of 'delightful curiosities'. So near to the border, the streets were still thronged with the brown faces and bowler hats of migrant Bolivian workers, but the pale, sleek tango dancers were asserting themselves at a wedding reception in the hotel. As I sat at my breakfast table on the first morning, a middle-aged couple entered the dining room. He was as slender as a willow wand, with glossy black hair and a black pencil-line moustache. Even on a Saturday morning, he was buttoned tightly into a black pinstriped suit, slightly waisted, while his dainty little feet twinkled in a pair of mirror-bright black patent-leather shoes. His partner was just as slender, and sleek as an otter. Embroidered Chinese mules peeped out from a long, sinuous silk dress patterned with pale turquoise and jade-green swirls, like an original Liberty art nouveau print. Most amazing of all, she was crowned in an emerald-green turban, which was decorated with such dramatic diamonds and strings of pearls that they had to be paste – but very good paste. With the utmost dignity, he acknowledged my presence with a slight bow from the waist upwards; she with a gracious nod of the head. Neither spoke, but I knew they could only be Argentines, and professional dancers. I felt distinctly underdressed in my travelling trousers and jersey.

I was back in the land of the ATMs, so I filled up my wallet with Argentine pesos and breathed a sigh of relief. I was planning to start off that afternoon down the dramatic Quebrada de Humahuaca (Humahuaca Gorge), which is known locally as *El Camino del Inca*, but first there was a church in Yavi that I particularly wanted to see. As time was short and taxis cheap, I stood on a likely corner until I was picked up by Pablo, a young Indian who called me '*Mami*' and addressed me with the familiar *Tu*, a form which is much more common between strangers in South America than in mainland Spain. He turned out to be an engaging companion, who chattered all the way to Yavi and back.

'What do your family think about you wandering around on your own in Argentina?' he asked. 'Aren't they worried? I should be worried stiff if you were my *mami*.'

'Yes. I suppose they do worry a bit, but I've been travelling around on my own for so long now that they've got used to it. Anyway, I've spent years worrying about them. Now it's their turn to worry about me.'

He laughed. 'My *mami* doesn't go travelling. If she goes to the corner shop, it's a big adventure for her, so she'd be terrified if I went travelling abroad. And my girlfriend! She worries so much, I have to keep ringing her on my mobile, to let her know that I'm still safe and haven't crashed the taxi. We're not married, but we've lived together for nine years. I don't know what it's like in England, but that arrangement is very usual these days in Argentina. We've got two children – a little girl of seven and a new baby boy, just five months old. Which reminds me. I'd better give Maria a ring now, as I'm driving out of town. I'll be gone longer than usual and she's bound to start panicking soon.'

We drove for about 15 km along a smooth strip of tarmac, through a valley sandwiched between extraordinary eroded hills. They were worn into narrow, uptilted strata, which swirled and swooped around their bare flanks. From the plain below, they looked like milk chocolate meringues, or brown Mr Whippy ice creams. Pablo told me they were called the Eight Brothers.

Yavi itself was a gem of a colonial village, with cobbled streets, brown adobe houses and a small white adobe church with a single sturdy tower, the Iglesia de Nuestra Señora del Rosario y San Francisco. I was expecting little from its modest size and plain exterior, but once my eyes had got used to the dimness, I was amazed at the treasures inside. Wood carving was a highly developed pre-Columbian art, which the local craftsmen brought to the service of the Church once they had been converted to Christianity by the Spaniards. But they had their own ideas about things. Their angels in the churches of the Quebrada de Humahuaca are famous. Not for them the plump little cherubim of Western religious paintings. Theirs are soldiers of Christ, dressed in full suits of Spanish armour. In Yavi church a beautifully carved angel stands guard to the right of the golden altar, resplendent in cuirass, greaves and helmet, with a pair of golden wings sprouting somewhat incongruously out of his back. There is a wonderfully rich gold-encrusted pulpit, carved with the four Evangelists and their symbols, its canopy topped with another martial angel brandishing a miniature sword. But my favourite was the statue of the pilgrim saint, San Rocco, with his dog. The saint is dressed in his wide-brimmed pilgrim's hat and a magnificent cloak of burgundy velvet, embroidered with real gold thread. He is lifting this cloak discreetly by the hem to reveal a hideously gory mess on his thigh, which his long-nosed dog is inspecting with prurient interest. The story is that San Rocco's dog saved him from death of the plague by licking his sores. All of these golden treasures are enhanced by the golden light filtering through the onyx window panes.

When I emerged from the empty courtyards and dusty bric-a-brac of the former owner of most of the province, the Marqués Campero y Toro – a sad anticlimax after the magnificence of the church – I found Pablo waiting for me and we set off back to La Quiaca, picking up a couple of dumbstruck locals on the way. The old man and his grandson were obviously not used to foreign women and thought it safest to keep quiet.

Like the taxi driver the night before, Pablo amazed me with his honesty. He'd started off by quoting me 18 pesos (about £6) for the journey to Yavi. On the way there, I asked him how much he would charge to wait for me and drive me back to my hotel. He quoted 25 pesos, provided he didn't have to wait for more than an hour. I took it that the 25 pesos was the additional charge for the hour's wait and the return journey, making a fare of 43 pesos in total. Tips to taxi drivers are not customary in Argentina, but Pablo had been such a good companion that I offered him 45 pesos.

'What's this?' he exclaimed. 'I said twenty-five pesos. That's for the lot, not in addition. I'm not a robber!' Indignantly, he handed back one of the 20 peso notes and no amount of persuasion would make him take any more than 25. He could so easily have profited from a foreigner's misunderstanding.

At one o'clock I boarded a gleaming Argentinian coach. It had treads on the tyres, air conditioning, windows without cracks and clean seats with no springs poking through them. We drove out of La Quiaca and started our long descent towards Buenos Aires and the sea.

I'm so used to being on a bicycle now, that I look at every landscape with a cyclist's eye. And if ever I regretted not being on my bicycle, it was on that journey down the Quebrada de Humahuaca. The colours of the rock were simply amazing. Beige, ginger, dark brown, bright crimson, the ferrous red of dried blood, terracotta, white, cream, burnt umber, pink, orange, grey and malachite green. The colours flashed past the bus windows and I had no time to take in one array before we rounded the next bend and the kaleidoscope shifted into another gorgeous pattern. Oh, to be on my bike! To be able to gaze on the changing moods of that landscape, as the sunlight varied in intensity, and to be able to do it at my leisure, stopping and starting where I pleased and savouring it all. And to add to the delight, it would all have been downhill! By the time I reached Uquía at 4.30, I was down to 2818 m, 600 m below La Quiaca. I had to carry my suitcase, because the village cobbles were too proud for its little wheels, but at that altitude, I already noticed the difference. I was no longer gasping like a salmon on a riverbank.

Uquía consisted of another fabulous church (the reason for my visit, but closed in the evening), a modern hotel, two shops for the tourists (also closed) and a few rows of adobe houses. I sat under a sunshade on the patio in front of the hotel and wrote up my notes in a warm, light breeze. The mountains were magnificent in the setting sun. The sprinkling of tall cacti threw ever longer shadows across the coloured rocks, whose shades deepened with the waning of the light. No one passed the hotel. It was utterly peaceful. Uquía was one of those small places I love, places where nothing happens and people just get on quietly with their lives.

I was the only guest in the hotel and while I waited for my delicious home-cooked dinner of braised beef with rice and plenty of wine, I sat on the settee and watched television with the three-year-old son of the house. He was watching a film about good and evil monkeys, with such a complicated plot that he kept getting lost. Being asked to explain what was happening was quite a test of my Spanish, but Juanito listened intently and seemed to understand me, though I couldn't myself understand a word of his comments. I just had to guess what he was saying. But we sat there very companionably and at least I kept him out of his mother's hair while she was cooking my dinner. When I sat down to my meal, Juanito entertained me by standing on his head on the settee, then clung to my leg and screamed when his mother suggested bed.

Next morning the Iglesia San Francisco de Paula y la Santa Cruz was open. On the outside, it was another plain white adobe church, this time with its campanile standing apart. One of the oldest churches in Argentina, built by the Jesuits in 1691, its walls, almost two metres thick, contain a spectacular series of seventeenth-century paintings by the Cuzco School of indigenous artists, *The Angels of the Arquebus*. Like the armoured angel of Yavi, these are soldiers of Christ, but in Uquía most of them are armed with guns. They are such a delight that I decided it would be worth travelling all the way to Argentina just to see this one set of angel portraits.

There are nine angels, dressed up as officers of Los Tercios, one of the first Spanish regiments to arrive in the New World. Elegant, even dandified, they pose in richly embroidered brocade cloaks and jackets, slit to reveal their wide-sleeved linen shirts with fancy lace cuffs. A rectangular bib of the finest lace decorates the front of their brocade tunics, which are short enough to reveal their elegant legs in skintight breeches, silk stockings and silver shoes with large pink pussy-cat bows. They have coy little pouting smiles on their rather androgynous faces and their flowing curly locks are crowned with wide-brimmed hats trimmed with red ribbons and multicoloured sweeps of plumes. Silver and red wings peep out from behind their shoulders.

Each angel is named and his portrait surrounded by a frieze of flowers. The captain of the squad, the only one to wear a helmet rather than a gorgeous hat, is obviously the Archangel Michael, though he is dubbed Uriel beneath his portrait. The Archangel Gabriel, who carries his arquebus over his shoulder in a jaunty manner, is draped in a regimental flag. The Archangel Raphael leans elegantly on his spear and gazes heavenwards. The names of the other six angels are taken from the Apocrypha, from the Book of Enoch. Salamiel, the Peace of God, holds his arquebus over his right shoulder, while carrying the rope that is used to fire the weapon in his left hand. A small box of gunpowder dangles from his belt. Oziel, the Sacrifice to God, stands ready to charge his arquebus, while Eliel, the Power of God, is portrayed actually charging it. Yeriel, the Fear of God, holds his arquebus in both hands, with the wick dangling down. Hosiel, the Strength of God, is marching along with his weapon in his right hand and the wick in his left. The only unarmed angel is Oziel, the Bravery of God. He too is marching along, with a particularly saucy smile on his face, beating a military drum. Despite their weaponry, a less martial squad would be hard to imagine. They are foppishness and swagger personified – an absolutely delicious combination.

Flash photography was obviously not allowed, so Mean Mustoe had to buy a book on the artistic heritage of the entire Quebrada de Humahuaca to have a record of the gorgeous band of angels. It was a purchase I resented at the time, as I rarely buy books. What are libraries and the internet for? But now I have it, I find myself looking at the pictures quite often and smiling. It was a good buy.

There were other famous early churches along my route, but time was not on my side. In any case, I'd already decided that one day I would return to the Quebrada with my bicycle and ride all the way down that fabulous road, visiting every church, pausing to gaze at every rainbow mountain and staying in every lovely village on the way. Now I had a plane to catch and a lot of ground to cover between Uquía and Buenos Aires.

There was just one short stop I wanted to make before I took to long-distance travelling – La Posta de Hornillos, one of the survivors of the chain of Spanish post houses which used to serve the road at regular intervals, all the way from Buenos Aires to Lima.

I was still in predominantly Indian and *mestizo* territory, much of it Quechua-speaking. When the Incas conquered an area, it was their practice to keep a grip on it by settling their own people there. Their expedient of establishing colonies rather than maintaining armies of occupation was being recommended at roughly the same time by Machiavelli, in *The Prince*. Although he was unaware of the Incas and took all his examples from Greek and Roman history, the principle was the same. 'Colonies,' he wrote, 'cost less than soldiers, are more faithful and give less offence, while those who are offended, being poor and dispersed, cannot hurt. And let it here be noted that men are either to be kindly treated or utterly crushed, since they can revenge lighter injuries, but not graver. Wherefore the injury we do to a man should be of a sort to leave no fear of reprisals.'

The Incas seem to have treated their subject peoples kindly on the whole, allowing them to follow their own customs. Their one stipulation was that they adopt the Inca religion and accept the Inca himself as the incarnation of the Sun God, Inti. They drafted families and sometimes whole communities into conquered territory for two main reasons. One was a Machiavellian determination to keep watch on the subject peoples and introduce them, by example, to the Inca language and the Inca ways of doing things. The other was to provide a reliable supply of the fresh produce and livestock which were not available in their stark mountain kingdom. When the Incas swept south and conquered the Chichas and Collas, they extended one of their main roads from Cuzco through the Quebrada de Humahuaca. It was this road, still called El Camino del Inca by the locals, which became the first leg of the Spanish Silver Road, La Via de la Plata, down from Alto Peru into Northern Argentina. It now bears the unromantic name of

Highway 9, but it follows what is even today the only practicable route through that cleft in the mountains.

On New Year's Eve, which also happened to be a Sunday, buses through the Quebrada were running on a limited schedule. After my visit to Uquía Church, I stood on the highway at the exit from the village and waited ... and waited ... and waited. Eventually, a private car, with Fangio at the wheel, screeched to a halt on the hard shoulder in a shower of gravel. There was no taxi sign or official disc on the car, but the driver assured me that it was a proper taxi and, in any case, I had few options that day. I climbed inside, wondering if I was lion-hearted or just plain mad. He told me the taxi was on its regular run from La Quiaca to Maimará. The Posta de Hornillos was just a little further on down the highway, but the driver agreed to take me there, then return to Maimará and drop me at the bus station.

We had only just got started when he was pulled in by a highway police car. The officer wanted to know who I was and where he was taking me. The driver produced his licence and explained. As I was sitting calmly on the back seat and not screaming for help, the police car and its occupants drove off with a cheery wave. The incident was immensely reassuring. The police had been alert, so I knew I was going to be safe in the unknown territory of Northern Argentina.

I was still travelling through the magnificent multicoloured Quebrada de Humahuaca, gouged out of the surrounding heights by the turbulent little Rio Grande. And running beside the road were the tracks of the old Panamerican Express, which Paul Theroux had ridden all the way from La Paz, through the border towns of Villazón and La Quiaca, to Tucumán, a journey of around 1600 km. The tracks were deserted. 'We haven't had trains along there for years,' said the taxi driver. 'There was talk of a Japanese company taking over and running passenger trains again, but nothing seems to have come of it.'

We crossed the Tropic of Capricorn just north of Huacalera. It was my fourth land crossing of the line. Flights and voyages don't count. The first time was in Rockhampton, Queensland, on my second cycle ride around the world. As it was Australia, with a highly developed tourist industry, there was a shop and café there, and a large carved TROPIC OF CAPRICORN sign in front of which people queued to be photographed. The Australians had turned the crossing into an event. By contrast, the monument near Antofagasta, which I reached with great difficulty, stood deserted opposite a Chilean airforce base; and the one in the Atacama Desert on the way to Calama was in such a desolate spot that I didn't even catch a glimpse of it from the bus. There was said to be a sundial beside Highway 9, marking the Huacalera crossing, but I didn't see that from the taxi either. And no one in South America seemed remotely interested. 'The Tropic of Capricorn? What on earth do you want to go and see that for?' What impressed me was the difference in landscape between the blazing desert coastline of the Chilean Tropic, which I had crossed less than three weeks before, and the cool green valley of the Rio Grande with its spectacular mountain backdrop. Both were in the same continent, but they couldn't have been less alike in climate or appearance.

La Posta de Hornillos was deserted, but its rough stone walls, topped with blobs of diabolically prickly cactus, were low enough for me to see the white adobe buildings inside and take a few photos of their solid exteriors. It was closed to the public on New Year's Eve, so I didn't see the bed where General Belgrano slept during Argentina's War of Independence.

We drove into Maimará, an oasis town in the shadow of a particularly colourful sweep of mountains called the Artist's Palette and a vast hillside cemetery, which looked almost cheerful with its bright paper and plastic flowers. It reminded me of Chinese cemeteries, always planted on hillsides, so that the dead may have a happy time, watching their families' activities in the houses below.

The bus station turned out to be another deserted spot, the ticket office locked and just one old man sitting behind the counter in his refreshment shed. 'No buses today,' he announced, before returning to his newspaper. But there was a young woman sitting patiently on a doorstep across the road. She had a suitcase beside her, so my hopes rose. I joined her on the doorstep and found that she was hoping to catch a bus to Jujuy. One was sure to come some time, she told me, but she had no idea when. There was a Sunday vegetable market in progress under the trees. Each pool of shade contained one or two ladies in the kind of beige bowlers worn in Potosí. They had arrived on tricycles with wooden platforms constructed at the rear, piled high with crates of tomatoes, onions and garlic. A public loudspeaker system blared out tangos and sambas at two million decibels. Women chatted over their vegetable purchases, men hid from their wives and the Sunday chores in the crowded bar, teenagers lounged on the police station walls, children rode their bikes in the empty bus station yard and I made desultory conversation with the girl on the doorstep. She had come from Jujuy to spend the weekend with her granny and was glad to be going home. She loved her granny, but there wasn't much to do in Maimará on a Saturday night. I could see her point. Maimará was another of those sleepy little places I love, where nothing much ever happens and there's no obligatory sightseeing to be done. I could have frittered away a week or so quite happily there, lodging in the village pension and just sitting around – but then, I'm not a pretty little teenager looking for romance.

Eventually, an elderly local bus came creaking down the main street, bound for Jujuy. I got a seat next to a blond, curly-haired boy of about eight and produced my map of Argentina to follow the route. Pancho was intrigued and eager to learn, so we spent a sociable journey poring over what he called *la cartita* (South Americans love diminutives), studying the geography of Argentina. Fortunately, the vocabulary required was not wide, so Pancho improved his knowledge of his native land, while I improved my Spanish. Buses on long journeys are excellent places to practise conversation.

Outside the bus window, the scenery remained superb. Purple-red mountains, now thickly forested on their lower slopes. I noted one stiff climb from the highway up to Purmamaca, with its exquisite church, which I didn't have time to visit. Then we sped down a tremendous winding descent between Volcán and Barcena. My cyclist's eye took in all this beauty, not to mention all the easy downhill riding, and for the fiftieth time since I left La Quiaca, I hated being stuck on a bus. Some day, I shall return with Condor and we will glide together down that fantastic Quebrada de Humahuaca.

When we rolled into the city of Jujuy, we had reached what was probably the end of the Camino del Inca and the southern limit of the Inca Empire in Argentina. From somewhere around that point, the Inca roads turned west and climbed over the Sierras into what is now Chile, while the Spanish Silver Road continued south towards Buenos Aires.

18. FULL CIRCLE

What we call the beginning is often the end
  And to make an end is to make a beginning.
The end is where we start from.

(T.S. Eliot)

San Salvador de Jujuy (pronounced Hoohooey) is a con-fusing place. Foreigners choose to call it Jujuy, while the locals all refer to it as San Salvador, to distinguish it from the province, which is also called Jujuy. This makes a minefield of asking directions or enquiring about buses.

'Does this bus go to Jujuy?'

'We're in Jujuy.'

'No. I want to go to the city of Jujuy.'

'Oh, you mean San Salvador. Why didn't you say so? Hop on board then.'

But it was a lovely city for all that. Lying at a comfortable altitude of 1260 m in a bowl of wooded hills, it had streets lined with orange trees, a luxuriant Parque San Martín and a gracious main square, the Plaza Belgrano, with an equestrian statue of the general at its heart. Everything was walking distance from everything else.

I checked into the Hotel International, where my double-glazed windows on the sixth floor gave me a stunning, yet silent, view over the tree tops in the plaza below and immediately went out in search of a supermarket. Having starved on Christmas Day in Potosí, I was running no risks ahead of New Year's Eve and New Year's Day in Jujuy! I found a branch of Norte in the main shopping street, the Calle Belgrano, and felt a much happier woman when I returned to my hotel with a bulging carrier bag.

I'd chosen the right city to stay in over the New Year holiday period. All the public buildings were closed, but that was no frustration, as there were no buildings of any historical significance to be seen. Jujuy had destroyed its past, not out of wantonness, but out of patriotic duty.

The city was one of the worst casualties of the War of Independence. Between 1810 and 1822, the Spanish Royalists launched no fewer than eleven invasions down the Quebrada de Humahuaca; and on one notable occasion, in August 1812, General Manuel Belgrano, who was Commander of the Republican forces, asked the people of Jujuy to make the supreme sacrifice – the total destruction of their city in the face of the invading Royalist army. They complied and to honour their loyalty to the cause, Belgrano presented them with one of the new Argentine flags which he had just designed. This sky blue and white banner is still on display in the city's Government Building. To those of us who were not involved in the independence struggle, a flag seems a pretty poor return for the loss of a city.

General Belgrano. The mention of that name in Argentina, and the sight of all the streets and squares named after him, always made me feel a little uneasy. It brought back all too vividly the Falklands War and the sinking of the *General Belgrano*. I don't pretend to know the rights and wrongs of that controversial issue. Was she carrying Exocet missiles? Was she therefore a grave threat to the British fleet? Or was she simply a cruiser on patrol, as the Argentine Junta claimed? All I know is that out of a crew of 1042 seamen, 368 were lost, most of them innocent young conscripts. As in any conflict, there were terrible losses on both sides. What makes the Falklands War so tragic is that it was a war between friends. In conversation with Argentines, I sometimes expected resentment, but I found only sadness. As Kemal Atatürk so rightly said, 'Do not bear a grudge against any nation. Our foes are not people, but politics.'

On my way back from the supermarket, I checked out the restaurants along Belgrano. They were either closed because it was Sunday, or open because it was New Year's Eve and they were putting on special gala dinners. I boggled. In Argentina, the helpings were so huge that I usually had to leave half of a simple one-course meal, so how on earth would I cope with five courses? I knew that the very sight of the menu would defeat me. In any case, it wouldn't be much fun going out to a gala New Year's Eve dinner on my own. I should have to find a café or bar which offered snacks – and even Argentine 'snacks' are sometimes unmanageable in size.

As evening fell, I strolled again through the plaza, heady with the scent of lilacs. I felt neither hot nor cold. The climate was so perfect that I was completely unaware of heat or humidity. My body seemed to float along, relaxed in its own element. Why endure winter in Europe, when such a lilac-scented paradise is available and costs less? I patrolled the streets, until I found a smart *café resto*, where my Argentine 'snack' consisted of a delicious toasted ciabatta, stuffed with lettuce, tomatoes and an entire sirloin steak, served with a large side salad, a basket of bread, olives and a carafe of wine. The waiter told me they would be open on the evening of New Year's Day as well, so everything was going to be fine. I wouldn't be dining on dry crackers in Jujuy.

Changing tastes and Argentina's recent economic crises had brought a decline in demand for the region's main products, tobacco and sugar, but tourism in the Quebrada was on the rise, and there was a lively buzz about the city. It still had its share of the exotic too. Its large indigenous population – Aymara-speaking Collas and Quechua-speaking Incas, along with migrant workers from Bolivia – were selling their carved, woven and knitted Andean handicrafts on pavement stalls and roaming the streets with baskets of home-baked *empanadas* and *tamales*. For me, Jujuy was an end and a beginning. An end to the bowler-hatted ladies, who had been my companions since Calama, and the beginning of white Europe in the major cities of the north.

I arrived in Salta in pouring rain. Although it was at roughly the same altitude as Jujuy, the humidity that closed in with the rain was unbearable. I was economising in a cheaper hotel and there was nothing I could do that afternoon but lie on my bed gasping. I'd chosen the wrong day to be without air conditioning.

The first Spaniard to pass through the area was probably Diego de Almagro, who wintered in the Salta Valley in 1535 on his monumental journey from Cuzco across the Andes into Chile. Like his fellow conquistadors, he was greedy for gold, which the Incas told him could be found in abundance among the peoples west of the Andes. He found no gold, and the tattered remnants of his expeditionary force, those who had not frozen to death in the mountains, died of thirst in the Atacama Desert or been killed by the fierce Mapuche, stumbled back defeated into Cuzco two years later.

The city of Salta itself was founded by the Spanish in 1582 and is one of the best preserved colonial cities in South America. Its smart shops were crowded with well-heeled Argentinians on their holidays. They were all white, or white with the barest touch of *mestizo*. This was a province where the local peoples had put up a fierce resistance to the Spanish conquistadors, but had inevitably lost the struggle. Today, their way of life and traditions survive in the mountains and the altiplano on either side of Highway 9, but there were few to be seen in the city.

It was not the colonial buildings that interested me so much as the role of Salta on the trade route to Buenos Aires, but my researches took me, as it happened, to one of the finest of them. The Cabildo of 1783 houses the Museo Historico del Norte in its elegant series of rooms set around two open courtyards and its first-floor balcony overlooking the tall palm trees of the Plaza 9 de Julio. One courtyard was tranquil and cobbled, with pink flowering bushes in its corners and a fine view of the Cabildo's unusual weathervane, which looked like a running child with a fire cracker in his hand. The other was a grassy space with a collection of old carriages and carts.

Such things don't normally interest me very much, but the information displayed beside these vehicles was fascinating. For instance, under King Philip II of Spain, that miserable monarch, a royal act prohibited the use of carriages in America, *para contener el lujo desmedido de los functionarios* (to control disproportionate luxury amongst the officials). But the ascetic king was too far away to supervise such austerity and his officials continued to travel in style – or at least in such style as the roads of the time allowed. Wheels got bogged down in the mud or were rattled to splinters over the rocks, and their progress was sadly impeded by the trains of bullock carts with their hard-bitten, obstinate drivers. These travelled in convoys of at least fifteen, so that they could defend themselves against Indian attack. Each cart was drawn by six oxen, with three spares walking alongside. Journeys that took five days on horseback took a month by bullock cart, and the trek from Salta to Buenos Aires took anything from two to five months, depending on the weather.

Charles Darwin travelled along this road from Buenos Aires to Santa Fe in September 1833. It had been raining, and he notes in his diary that the surface was 'extraordinarily bad. I should never have thought it possible for a bullock-waggon to have crawled along: as it was, they scarcely went at the rate of a mile an hour, and a man was kept ahead, to survey the best line for making the attempt. The bullocks were terribly jaded . . .'

Livestock was easier and cheaper to trade, as the herds could be driven along. But whether the goods travelled by cart or on their own hooves, they blocked up the roads and obstructed everyone's progress. It amused me to think of the Spanish noblemen in all their finery, leaning out of their coach windows, fuming at the traffic jams. It must have given the waggoners the same smug satisfaction I often feel, when I'm cycling peacefully along and there's no room for an aggressive Mercedes or Chelsea tractor to overtake me.

Things improved in 1770, when the Spanish began to establish post houses along the route. In 1776, the city of Buenos Aires was elevated to the Viceroyalty of the Rio de la Plata, and by 1791 its go-ahead governors had regularised the system, with an unbroken chain of posts throughout their domain no more than 4 leagues (16–20 km) apart.

There was a trade map on one of the walls of the Cabildo, listing the goods exchanged: coca from Peru, silver from Potosí and European manufactured goods from Buenos Aires, usually in return for mules, livestock and agricultural produce. According to Fabiola Mitru T. de Sánchez, between 1740 and 1810, a river of mules, more than 70,000 a year, travelled north from Salta to Tupiza. The luckier ones were beasts of burden, carrying goods in mule trains to Potosí; the rest were destined to die of ill-treatment and exhaustion after a few short months of savage toil in the Mint and the silver mines. But all enjoyed a few days' respite, as they were rested, fed and watered in the lush grass by the Rio Tupiza.

Salta was undeniably elegant, but I didn't like it very much. Big cities are impersonal and I was just one addition to the horde of tourists – and an uninteresting addition too, as I'm a non-shopper. I wasn't like the North American girl who was shouting excitedly into her mobile that she was doing some 'mega power shopping'. I couldn't even be persuaded to buy one of the scarlet ponchos, sold in all the tourist shops as a tribute to General Güemes' gaucho army. These guerrilla fighters in their red ponchos used their intimate knowledge of the terrain to smash the Spanish Royalist forces in the War of Independence. Legend has it that the general dressed up giant cardoon cacti in the gauchos' distinctive red ponchos and broad-brimmed hats to trick the Spaniards into believing that his forces were stronger than they were. I liked the story, and the ponchos were lovely, but what would I do with such a garment in London?

The one thing I really wanted to arrange in Salta was a ride on El Tren a las Nubes, the famous Train to the Clouds. Built between 1921 and 1941, this narrow-gauge line is the phenomenal achievement of Richard Maury, a Pennsylvania engineer. It climbs up from Salta to an altitude of 4475 m at the Chorrillos Pass, negotiating 21 tunnels, 13 viaducts, hairpin bends, zig-zags and even one or two 360-degree turns along the way. Oxygen is available for those who suffer from altitude sickness. Goods trains, which serve the borax, salt and copper mines, go all the way across the salt flats to the border at Socompa, where they join up with the Chilean freight network, but passengers travel only as far as the dramatic Polvorilla Viaduct. With my vertigo, that was not a crossing for me and I was planning to get off there and wait for the train to come back. I'm told that a terrifyingly slender pair of rails, 224 m long, span a gorge with a 63 m drop. Not a ride for the faint-hearted! But I was not to be tested. The passenger train was scheduled to run only on Saturdays and only between April and November. And because of a recent breakdown, even that limited timetable was in doubt. The tourist office was crowded and uninformative. They just tried to sell me an excursion on one of their buses up the parallel road to the Polvorilla Viaduct, but that would have been a mundane and very dusty experience by comparison. It was the train I wanted, not yet another long day spent gazing at featureless altiplano and salt pans. Now that I was down in the lush valleys, I intended to stay there.

To while away the morning before my intercity coach left for Tucumán, I visited the Mercado Artesanal, the highly publicised indigenous craft market in an elegant old mill on the outskirts of Salta. I'd read that the hand-knitted llama wool socks were wonderfully warm and thought they would make good presents, but they were so thick that they would never have fitted into normal shoes. I wandered through the many rooms at least half-a-dozen times, looking for something – anything – I could reasonably buy to help the local economy along. The stalls were all piled high with Andean handiwork, lovingly crafted, but what could I do with a set of pan pipes, a woolly hat with ear flaps, a red poncho or socks that were too bulky for shoes? In the end, I found two little dishes, beautifully carved in local wood in the shape of flat fish, which would be useful at drinks time for peanuts or crisps.

It rained again on the way to Tucumán. I sat on the front seat upstairs, watching the tropical downpour with mixed feelings. The road ran downhill all the way from Salta and the landscape gradually opened out from a cleft in the coloured mountains to become the 'Garden of the Republic'. There were wide green riverbanks dotted with thoroughbred chestnut horses, orchards of lemons and avocados, and fields of everything from sugar cane, maize and tobacco down to the humble potato. Another fantastic stretch of the Silver Road to cycle along, but not in torrential rain. I must be sure to pick the dry season for my ride.

Tucumán Province is said to be so fertile because it has nine months of unbroken sunshine each year and reliable heavy rains between January and March. I think the whole of the annual average for 2007 must have fallen during my two days' stay there. It rained while I sat on the bus, it rained on my arrival in the city, it rained when I went out to dinner and it rained when I visited museums. And at only 450 m, in midsummer it was very hot and sticky. Bundled up in my anorak, with the hood tied under my chin, I felt like a steamed cauliflower.

I'd been looking forward to San Miguel de Tucumán, as it was one of the main commercial centres on the Silver Road between Buenos Aires and Potosí, with a particularly brisk trade in mules. But its glory days were over. The largest city in the north of Argentina, its economy had collapsed in the recent recession. It was the capital of a virtually bankrupt province, with a distinctly scruffy, down-at-heel appearance, not helped by the rain which streaked endlessly down its peeling walls.

The pavements were crowded and noisy. As for the roads, they were jammed with clapped-out cars, stuttering and juddering along in clouds of black exhaust fumes, like mobile factory chimneys. Some of the city's tradesmen were having such a hard time that they had even been forced back to their old horses and carts. Unemployment was running at record levels and there was talk of child poverty, a blight unknown in the years of Argentina's prosperity. It was not a happy city, but it was a proud one.

It was in Tucumán, in what is now called the Casa Historica, that the representatives of fourteen provinces (three of them now in Bolivia) met at the Congress of Tucumán and signed the Declaration of Independence of the Argentine Republic on 9 July 1816 – the reason for all those Plazas 9 de Julio. Portraits of the signatories line the walls of the actual chamber where the meeting took place and gaze down on rather spooky waxwork dummies of themselves. People in Argentina are usually pretty voluble, so it was interesting to note the reverential hush in that particular room, even though it was full of teenaged visitors.

From Tucumán, there was actually a real, live regular train service, operated by TUFESA (Tucumán Ferrocarriles, SA), to Buenos Aires, via Rosario. As far as I could make out from the internet, one railway company along that line, the NOA Ferrocarriles, had been declared bankrupt in 2004, but capital had obviously been raised to form another company and reopen the line to passengers. I arrived in Tucumán too late to do anything about a booking on Thursday afternoon, but immediately after breakfast on Friday morning, I shrouded myself in my anorak and hurried to the station.

'Do you want to travel on Sunday or next Thursday?' asked the ticket clerk. Just my luck! I had missed the Thursday morning train by a few hours; and if I hung about in Tucumán, then spent most of Sunday on the train journey to Rosario, I should run out of time for what I still needed to do in Argentina. It seemed I was not destined to ride the South American trains.

What with the rain, the noise, the dreary streets and my disappointment over the trains, my journey in Argentina seemed to be going downhill in more ways than one. And to add to the general misery, for the first time ever in South America I had a desperate attack of Montezuma's revenge. Twice in the Casa Historica I was on the verge of disaster and only just managed to get to the ladies' room in time. After that, I played safe and kept to my hotel room, brewing myself endless cups of black Earl Grey tea, which I drank on my bed with the bathroom door wide open, at the ready. I wanted to go home!

On the rare occasions when I've suffered from diarrhoea in the past, I've never taken drugs for it. Not travelling in a group, I haven't been forced to move on. I've been able to stay put, take it easy, drink plenty of liquids and wait for the problem to solve itself. But on this journey, I had to move on swiftly to Rosario, and the only buses were at night. Fearing the worst, I got out the Imodium and dosed myself heavily.

When I reached Rosario (still in the rain!), I was back in the pampas. I checked into the run-down magnificence of the Hotel Savoy, an art deco gem, once the finest hotel in Rosario. My bathroom had all the original fittings and tiles, and my enormous, sparsely furnished bedroom looked out over a glassed-in courtyard with potted plants. Among the common rooms I was amused to find an old-fashioned gentlemen's smoking room, with great squashy leather armchairs and its *FUMOIR* sign still proudly displayed. Despite being neither a gentleman nor a smoker, I found it a very agreeable place to sit and read. The staff too were old fashioned and courteous, in keeping with the style of their hotel. In fact, throughout northern Argentina, I was always very courteously treated. Young men rushed to carry my bags and help me onto buses, usually calling me *Mami*.

It was Sunday and the streets were deserted, but I walked around in the rain to get my bearings. Rosario was the city where my two stories came together. It was the birthplace of

Ernesto Che Guevara and also the major port along the Silver Road. In Rosario, the precious metal could be loaded onto ships sailing down the wide and lazy Paraná River to Buenos Aires – an easier journey than the arduous overland haul.

Monday dawned gloriously sunny, just the day for sightseeing. I walked down to the Rio Paraná, whose waters drift idly by like thick Brown Windsor soup. The city's grandiose Monumento a la Bandera (Monument to the Flag) towers over the sward of the Parque a la Bandera which carpets the riverfront with acres of green. It was on this spot in Rosario in 1812 that General Belgrano, on his way to fight the Royalists in Jujuy, first unfurled his newly designed Argentine flag, of which a gigantic version dominates the monument. I climbed the hill to see the complex at close quarters and was immediately struck by its resemblance to the Anit Kabir, Atatürk's mausoleum in Ankara. Both are statements of patriotic pride. Both stand on hilltops. Both ascend by broad flights of marble steps to a vast open courtyard flanked by colonnades. And both hold the tombs of their country's great revolutionary leaders – Kemal Atatürk, 'Father of Turkey', in Ankara's Anit Kabir and in Rosario, General Manuel Belgrano, the second most famous of the Argentine commanders (after General Jose de San Martín) who wrested independence from Spain. The Monumento a la Bandera has more of a Greek feel, with its propylaeum housing the eternal flame in a circle of columns and torches. It also has a dash of Italian showmanship, not quite up to the wedding cake standard of the Victor Emanuel Monument in Rome, but still a little on the flashy side when compared with the sober grandeur of Atatürk's monument. But it's a moving and impressive memorial for all that, and the view from its summit across the Rio Paraná is unbeatable.

Che Guevara's birthplace was harder to find. I knew roughly where it was, but there was no plaque on the wall. I had to go to the tourist office to get the exact address. When I found the block of flats in Los Rios, I could see why the city was playing down the connection. The block was a substantial brick building on four floors, with gold-painted ironwork and smart black double doors. It was obviously home to some of Rosario's well-established families. I smiled at the thought of droves of long-haired students in Che Guevara T-shirts and berets besieging the block and hammering to be let into their revolutionary hero's flat. That was obviously the last thing the present inhabitants would want. Out of deference to their wishes, I shall keep the address to myself.

Once again, Fate was against me. The TUFESA train passed through Rosario at a totally unacceptable hour of the morning, so I had to take the bus down the remainder of the Silver Road, now a boring flat motorway. At least it was quick.

The guidebooks were warning against picking up taxis in the streets of Buenos Aires. Since the economic crisis of 2001, there was so much dishonesty, they said – even downright robbery – that visitors were advised to ring up a reputable taxi office or book a *remise* at one of the official desks in the airports and stations. On my previous visit to Buenos Aires, I'd had no problems at all with taxis and taken them without a care in the world, but then I had not been on my own. Julian and Katherine were with me, and Julian knew the ropes. This time, on my own, I decided to play safe. With uncharacteristic chicken-heartedness, I went to the *remise* desk at the terminus.

A driver was summoned to escort me to my car. He was a very trim elderly man in a smart grey suit.

'This isn't my real job, you know,' he declared, as soon as I was seated in his equally smart grey Renault. 'I'm not a taxi driver. I own this car and I just drive it in the daytime to earn a bit of extra money. Times are hard in Argentina. I'm really a dancing teacher and I do that in the evenings.'

'What sort of dancing?' I asked. 'What do you teach?'

He looked at me with a mixture of pain and bafflement. 'The tango, of course! What else would I be teaching in Buenos Aires?' I should have known better than to ask.

There were outdoor tango dancers in the Calle Florida, an exotic couple dancing to the music of an accordion, while a distinguished old man in the traditional black pinstriped suit with as narrow a waist as his girth would allow was going round with the hat. A crowd had gathered to watch in the shade of the old Harrods building, now sadly deserted. Later that evening, the *cartoneros* were going about their work in that same fashionable shopping street. They were mostly young teenagers, neatly dressed, who were rummaging through the rubbish bins, sorting out the cardboard, glass and plastic, and loading it onto little makeshift trolleys. Although there seemed to be plenty of money around for jewellery, Rolex watches, Mont Blanc pens and luxury leather goods, there were many middle-class families in Buenos Aires who had obviously fallen through the bottom of the net.

The shops in Buenos Aires are so wonderful that even I, a non-shopper, finally succumbed. I bought a ring, a great rectangular object made of amethyst, aquamarine, garnet, tourmaline and quartz, all Argentine semi-precious stones, set in gold. I have two weaknesses – rings and oriental rugs – and this was a ring I simply had to have. I'd never seen one like it. If I didn't buy it, I knew I would regret it all my life. So, after a night spent tossing and turning, wondering if the expenditure was justified, I steeled myself to the extravagance and marched boldly into the shop. Whatever it cost, I would buy it. After all, jewellery is an investment, isn't it?

The ring brought me luck. I wore it out to dinner on my last night in Buenos Aires and had one of my best meals ever. A simple dinner of steak, potato pureé, salad and Argentine Malbec, yet every ingredient was perfection. I glowed into my plate. Then, to add to the pleasure, a handsome young man on the next table asked me if I could help him with the menu, as his Spanish wasn't up to it. He spoke good English and together we ordered him a mountainous meal. I couldn't place his accent, so I had to ask where he came from. He was from the Ukraine.

'What are you doing in Buenos Aires?' I asked.

'I've got an evening's shore leave from my ship. I've just been promoted to chief engineer, so this dinner is a sort of celebration.'

Igor couldn't believe his luck that he had managed to get an engineering job with an Irish shipping company and had been promoted so soon to a well-paid senior position. He was currently working on a vessel which was spending the northern winters cruising between Salvador in Brazil and Buenos Aires.

'From May to October, we cruise around Europe. Then we sail in South American waters from November to April. So I have summer all the year round. You probably don't know what winter's like in the Ukraine, but I tell you it's hard, very hard. Snow and ice for months on end, and we often can't afford to heat our apartments. I've escaped all that. Cruising's the life for me! We're a mixed bunch on the ship – all nationalities – but we get on well enough together. I just wish I was earning enough to bring my mother out here on a cruise, away from the cold. Perhaps next winter. Who knows?'

It was good to be speaking English again and Igor seemed happy to tell me about his life and his hopes for the future over dinner. For the thousandth time, I thought what an advantage it was to be travelling alone. Had I been there with a friend, we would have talked together and I should probably not have got into conversation with the interesting stranger at the next table. I should have missed so much.

For me, as for Ernesto Che Guevara, Buenos Aires was the end and the beginning. He had set out from the city, a carefree young man on the back of his friend Alberto's Norton, La Ponderosa II, and I had set out to follow in his wheel tracks on my Condor. We had both ended our respective adventures, arriving back in the same place on public transport, he to resume his studies as a medical student and I to catch a plane and pick up the threads of my life in London.

Che's journey in South America saw the start of his political awakening, the first stages of his conversion from privileged boy to communist revolutionary. So it was very appropriate that my last conversation in Buenos Aires should range over South American politics.

I was on my way to the airport in a taxi. 'Where do you come from?' (The usual opening.)

'From England. I live in London.'

'Ah, Señora Thatcher. The Iron Lady.' (The usual response.) 'She's not a very popular person here. But then, neither is General Galtieri. Politicians! They're all the same, even the women. Chile's got a woman president now, you know.'

'Yes. I've just been travelling in Chile. From what I could gather there, Michelle Bachelet seems to be doing a good job. She seems to be steering a clever course between the Left on the one hand and the Pinochetistas on the other. How are things going in Argentina now?'

'They're getting a little bit better all the time. I think we're over the worst. Inflation's down and the unemployment figures are just starting to fall. We've been through a bad patch though, what with Galtieri and his military junta, then that crook Menem. Kirchner is straighter. He's brought back some stability. And we might even copy you and Chile, and have a woman next.'

'I haven't heard of a particularly strong woman candidate here. Who is she?'

The taxi driver laughed. 'Señora Kirchner! Kirchner can't be re-elected himself, so some people are saying that his wife may stand for president instead.'

'That's happened out in the east – in Sri Lanka, Pakistan and Bangladesh. Wives and daughters have taken over when their husbands or fathers have died. But I can't think of a case where a wife has taken over so that her husband can continue to govern through her.'

'Well, we like to be inventive in Argentina. We like to try something different. But Señora Kirchner is a strong woman. Her husband might find that she shows more independence than he's bargained for. It will be fascinating to see how it all turns out.'

BICYCLE SPECIFICATIONS

I am still riding my old faithful Condor, bought for me by the staff and girls at my school and built specially by Monty Young and his team for my first cycle ride around the world.

Frame	Reynolds 631 Mixte, butted tubes
Transmission	Shimano Deore. Front 28-38-48
Rear	13-15-17-20-23-26-30
Wheels	Deore LX hubs
	Mavic TS19 rims
	DT stainless steel spokes
Tyres	Continental Top Touring 2000
Handlebars	Humpert Pro Bars
Pedals	Shimano M324 SPD
Saddle	Brooks B17 STD
Mudguards	SKS
Pannier rack	Blackburn Ex1
Rear panniers	Karrimore Iberia
Colour	Bright orange

INDEX

INDEX